LANGUAGE AND SOCIAL CHANGE IN CHINA

Language and Social Change in China: Undoing Commonness through Cosmopolitan Mandarin offers an innovative and authoritative account of the crucial role of language in shaping the sociocultural landscape of contemporary China. Based on a wide range of data collected since the 1990s and grounded in quantitative and discourse analyses of sociolinguistic variation, Qing Zhang tracks the emergence of what she terms "Cosmopolitan Mandarin" as a new stylistic resource for a rising urban elite and a new middle-class, consumption-based lifestyle. The book powerfully illuminates that Cosmopolitan Mandarin participates in dismantling the pre-reform, socialist, conformist society by bringing about new social distinctions. Rich in cultural and linguistic details, the book is the first of its kind to highlight the implications of language change on the social order and cultural life of contemporary China. *Language and Social Change in China* is ideal for students and scholars interested in sociolinguistics and linguistic anthropology, and Chinese language and society.

Qing Zhang is Associate Professor in the School of Anthropology at the University of Arizona, USA.

LANGUAGE AND SOCIAL CHANGE IN CHINA

Undoing Commonness through Cosmopolitan Mandarin

Qing Zhang

Routledge
Taylor & Francis Group
NEW YORK AND LONDON

First published 2018
by Routledge
711 Third Avenue, New York, NY 10017

and by Routledge
2 Park Square, Milton Park, Abingdon, Oxon, OX14 4RN

Routledge is an imprint of the Taylor & Francis Group, an informa business

© 2018 Taylor & Francis

The right of Qing Zhang to be identified as author of this work has been asserted by her in accordance with sections 77 and 78 of the Copyright, Designs and Patents Act 1988.

All rights reserved. No part of this book may be reprinted or reproduced or utilised in any form or by any electronic, mechanical, or other means, now known or hereafter invented, including photocopying and recording, or in any information storage or retrieval system, without permission in writing from the publishers.

Trademark notice: Product or corporate names may be trademarks or registered trademarks, and are used only for identification and explanation without intent to infringe.

Every effort has been made to contact copyright holders. Please advise the publisher of any errors or omissions, and these will be corrected in subsequent editions.

Library of Congress Cataloging in Publication Data
A catalog record for this title has been requested

ISBN: 978-0-415-70807-4 (hbk)
ISBN: 978-0-415-70808-1 (pbk)
ISBN: 978-1-315-88625-1 (ebk)

Typeset in Bembo
by codeMantra

 Printed in the United Kingdom by Henry Ling Limited

This book is dedicated to Dan and Jing-yi.

CONTENTS

List of Illustrations	*viii*
Preface	*ix*
Notes on Chinese Names and Transcription Conventions	*xiii*
List of Abbreviations	*xv*

	Introduction: Emerging Social Distinctions and the Semiotic Inadequacy of the "Common Speech"	1
1	Sociolinguistic Change, Style, and Ideology	20
2	Beijing Yuppies: The New Business Elite	46
3	Cosmopolitan Mandarin in the Making of Beijing Yuppies	61
4	Cosmopolitan Mandarin in the Making of a New Chinese Middle-Class Consumer	105
5	Warring Standards: Contesting the Enregisterment of Cosmopolitan Mandarin	134
6	A Style-Based Approach to Sociolinguistic Change	177

Index	*191*

LIST OF ILLUSTRATIONS

Figures

0.1	Enjoy the same class of private	3
0.2	Let the era of no individuality be gone forever!	6
3.1	Gender Variation in Each Professional Group	78
3.2	Topic Variation in Each Professional Group	79
3.3	Contrast in Styles	81

Tables

3.1	Summary of Linguistic Variables	76
3.2	Effects of Professional Group, Gender, and Topic on Variation	77
3.3	Effects of Gender and Topic in Yuppie Group	77
3.4	Effects of Gender and Topic in State Professional Group	77
4.1	Vocabulary of New Urban Lifestyle	111
4.2	"Trendy" Expressions	113
4.3	English Expressions	115
4.4	Limited Use of Rhotacization	116
4.5	Locative Particles with Non-rhotacized Suffixes	118
4.6	Most Frequent Lexemes in *S Information Station*	125
5.1	Contrasting Indexical Values of Standard *Putonghua* and Cosmopolitan Mandarin	137
5.2	State's Construals of *"Gang-Tai Qiang"* vis-à-vis Standard *Putonghua*	155
5.3	N-th and *n*+1st Order Indexicality of Standard *Putonghua* and Cosmopolitan Mandarin	166

PREFACE

The seeds of my research in this book were sown at the end of my master's study in China, when I went on job interviews with foreign companies in Beijing and Shanghai and at the same time was awaiting admission letters from graduate schools overseas. With a bachelor's degree in English and a master's in linguistics, and no background in business, I crafted myself in the interviews as a linguistic and cultural intermediary for foreign businesses in China. Eventually, I received offers from three multinational corporations and admissions with financial support from several universities in the United States and the United Kingdom. My interest in pursuing graduate studies in linguistics overpowered my desire to join a new breed of Chinese business professionals. That decision shaped the trajectory of my professional and personal life: I have become an academic specializing in language and social change in China rather than one of the Chinese yuppies whom I studied for my dissertation research. I started my graduate studies in linguistics at Stanford University, knowing that I wanted to focus on the relation between language and social change, and where else is a better place to examine the relation than China?

People of my age cohort—starting primary school in the late 1970s when China initiated the opening-up policy and economic reform—have grown up with and lived the drastic socioeconomic and ideological changes that have profoundly transformed Chinese society. The power of language in such transformations has always fascinated me. The Department of Linguistics at Stanford University was where this passion of mine grew from a rudimentary interest articulated in my application statement in terms of speech act theory and cross-cultural communication to a deepened understanding of language as social action and meaning-making resource. Specifically, I became interested in examining the inextricable link between language and social change grounded in rigorous linguistic analysis and cultural theories.

x Preface

I began to find my own intellectual voice during the writing of my dissertation. I am grateful for three people who helped nurture the voice and shape my intellectual trajectory at its early stage. I owe a tremendous intellectual debt to Penny Eckert, my doctoral adviser at Stanford University. Taking me on as her advisee from the very beginning of my graduate studies, she has encouraged and supported my interest in language and social change throughout my academic career. I draw inspiration from her work on style and sociolinguistic variation and from her encouragement to expand my intellectual horizon, integrating scholarship from other related fields to make greater waves in advancing sociolinguistic theory on language and social change. I am grateful for her unwavering encouragement and enthusiasm in my work, and her comments on Chapter 1 and earlier drafts of Chapter 2 and 3 of this book. I have also benefited tremendously from Miyako Inoue's advice and insights on seeing the broader picture: How linguistic issues come to stand in for larger social and political projects and processes, and how a deep understanding of the local political economies can shed light on the intricacies of linguistic practices. John Rickford, another mentor and member of my dissertation committee at Stanford, whose earlier work on linguistic variation and change in a non-Western, non-industrialized community, inspired me to pursue my research in China. Research on sociolinguistic variation and change has continued to be dominated by studies in Western societies and on English. More research in other societies and on other languages is needed to not only expand the empirical breadth of the discipline but also to strengthen the methodological and theoretical rigor in investigating sociolinguistic change in diverse contexts. This book seeks to offer such a contribution.

The project on the emergence of Cosmopolitan Mandarin at its various stages has benefited from the support of many people. I extend my greatest appreciation to the yuppies and state professionals in Beijing. I am most grateful to them for finding time from their busy schedules to participate in my study. I thank them for sharing with me their professional experiences and their views on the effects of social and economic changes on their lives and their city. Particularly, I would like to thank "Mr. Wang," my point of contact and friend, for his enthusiasm in my project and for introducing me to the first six yuppie participants, and I thank "Ms. Jiang" for getting me into contact with managers in the state sector. I am deeply grateful to Liu Ling of Tianjin Television Station, one of the hosts of the program *S Information Station*, for allowing me to analyze her program and helping me obtain recordings of the show.

Friends, colleagues, and mentors at the University of Arizona whose friendship, encouragement, and support have enriched my academic and personal life. My deepest appreciation goes to Dianne Austin, Anita Bhappu, Wenhao Diao, Tami Draves, Perry Gilmore, Jane Hill, John Olsen, Susan Philips, Barney Pavao-Zuckerman, Jen Roth-Gordon, and Stacey Tecot. Senior colleagues and peers, Asif Agha, Susan Gal, Barbara Johnstone, Bonnie McElhinny, Norma

Mendoza-Denton, Rob Podesva, Michael Silverstein, Keith Walters, and Kathryn Woolard have offered me insights and comments on various issues and versions of the chapters in this book. I am deeply grateful for their interest in my work. I am particularly thankful to Andrew Wong, my colleague, friend, and sounding board, for spending time on reading and commenting on Chapters 1, 5, and 6.

Earlier versions of chapters of this book were read and discussed at my graduate seminar "Linguistic Analysis of Social Meaning" and at Norma Mendoza-Denton's graduate seminar "Genealogies of Language and Power" at the University of California, Los Angeles. I am thankful for the students' questions and comments. I am thankful for Bill Cotter and Priscilla Shin for their assistance at the final editing stage of the book. Earlier sections of the book were presented at lectures and workshops at the following universities: National Taiwan Normal University (English); Tianjin Foreign Studies University (English and Semiotics); Stanford University (Linguistics); University of Chicago (Anthropology); University of California, Los Angeles (Center for Chinese Studies); University of California, San Diego (Anthropology); and University of Virginia (Anthropology and East Asian Studies). I extend my appreciation to the student and faculty audiences for offering me valuable insights and suggestions.

I would also like to extend my special appreciation to Nikki Seifert for her incredible editing work that helped shape the final product and made the book more readable for a general audience. I am deeply grateful for the editor at Routledge, Rebecca Novack, and editorial assistant, Kathrene Binag, for their support and patience that helped me carry the project to its completion.

I gratefully acknowledge the financial support and research leave time at various stages of my research offered by Stanford University, University of Texas at Austin, and University of Arizona. I am also thankful to Cambridge University Press for allowing me to reuse portions of my 2005 article published in *Language in Society* 34 (3):431-466, "A Chinese Yuppie in Beijing: Phonological Variation and the Construction of a New Professional Identity" in Chapter 3 of this book. Parts of my 2012 article, "'Carry Shopping through to the End': Linguistic Innovation in a Chinese Television Program" in *Style-Shifting in Public: New Perspective on Stylistic Variation*, edited by Juan Manuel Hernández-Campoy and Juan Antonio Cutillas-Espinosa, 205-224 (Amsterdam: John Benjamins), were significantly modified and incorporated in Chapter 4 of this book.

My deepest appreciation goes to my family—my parents, my sister, and my brother-in-law on the other side of the Pacific; my husband, Dan; and our six-year-old daughter Jing-yi. I owe the greatest debt to my parents, for their unconditional love, for being my ardent supporters, and for their faith in my ability to accomplish whatever I dedicate myself to. I am also forever grateful for their love and support of my whole family: Taking care of Jing-yi and me when we go back to China on my research trips, and traveling to the United States to

xii Preface

support all three of us when we need their help. I am also grateful for my sister and brother-in-law for taking good care of our parents when I am thousands of miles away from them. Finally, I am tremendously indebted to Dan and Jing-yi, who lived the book project with me. The book would not have been possible without Dan's support and love. I am grateful for him sharing my academic life and always being there for me. To our daughter, Jing-yi, I deeply appreciate her understanding at such a young age that sometimes I have to prioritize the book over spending time with her. Her sunny smile and laughter are the best de-stressors after long hours of work, and her self-made congratulation card for the completion of my book manuscript is the best reward I could ask for. This book is for you, Dan and Jing-yi!

NOTES ON CHINESE NAMES AND TRANSCRIPTION CONVENTIONS

In this book, Chinese names are presented with the family name (*xing*) followed by the given name (*ming*). Original Chinese expressions and utterances are represented in *italics* in *pinyin*, the official phonetic alphabet system of mainland China, and English translation is enclosed in single quotation marks. All English translations are mine unless otherwise noted. The *pinyin* transcription does not include tone marks except for examples used to illustrate variation in tones. In such examples, the four Beijing/Standard Mandarin tones are marked by numbers: 1 for the high-level tone; 2 for the rising tone; 3 for the falling–rising tone; 4 for the falling tone; and 0 for the neutral tone, for example, *piao4liang0* versus *piao4liang4* 'pretty'. The International Phonetic Alphabet is used to transcribe particular sounds, specifically in Chapter 3 in the description of linguistic variables.

The following symbols are used in the transcription of speech:

<u>Underline</u>	Words originally spoken in English are underlined
EMPHASIS	Capitalization indicates emphasis, which may be signaled by increased amplitude or careful articulation
h	laughter, each token marks one pulse
[ ]	overlapping speech
:	Lengthening
–	Self-interruption
.	end of an intonation unit with a falling contour
?	end of an intonation unit with a rising contour
,	a pause shorter than 1 second
(n)	A number enclosed in parentheses, e.g., (2), indicates a longer pause
(( ))	transcriber's comments

xiv Notes on Chinese Names and Transcription Conventions

Boldface highlights linguistic features and content that are significant and receive special attention in analysis. Bold capitalized letters in square brackets represent the following types of linguistic feature:

[+R]: -*r*, rhotacization; **[-R]**: de-rhotacization

[+lenition]: lenition of *zh* /tʂ/, *ch* /tʂʰ/, and *sh* /ʂ/ as *r* [ɻ]; **[-lenition]**: *zh* /tʂ/, *ch* /tʂʰ/, and *sh* /ʂ/ realized as [tʂ], [tʂʰ], and [ʂ] respectively

[+interdental]: interdental realization of *z* /ts/, *c* /tsʰ/, and *s* /s/ as [tθ], [tθʰ], and [θ] **[-interdental]**: *z* /ts/, *c* /tsʰ/, and *s* /s/ realized as [ts], [tsʰ], and [s] respectively

[T0], **[T1]**, **[T2]**, **[T3]**, **[T4]**: represent the tone realization of the syllable: **[T0]** = neutral tone; **[T1]**, **[T2]**, **[T3]**, and **[T4]** each represents a full tone in a conventionally neutral tone environment

[E]: use of English

[L]: innovative lexical item

LIST OF ABBREVIATIONS

BM	Beijing Mandarin
CCP	Chinese Communist Party
CCTV	China Central Television
CM	Cosmopolitan Mandarin
IPA	International Phonetic Alphabet
KMT	Kuomintang, the nationalist party
MSP	Mainland Standard *Putonghua*
PRC	People's Republic of China
PSC	*Putonghua Shuiping Ceshi* 'Putonghua Proficiency Test'
PSCSG	*Putonghua Shuiping Ceshi Shishi Gangyao* '*The Implementation Guidelines for the Putonghua Proficiency Test*'
PTH	*Putonghua*, the name of the standard language in the People's Republic of China
RMB	*renminbi* 'Chinese *yuan*'
SARFT	*Guojia Guangbo Dianying Dianshi Zongju* 'State Administration of Radio, Film, and Television'
XHC	*Xiandai Hanyu Cidian* '*Modern Chinese Dictionary*'
XXCC	*Xinhua Xin Ciyu Cidian* '*Xinhua Dictionary of New Expressions*'

INTRODUCTION

Emerging Social Distinctions and the Semiotic Inadequacy of the "Common Speech"

It is our policy to let some people and some regions prosper before others, so that they can bring along the backward regions. ... The [economic] reform is designed, first and foremost, to break with egalitarianism, and to break with the practice of having everyone "eat from the same big pot."

(Deng 1994 [1986], 169)

我们的政策是让一部分人、一部分地区先富起来，以带动和帮助落后的地区… 改革首先要打破平均主义，打破"大锅饭"

(Deng 1993 [1986], 155)[1]

0.1 The Power of Language in Social Change

The opening quote from Deng Xiaoping, often referred to as the chief architect of China's economic reform, offers perhaps the most convincing example of the power of language in transforming Chinese society. In an Austinian sense, Deng's declaratives perform a powerful speech act that has fundamentally reshaped the country's socioeconomic trajectory. However, the power of language resides not just in such speech acts performed by powerful leaders. The focus of this book is that changing ways of using language—even at the micro level of innovative ways of using sounds and words—can bring about social change. The central theme of this book is about the mutually constitutive relation between language and social change. Linguistic innovation and change are not merely the reflexes and effects of social change but are among the very forces and resources for reconfiguring sociopolitical landscapes. I argue that sociolinguistic investigation of language change needs to look beyond the linguistic system to locate it within broader cultural political processes. This book thus examines language change in China as a tool to dismantle a pre-reform socialist

2 Introduction

egalitarian society that upheld political and cultural conformity and suppressed expression of difference. It tracks the emergence of a new linguistic style, "Cosmopolitan Mandarin," and how it is used to bring about new social distinctions. In doing so, the book develops a style-based approach to sociolinguistic change that treats linguistic change and innovation as emerging stylistic resources for effecting social change.

Ultimately, the book seeks to illuminate how Cosmopolitan Mandarin participates in the emergence of a postsocialist stylistic regime that valorizes differentiation. The social-ideological upheaval of Chinese society over the past four decades makes China one of the most fecund sites for examining the inextricable relation between language and social change. The investigation of linguistic innovation in this book is not only timely but also contributes more broadly to the development of sociolinguistic change that embeds language change in the broader processes of sociopolitical transformation—and this book looks in detail at the ways in which style has a particular role to play in effecting this change (Coupland 2014).

The rest of this chapter provides the sociolinguistic context for the book. Following a short description of an ideological shift from socialist egalitarianism to valorization of difference, Section 0.3 discusses tidbits of innovative language use as an example of the kind of linguistic analysis developed in the rest of the book. Section 0.4 explains the various language-related terms used in this book. Section 0.5 offers a historical overview of language standardization in the People's Republic of China (PRC). The chapter ends with an overview of the book.

0.2 Abolishing Socialist Egalitarianism and Valorizing Difference

"Let[ting] some people and some regions prosper before others" and abolishing egalitarianism became a central guiding principle of economic reform initiated in the late 1970s. The seismic socioeconomic change over the past four decades has led to the advent of consumerism and increased socioeconomic stratification, including the burgeoning Chinese middle classes (e.g., Bian 1994; Bian et al. 2005; Croll 2006; Davis 2000; Griffiths 2013; Hanser 2008; Pun 2005; Woronov 2016; Zhou 2004). Emergent social groups draw on linguistic and other semiotic resources and engage in practices that forge new cultural identities and (life)styles (e.g., Dong 2016; Farquhar and Zhang 2012; Goodman 2008; Hoffman 2010; Hsu 2007; Ren 2013; Zhang 2010). The diversification of the contemporary Chinese society would not have happened without the fundamental ideological shift away from socialist egalitarianism, captured in the opening quotation. As Dirlik observes (2001, 16):

> The most important contrast between the capitalist present and the socialist past is the valorization of difference, which provides a radical departure

from the days of socialist frugality and control which dressed everyone in sexless green and blue in the name of socialist equality. Socialism, at least as it was understood then, required homogeneity of values as well as of representations. Capitalism, and the consumer revolution, require for their sustenance the production of heterogeneity, however superficial and symbolic.

Valorization of difference legitimizes overt display and expression of difference, which requires the use of semiotic resources to create meanings of distinction. Language thus comes to serve as a vital tool in the making of new social distinctions. Examples of language being used to effect differentiation are ubiquitous. The next section introduces the reader to a few tidbits of innovative ways of using language to bring about distinction.

0.3 Tidbits of Language and Social Change in China

A large billboard real estate advertisement across the top of a five-story commercial building reads 同一个圈层的私享, *Tong yige quanceng de sixiang*, 'the same circle-stratum's private enjoyment', or more idiomatically, 'private enjoyment for the same stratum' (see Figure 0.1). The original English—or rather Chinglish—translation, "ENJOY THE SAME CLASS OF PRIVATE," is printed in a much smaller size, so small that it is barely visible from across the street.

The advertisement is for Hai Yi Chang Zhou, a luxury residential real estate development in the city of Tianjin. The expression *si-xiang* 私享 'private-enjoyment' is a nonce compound noun and a creative antonym to an established

FIGURE 0.1 Enjoy the same class of private

4 Introduction

compound *gong-xiang*共享 'shared-enjoyment', meaning enjoying together or sharing with others. Furthermore, 'private-enjoyment' is homophonous with the noun *sixiang* 思想 'thought, thinking'. Hence, at least two layers of meaning are created simultaneously in this advertisement: (1) The denotational meaning expressed through the characters of the phrase "private enjoyment [shared among members] of the same stratum," and (2) a meaning created through the sound of the characters "thought/thinking [shared among members] of the same stratum." Another potential meaning can be created by linking the ownership and owner of a property in this development to belonging to "the same stratum," which is the intended message of the advertisement. In other words, the real estate property is intended to serve as a social index, linking a commodity to a social class of people and the privacy and exclusiveness offered by the property. Language is used in this case to produce this message about class privilege and distinction.

About a kilometer to the north, at the end of a busy thoroughfare, stands another large billboard with an advertisement for the 八里台新文化广场：三百万新青年的 Shopping Mall '8 Miles New Culture Plaza: The Shopping Mall for three million new youth'. In this advertisement, the English expression "shopping mall" is perfectly mixed with Chinese, which violates the official mandate that prohibits mixing of "scripts and words from foreign languages with Chinese in the same sentence in an advertisement" (State Administration for Industry and Commerce 1998). Rather than using the Chinese expression for shopping mall, *gouwu zhongxin*, the English "shopping mall" adds a linguistic fashion element to the advertisement and creates the meaning of *yangqi* 'Western', 'stylish', and 'newness'. This is in accordance with the intended consumers of 8 Miles New Culture Plaza, who are fashion-conscious young urbanites.

Upon entering the shopping mall, one is greeted with a mural of sharp contrasting colors of red, black, and white (see Figure 0.2). In the middle frame is an apparently old black-and-white photo of three rows of young women and two men in the mid-front row wearing the same People's Liberation Army-style uniform. The uniform and unisex style of the people in the photo immediately evokes a connection to the pre-reform era. A closer look at the faces reveals that the images are actually reproductions of the same woman and man. The caption at the bottom of the photo reads "Chinese clone technology in 1949," written in standard, i.e., simplified, characters. Below the picture, in a much larger font size, a slogan reads *Rang meiyou gexing de niandai yiqu bu fufan!*, 'Let the era of no-individuality be gone forever!' In contrast to the photo caption, the slogan is written in traditional Chinese characters, a script officially prohibited in advertisements in mainland China (State Administration for Industry and Commerce 1998), but in use in Hong Kong, Taiwan, and many diaspora Chinese communities.[2] The middle frame is bordered on each side by the image of two cultural icons, on the left, the image of Che Guevara reminiscent of the famous portrait by Jim Fitzpatrick and on the right, that of Lei Feng in a similar style. Lei Feng

(1940–1962) was a soldier of the People's Liberation Army. After his death on duty, a national "Learn from Lei Feng" campaign was initiated, and March 5 is designated the "Day of Learning from Lei Feng." As a model soldier and Communist Party member, he is an emblem of altruism and collectivism; loyalty to the Party, the people, and the country; industriousness; and plain-living (*jian-ku-pu-su*). Both Lei Feng and Che Guevara were communist soldiers, but Lei was a loyal and dutiful servant of an established communist regime, whereas Guevara was a communist rebel-revolutionary participating in overthrowing an oppressive capitalist government. Particularly in Jim Fitzpatrick's rendition, he "has become the romantic embodiment of youthful idealism and passionate rebellion" (Kemp 2012, 167). Lei Feng is the antithesis of individualism, individuality, rebellion, and consumerism. Thus, Lei represents the bygone era of no-individuality. Juxtaposing the Chinese domestic communist icon of Lei Feng with the global icon of Che Guevara in this shopping mall targeting youth consumers, the message cannot be clearer: Guevara stands in defiance of all that Lei represents, and the consumers are invited to align with the former and join in a consumer revolution to dismantle the bygone world of "no individuality." This is the denotational meaning of the slogan.

In a parallel way, the contrast between the two types of scripts creates a corresponding message. The simplified script used in the caption is linked to the pre-reform era portrayed in the photo, one of homogeneity and no individuality. Not only is the traditional script the medium through which the defying slogan is written but also the use of the script itself performs simultaneously an act of breaking the norm—that is, the norm would be to use the standard, simplified script—and an act of breaking away from a past of homogeneity. In addition to the temporal contrast just described, the two sets of juxtaposition (simplified vs. traditional script and Lei Feng vs. Che Guevara) index a spatial contrast between a mainland China territorial orientation and a transterritorial, global orientation and connection.

In this example, we see that multiple kinds of semiotic resources work together to create social meanings through contrast. We also see that contrast at one level is projected onto other levels (Irvine and Gal 2000): On one level, homogeneity and collectivism contrast with individualism; this contrast is mapped onto one on the temporal level between the past and the present and a spatial contrast between a mainland China orientation and a supraregional orientation.

The three examples show that linguistic and other semiotic resources from both regional sources (simplified Chinese script, black-and-white photo of clones, and image of Lei Feng) and extraregional sources (traditional Chinese script, English, and image of Che Guevara) are combined to create social meanings. Furthermore, multiple layers of meaning are created through the content of the message as well as variation in the form of the semiotic resources employed, including the juxtaposition of contrasting linguistic forms. Innovative language—at the morphological level (creative nonce compound noun

6 Introduction

FIGURE 0.2 Let the era of no individuality be gone forever!

'private-enjoyment'), choice of scripts (traditional and simplified characters), and choice of languages (Chinese and English)—expresses the social meaning of newness and differentiation.

The use of "new" linguistic elements in the above examples indicates that the creators of the advertisements seemed to find the standard language, *Putonghua* 'common speech', lacking as a meaning-making resource in the present socioeconomic context. To better understand the intimate relation between linguistic innovation and social change presented in the upcoming chapters, it is necessary to explicate a cultural and political understanding of what I refer to as the semiotic inadequacy of the "common speech."[3] With an emphasis on the *cultural* and the *political*, the following short historical overview of the standardization of Modern Standard Chinese, and *Putonghua* in particular, highlights the politics of language standardization whereby Standard Chinese, as standard languages elsewhere, is vested as a sociopolitical tool in national and political endeavors. But before the discussion on Standard Chinese, a clarification of terms referring to language varieties that are relevant to this book is necessary.

0.4 Clarification of Terms[4]

Chinese, or Chinese language, *Zhongwen*, in its singular form, implies a monolithic linguistic entity, whereas in reality, the so-called "Chinese language" consists of numerous *fangyan*, or groups of regional varieties, some of which can be as different as the Romance languages of Europe (e.g., Norman 1988). Thus,

Introduction **7**

a Chinese speaker from the northern part of the country, such as the capital city of Beijing, is unlikely to understand a Chinese speaker from the south, such as the city of Guangzhou. Linguists usually classify the Chinese varieties into seven or eight regional groups, *Beifanghua* 'Northern varieties' also known as *Guanhua* 'Mandarin', *Wu, Gan, Xiang, Yue* 'Cantonese', *Kejia* (Hakka), and *Min*, which some scholars further divide into Northern Min and Southern Min (e.g., De Francis 1984; Ramsey 1987). Mandarin is the largest dialect group, with more than eight million speakers (e.g., Shen 2015). The non-Mandarin varieties are also commonly known as Southern dialects. Furthermore, many linguists identify four major dialect groups within Mandarin: Northern Mandarin, Northwestern Mandarin, Southwestern Mandarin, and Eastern or Jiang-Huai Mandarin (e.g., Norman 1988; Ramsey 1987). One Northern Mandarin dialect, Beijing Mandarin, is officially designated as the phonological basis for the standard language of the PRC, i.e., *Putonghua*. Hence, according to a linguistic view of Chinese languages and dialects, the term "Chinese" masks linguistic diversity and complexity among and within regional language varieties. By associating the term "Chinese" or the "Chinese language" with the people(s) of China and those of Chinese origin, the singular label makes invisible, or rather erases, the vast number of languages used by ethnic minority groups living in Han Chinese dominant territories, namely, the PRC and Taiwan,[5] and non-Chinese languages used in Chinese diaspora communities around the world. However, the reader needs to be aware of a difference between the above *linguistic* description of what constitutes Chinese and a widely shared view among many native Chinese speakers that the various *fangyan* are subvarieties of a single language called "Chinese" (e.g., Chen 2007; De Francis 1984). The fact that speakers of diverse, even mutually unintelligible *fangyan,* share a standard Chinese writing system further strengthens this belief in a shared Chinese language among speakers of regional varieties. The Chinese script, or *Hanzi* 'Chinese characters' as it is called in Mandarin, is believed by many to be a unifying emblem of Chinese culture that transcends linguistic, geographic, and temporal divides. However, as De Francis (1984) points out, the appearance of uniformity and universality of the written Chinese script across space and time is also largely an illusion.

The term *Zhongwen*, literally 'Chinese language', is used to differentiate Chinese from non-Sinitic languages. *Hanyu,* the 'language of the Han people', the majority ethnic group in PRC and Taiwan, is often interchangeable with *Zhongwen*. Both *Zhongwen* and *Hanyu* are often used to refer to Mandarin, and specifically the standard language of China. For example, the official dictionary that codifies the pronunciation of the standard language is titled *Xiandai Hanyu Cidian* '*Modern Han Language Dictionary*', commonly translated as the *Modern Chinese Dictionary,* and the official standard alphabetical system is called *Hanyu Pinyin* 'Han Language Spelling-Pronunciation', or *Pinyin* for short, commonly translated as the Chinese Spelling System. *Zhongwen* and *Hanyu* are also used

8 Introduction

in contexts of language teaching. *Zhongwen* often refers to Chinese taught as a foreign language outside of the PRC whereas *Hanyu* is the preferred appellation by the Chinese government and institutions for Chinese taught as a second and foreign language. For instance, the national standardized test for proficiency in Chinese is called *Hanyu Shuiping Kaoshi* 'Han Language Proficiency Test', commonly translated as Chinese Proficiency Test. *Hanban* 'Hanyu Office' is the abbreviation of the China National Office for Teaching Chinese as a Foreign Language. *Putonghua* 'common speech' is the term for the standard language in the PRC. It is commonly translated as Standard Chinese or Standard Mandarin. The former emphasizes its distinction from standard languages of other countries. The latter English term specifies Mandarin as its dialectal basis (see definition in the next section).

In this book, I use "Standard Chinese" or "Modern Standard Chinese" in general discussions about the national standard language, as in the next section, including its spoken and written forms. I use "Standard Mandarin," "Mainland Standard *Putonghua*," "Mainland Standard Mandarin," and "Beijing-Mandarin-based *Putonghua*" in discussions highlighting the phonological basis of the spoken standard language in mainland China. Furthermore, *Guoyu* 'national language' and *Huayu* 'Chinese language' are the terms for standard Chinese used in Taiwan and Singapore, respectively. The two terms are also used among Chinese diaspora, referring to Mandarin as a lingua franca among speakers of Chinese origin who may not otherwise share a Chinese language. It should be noted that the specific cultural meaning of any one of the above terms is determined by who uses it, when, and where it is used. Their use in context often reveals underlying beliefs about the "Chinese language," the standard language, and the attitude and stance of the user of a particular term vis-à-vis broader sociopolitical considerations.

0.5 Modern Standard Chinese and the Semiotic Inadequacy of the "Common Speech"

The standardization of Modern Chinese in mainland China from the late 19th century, through the Republican era (1911–1949) and the People's Republic under the Chinese Communist Party (CCP) is a process of popularization, and in effect, de-eliticization to form a modern standard language that is accessible to the masses. The outcome of the process is a standard language based on Northern Mandarin—known as *Putonghua* 'common speech'—that symbolizes a modern Chinese nation as well as socialist egalitarianism. This section focuses on the development of *Putonghua* (here in after PTH) in the PRC, showing that language standardization is part of the social-ideological transformation from an old society under "the rule of imperialism, feudalism and bureaucrat-capitalism" (China 1983, 3) to a new socialist state under "the dictatorship of proletariat" (ibid., 4).

Introduction **9**

0.5.1 Modern Standard Chinese for a Modern Nation-State

Two regime changes in the history of modern China have shaped the course of the development of Modern Standard Chinese: the imperial Qing Dynasty (1644–1911) overthrown by the nationalists (Kuomintang) in 1911 and the defeat of the latter by the CCP in the mainland in 1949. Modern China began in the mid-19th century with a series of humiliating military defeats of the Qing Dynasty by foreign powers. These defeats engendered a keenly felt national crisis and an urgent need to modernize the country. A strong negative perception of the Chinese language as a major culprit for the backwardness of the country and ill suited for a modern nation-state was shared among progressive, prominent intellectuals and nationalist revolutionaries at the time (Chen 2007; Ramsey 1987). Advocates of language reform at the turn of the 20th century viewed the Chinese language as impeding modernization and unification in three main areas: (1) lack of a unified spoken standard language serving as a lingua franca among mutually unintelligible regional varieties, (2) lack of a modern written language closer to the daily vernacular, and (3) a traditional character-based script too difficult to acquire. The last two were considered responsible for the low literacy rate among the vast Chinese populations (Chen 1999). Hence, language reform became part of the efforts to modernize the country.

After the nationalists overthrew the imperial Qing regime and founded the Republic of China (1912–1949 in mainland China), *Guoyu* was established in 1926 as the national standard language. It was defined as "the speech of natives of Peking who have received a middle-school education" (De Francis 1950, 76). A phonetic alphabet system based on the pronunciation of Beijing Mandarin was also created, which was called *Guoyu Luomazi* 'National Language Romanization'. It served as an auxiliary tool for learning the written script. To reform the written language, the traditional *wenyan* 'classical literary Chinese', which had been the most prestigious style of written Chinese up to the beginning of the 20th century but did not resemble any of the contemporary spoken vernaculars, was replaced by *baihua* 'vernacular-based literary Chinese'.[6] By the 1930s, *baihua* was established as the basis for the standard written language for all purposes and occasions (Chen 1999). Little progress was made in script reform, however, in the Republic era (ibid.). Thus, language reform and standardization in the first half of the 20th century under the Kuomintang (KMT) regime was intended to modernize the standard language so that it became compatible with a modern, unified nation-state.

0.5.2 The Rise of Putonghua in the PRC

The defeat of the KMT regime by the CCP marked the bifurcation of the development of standard Chinese in the mainland and in Taiwan. Language standardization and reform remained a priority in building a new unified

10 Introduction

and socialist People's Republic (Zhou and Sun 2004). Guided by the political agenda to eradicate social inequality, language—particularly the standard language—is treated as a tool to transform China from an old society marked by socioeconomic inequality to a new socialist egalitarian People's Republic under the rule of the proletariat. The equalizing function of the standard language was evident in the designation of PTH 'common speech' as the standard language of the PRC in 1956 (Guojia Yuyan Wenzi 1996, 12):

> The standard form of Modern Chinese with the Beijing Mandarin phonological system as its norm of pronunciation, Northern Mandarin as its base dialect, and the exemplary works of modern *baihua* [vernacular literary language] literature as its grammatical norms.

In contrast to the 1926 definition of the standard pronunciation of *Guoyu* cited earlier, the above definition of PTH left out any overt status-marking descriptor of Beijing Mandarin. The change in the appellation of the standard language from *Guoyu* 'national language' to PTH 'common speech' is also politically significant. The new name not only specifies the instrumental function of the standard language as a shared lingua franca among speakers of diverse varieties but also, and more important, an ideological shift to privilege the language of the common people rather than that of a minority educated elite (see also Dong 2010; Li 2004). Thus, the connotation of the newly designated PTH stands in sharp contrast to its early uses in the late 19th century, which associated *putong*, 'common' or 'general', with "being adulterated and substandard" (Chen 1999, 25).[7] The political implication of the term PTH can be traced back to the writings of Qu Qiubai in the 1930s. A prominent leader of the Communist Party and an advocate of language reform at that time, Qu proposed PTH as "a new modern vernacular of the urban proletariat" (1953 [1932], 889). Distinguishing the new "common speech" from "the so-called national language [*guoyu*] of the officials" (ibid.), Qu argued that PTH should be the new common language used in the revolutionary popular literature so that it would be accessible to the masses.[8] Thus, at its inception, the standard language of the PRC takes on a distinctly class-based connotation, that is, the proletariat, the new ruling class who stood in opposition to the old *guanliao zichanjieji* 'bureaucrat-capitalists' overthrown by the communist revolution.

0.5.3 Script Reform

In the area of script reform, the traditional characters were seen as not only a great barrier to mass literacy but also a means to sustain the privilege and power of the former ruling classes (Zhao and Baldauf 2008). Hence, to make the written standard language more accessible to the masses, efforts were carried out in the early 1950s to simplify the characters by reducing the number of strokes. In 1964, the General List of Simplified Characters (*Jianhuazi Zongbiao*) was published, providing a comprehensive list of 2,236 simplified characters (Chen 1999, 154). Reducing the average number of strokes of the most commonly used 2,000 characters from 11.2 to 9.8, the list became the standard for all publications in mainland China (ibid., 157). Take the verb *xuexi* 'study' as an example, the number of strokes of the two characters in the traditional script, 學習, is 15 and 11 respectively, whereas the two simplified characters 学习 have 11 strokes combined. A new phonetic alphabet called *Hanyu Pinyin* (*Pinyin* for short) was officially published in 1964 to serve as a sound annotation tool that provides the standard pronunciation for Chinese characters. Since the mid-1960s, simplified script *jianti zi* or *jianhua zi* and *pinyin* have come to take on a territorial and potentially political association with socialist mainland China but traditional characters *fanti zi* and non-*pinyin* alphabet systems with Hong Kong, Taiwan, and other overseas Chinese communities.[9] Hence, the traditional script and non-pinyin spelling convention can be employed to signal an extra-mainland association or orientation, as demonstrated in the example of the mural in the 8 Miles New Culture Plaza.

0.5.4 De-eliticization and Conformity during the Great Proletarian Cultural Revolution

The de-eliticization of the standard language took another drastic turn during the Great Proletariat Cultural Revolution (1966–1976). Just like androgynous clothing styles in green, blue, and grey were used to represent and express cultural and political conformity at that time, drastic linguistic changes took place as language served a similar political function erasing social differentiation and producing conformity in the name of socialist egalitarianism. It is thus no surprise that one of the most drastic changes in language use happened in the area of address terms. All traditional honorific titles, terms that marked superior status in pre-revolutionary time and those with gender marking became obsolete, for example, *laoban* 'boss', *laoye* 'master', the patriarch of a prestigious family, *taitai* 'madam or Mrs.', *xiaojie* 'miss', a young woman or daughter of a prestigious family, *shaoye* 'junior master', a young man or son of a prestigious family, and *xiansheng* 'mister'. In their place, the government promoted the use of *tongzhi* 'comrade' as a general neutral term that **"implies no social or economic distinctions** but which unites all as sharing the same political goals" (Scotton and Zhu 1983, 479; emphasis added). In addition, the prestigious status of the proletariat gave rise to the popularity of another term, *shifu*. Originally used to address senior skilled tradesmen and craftsmen, during the Cultural Revolution, its use was extended to address all workers to express deference to the proletariat and solidarity among those identifying with the workers (Scotton and Zhu 1984).[10] Other explicit ways of signaling status differentiation and social privilege were also masked through changes in language use.

12 Introduction

For example, in the description of his visit to China in 1972, Simon Leys, a Belgian art historian and Sinologist, observes (1977, 117 cited in Evans 1978, 85):

> In trains ... first, second, and third classes have disappeared *in name*, but you have now "sitting hard"(*ying tso*) [hard seat], "sleeping hard" (*ying wo*) [hard sleeper], and "sleeping soft" (*ruan wo*) [soft sleeper], which are exactly the same classes as before and with the fares, as before, ranging from single to triple prices.

More totalitarian attempts to control language use in the public sphere were made through what is called "linguistic engineering" during the Cultural Revolution (Ji 2004). Linguistic engineering refers to processes and attempts to control and change language to affect beliefs and attitudes. The strict central control and enforcement of revolutionary discourse, including "carefully crafted words, phrases, slogans, and scripts expressing politically correct thought" (Ji 2004, 2), reached its zenith in that period. The goal of such rigorous control on language was to produce political conformity and consent among the Chinese people. Thus, the ability to produce "correct" revolutionary speech demarcated revolutionaries from their enemies. Failure and "incorrect" use of revolutionary speech would lead to draconian punishments. As vividly demonstrated in Ji (2004), the Cultural Revolution exerted a tremendous impact on the Chinese language not only in public life but also in private communication "as people resorted to safe formulae because they were uncertain about whom they could trust" (Ji 2004, 155). Under such circumstances, Mao's words, as published in *Mao Zhuxi Yulu* 'Quotations from Chairman Mao', or the *Little Red Book*, were taken to be the source for the safest and most revolutionary way of speaking and writing (ibid.). According to Ji (ibid., 155):

> The result was a profound, if temporary, impoverishment of the Chinese language, which became repetitive, narrowly political, and cliché ridden. Newspapers and journals that had once catered to intellectuals were now written in the language of political talks Mao had given with the needs of illiterate soldiers and peasants in mind.

0.5.5 The Semiotic Inadequacy of "Common Speech"

The preceding discussion shows that language in the Cultural Revolution era served as a tool to erase or mask social inequality and produce cultural and political conformity. At the same time, it was deployed to articulate dichotomizing political differentiation, or *huaqing jiexian* 'demarcate a clear line', between the proletariat revolutionaries and their enemies (Dittmer 1977; Ji 2004). As Chuang observes, since the CCP came to power, "every political campaign in China has been simultaneously a semantic campaign as well, introducing

Introduction **13**

or reviving a plethora of shibboleths and slogans with such determination and concentration...." (1968, 47; quoted in Ji 2004, 150). By the end of the Cultural Revolution, the legitimate language in the PRC, that is, 'common speech' used in public domains and in the state controlled media, had evolved into an excessively politicized language (Dittmer and Chen 1981; Ji 2004) and an icon of socialist egalitarianism and conformity. Such drastic changes in PTH led to further differentiation between the "common speech" and (standard) Mandarin varieties used elsewhere outside of mainland China. The linguist Robert Ramsey describes his impression of the contrast between news reading in PTH heard on the central radio station in the mainland and that in *Guoyu* of Taiwan[11] in the early 1980s not long after the Cultural Revolution (1987, 47; emphasis added):

> All Radio Peking announcers, both men and women, broadcast in a pitch range noticeably higher than that of their normal speaking voices. Each sentence begins high and shrill. Then pitch falls gradually, reaching a lower key by the end of the sentence. Pauses are exaggerated, and the normal rise of a nonconcluding clause becomes longer and more drawnout. The devices of this strident intonation may well be borrowed, in part, from traditional Chinese drama and opera; but **their use in the media today seems intended to arouse in the audience an impression of struggle and determination. In Taiwan, by contrast, announcers usually do not affect such deliberate intonation and instead broadcast in a lower, more conversational speaking voice.**

In summary, the development of Modern Standard Chinese, from *guoyu* 'national language' to PTH 'common speech', is part of the social-political transformations of China from an imperial and semi-colonial society in the early 20th century to a socialist society up to the 1970s. Language standardization and the standard language itself serve as tools to carry out national and political agendas; at the same time, such agendas are instantiated in the process of standardization (as shown in the vernacularization of written, literary Chinese and the simplification of the Chinese script), as well as changes in the use of the standard language (as shown in changes in language use during the Cultural Revolution).

Against this backdrop, the overly politicized, shrill, determined, and strident "common speech," adept at expressing conformity and proletarian distinction and authority, becomes severely inadequate in creating meanings of new social distinctions that are not along the single political line of separating the proletariat and their allies from their enemies. It follows that language change, including innovative ways of using language as illustrated earlier, is an inevitable and inseparable part of the ideological change to valorizing distinction and socioeconomic transformation to increasing and intensified social stratification.

14 Introduction

0.6 Overview of the Book

This book examines the emergence of an innovative linguistic style, which I call "Cosmopolitan Mandarin," and how it is used to construct new social distinctions. Taking an integrated approach to language change that treats linguistic and social change as mutually constitutive, I show that "Cosmopolitan Mandarin" (hereinafter CM) is not simply a linguistic "effect" of, or response to, the socioeconomic transformation. Rather, the emergence of CM is itself both (a) part of the social change and (b) a resource that brings about change through creating meanings of distinction that dismantle the pre-reform socialist egalitarianism, of which the conventional Beijing-Mandarin-based "common speech" is a part. The present chapter lays out the social historical context in which the research on CM is situated.

Chapter 1 discusses the theoretical underpinnings and the methodology of the study. Building on recent developments in linguistic anthropology and variationist sociolinguistics, I propose a style-based approach to the investigation of CM as an emergent stylistic resource. CM and its salient linguistic components are treated first and foremost as a meaning-making resource for the construction of styles. I specifically consider the form, content, and meaning of style and how micro-level and discourse-level variation is linked to macro-level social and historical processes. Building on and expanding linguistic anthropological conceptualizations of language ideology, bricolage, dialogism, and enregisterment, I reformulate style as a sociohistorical process mediated by ideologies of differentiation. In so doing, I develop a style-based approach to analyzing sociolinguistic change and show how such an approach illuminates the interconnectedness of social change and linguistic change.

Chapters 2, 3, and 4 locate the making of social distinctions through CM in two central sites, in businesses and in television programs, for the production of a new cosmopolitan professional identity and a new middle-class consumption-based lifestyle. Chapters 2 and 3 examine the construction of a Chinese yuppie style among the top echelon of local Chinese professionals working for international businesses. As members of a new urban elite, the yuppies epitomize China's drastic transformation. Chapter 2 provides a general description of a group of Beijing yuppies in foreign-owned businesses, or *waiqi*. The chapter highlights the difference between *waiqi* and *guoqi* 'state-owned enterprises', particularly in the different gender dynamics in the two sectors, which contributes to contrasts in language use examined in Chapter 3. Keenly differentiating themselves from the newly rich, local private entrepreneurs who are considered lacking taste and ostentatious, the yuppies present themselves as cultured cosmopolitans.

Building on the discussion of the yuppies as cultured cosmopolitans, Chapter 3 provides an in-depth analysis of the linguistic construction of the Beijing yuppies. The chapter examines the use of four linguistic features, or

Introduction **15**

variables: three local Beijing features and an innovative extralocal feature. I trace the social provenance of the four variables through recent history, connecting them to three prominent character types.

Quantitative analysis comparing the use of the linguistic variables between the *waiqi* yuppies and their counterparts in *guoqi* reveals a stark contrast in their linguistic styles. The yuppies combine nonlocal variants to construct an innovative cosmopolitan Mandarin style, whereas the *guoqi* professionals' Mandarin carries a prominent Beijing accent. Within the *waiqi* group, the gendered character of recruitment and work described in Chapter 2 imposes more constraints on women's use of Cosmopolitan Mandarin than on that of their male colleagues. Furthermore, discourse analysis demonstrates the variable ways in which female and male yuppies enact their professional persona.

Chapter 4 examines the use of CM in another prime locale of rising social distinctions: television programs promoting a new middle-class cosmopolitan lifestyle. Linguistic analysis in this chapter focuses on the speech of two trendy hosts of *S Information Station* of Tianjin Television Station, a fashion and lifestyle show targeting white-collar professionals. The hosts combine CM with other semiotic resources to create a trendy, ebullient, and convivial persona. The chapter further reveals that the making of distinction is a process of mediation whereby, through metasemiotic discourse, signs, stylistic ensembles of consumer products and practices are interpreted, evaluated, and connected to (un) desirable social images and characters. This chapter demonstrates that CM is taken up as a crucial component in the media's representation of socioeconomic change. Furthermore, the rendering of CM as indexical of a trendy cosmopolitan persona and *simultaneously* affective attributes of youthful ebullience and conviviality offers strong evidence that the emergent indexical field of CM expands to a meaning area that is not typically indexed through conventional PTH.

Chapter 5 deepens the analysis of CM through examining it as a sociohistorical process of enregisterment, addressing the question, How is CM interpreted and evaluated across a wide range of speakers? Based on a large body of metalinguistic data accumulated since the 1990s, the analysis reveals the highly contested nature of the process and a more complex picture of the social meanings of the emergent stylistic resource. As a variety of social actors participates in the evaluation and construal of Cosmopolitan Mandarin, linguistic variation at the micro level becomes a battlefield where larger cultural conflicts and tensions are fought out among individuals and between individuals and the Chinese state. The linguistic-ideological battle over enregisterment reveals that what is really at stake is the location of the evaluative center of a modern, globalizing China and what gets to be its legitimate voice.

Based on the analyses developed in Chapters 2 through 5, the concluding chapter elaborates on a style-based approach to sociolinguistics change and discusses the future of Cosmopolitan Mandarin and Standard PTH.

16 Introduction

Notes

1 The quotation is from "Let the Facts Speak for Themselves," an excerpt from Deng Xiaoping's speech given at the meeting with the Prime Minister of New Zealand, David Lange, on March 28, 1986 (Deng 1993, 1994).
2 Traditional script was in use in mainland China up to the mid-1960s when script reform began to introduce simplified characters to replace traditional characters. Simplified script is the standard written script in mainland China. See Section 0.5.3 for details on script reform. The slogan as shown in the photo is written in traditional characters: 讓沒有個性的年代一去不復返! It would look like this in simplified characters: 让没有个性的年代一去不复返!
3 By saying "semiotic inadequacy of the 'common speech'" I do not intend to make a judgment of *Putonghua* as an "inadequate" language. Nor do I embrace a static view of language that assumes the existence of a *Putongua* in the socialist past, which has now become "inadequate" in making social meanings relevant to the postsocialist present. Such views on *Putonghua* do exist, as revealed in the metapragmatic discourses analyzed in Chapter 5.
4 Readers who are interested in the linguistic complexity of Chinese can refer to works such as De Francis (1984) and Norman (1988). Chen (1999) offers a sociohistorical account of the development of Modern Standard Chinese and its relation to other regional Chinese varieties. Ramsey (1987) provides a classic overview of the languages of China.
5 The number of languages in China ranges from the official number of 80 to 120 (Sun 1999 cited in Bradley 2005) to 298 in *Ethnologue* (Lewis, Simons, and Fennig 2016).
6 Before the development of *baihua*, the relation between the most prestigious form of written Chinese and the diverse varieties of spoken vernacular likened that of Classical Arabic to spoken regional Arabic varieties.
7 According to Chen (1999, 25), the earlier term *guoyu* 'national language' established in the preceding Republic government was abandoned allegedly because the former sounded somewhat Han-chauvinistic in taking the language of one ethnic group, the Han, as the national language, ignoring the fact that there are more than 50 officially recognized ethnic groups in China, which speak over 80 different languages ....
8 I am grateful to Jin Liu for bringing to my attention the writings of Qu Qiubai on *Putonghua*.
9 Thus, for example, my name in simplified characters 张青 and its spelling as Zhang Qing can identify my mainland China origin. To obscure such a connection, I may use traditional characters and a spelling not following the *pinyin* convention, 張青 Chang Ching or Ching Chang.
10 After the Cultural Revolution in the 1980s, *shifu* was widely used to address adults regardless of their occupations (Scotton and Zhu 1984). In the early 1990s, it had lost its political connotations and was used as a general term of respect to service personnel and strangers (Lee-Wong 1994).
11 In this book Taiwan *Guoyu* is equivalent to Taiwan Mandarin.

References

Bian, Yanjie. 1994. *Work and Inequality in Urban China*. Albany, NY: State University of New York Press.

Bian, Yanjie, Ronald Breiger, Deborah Davis, and Joseph Galaskiewics. 2005. "Occupation, Class, and Social Networks in Urban China." *Social Forces* 83 (4):1143–1167.

Bradley, David. 2005. "Introduction: Language Policy and Language Endangerment in China." *International Journal of the Sociology of Language* 173:1–21.

Chen, Ping. 1999. *Modern Chinese: History and Sociolinguistics*. Cambridge: Cambridge University Press.

Chen, Ping. 2007. "China." In *Language and National Identity in Asia*, edited by Andrew Simpson, 141–167. Oxford: Oxford University Press.

China. 1983. *The Constitution of the People's Republic of China: Adopted on December 4, 1982 by the Fifth National People's Congress of the People's Republic of China at Its Fifth Session*. Beijing; New York, NY and Oxford: Pergamon Press.

Chuang, Hsin-Cheng. 1968. *The Little Red Book and Current Chinese Language*. Berkeley, CA: Center for Chinese Studies, University of California. Monograph No. 13, Studies in Chinese Communist Terminology.

Coupland, Nikolas. 2014. "Language Change, Social Change, Sociolinguistic Change: A Meta-Commentary." *Journal of Sociolinguistics* 18 (2):277–286.

Croll, Elisabeth. 2006. *China's New Consumers*. New York, NY: Routledge.

Davis, Deborah S., ed. 2000. *The Consumer Revolution in Urban China*. Berkeley, CA: University of California Press.

De Francis, John. 1950. *Nationalism and Language Reform in China*. Princeton, NJ: Princeton University Press.

De Francis, John. 1984. *The Chinese Language: Fact and Fantasy*. Honolulu: University of Hawaii Press.

Deng, Xiaoping. 1993. *"Na Shishi lai Shuohua"* ("Let the Facts Speak for Themselves"). *Deng Xiaoping Wenxuan, Disan Juan (Selected Works of Deng Xiaoping, Volume III)*. Zhonggong Zhongyang Wenxian Bianji Weiyuanhui (Compiled by The Communist Party Central Documents Compilation Committee), 155–156. Beijing: Renmin Chubanshe (People's Publishing House).

Deng, Xiaoping. 1994. "Let the Facts Speak for Themselves." *Selected Works of Deng Xiaoping, Volume III (1982–1992)*. Translated by The Bureau for the Compilation and Translation of Works of Marx, Engels, Lenin and Stalin Under the Central Committee of the Communist Party of China, 169–171. Beijing: Foreign Languages Press.

Dirlik, Arif. 2001. "Markets, Culture, Power: The Making of a 'Second Cultural Revolution' in China." *Asian Studies Review* 25 (1):1–33.

Dittmer, Lowell. 1977. "Thought Reform and Cultural Revolution: An Analysis of the Symbolism of Chinese Polemics." *The American Political Science Review* 71 (1):67–85.

Dittmer, Lowell, and Chen Ruoxi. 1981. Ethics and Rhetoric of the Chinese Cultural Revolution. Berkeley, CA: Center for Chinese Studies, Institute of East Asian Studies, University of California.

Dong, Jie. 2010. "The Enregisterment of Putonghua in Practice." *Language & Communication* 30 (4):265–275.

Dong, Jie. 2016. *The Sociolinguistics of Voice in Globalising China*. Milton Park, Abingdon, Oxon and New York, NY: Routledge.

Evans, Leslie. 1978. *China after Mao*. New York, NY: Monad Press.

Farquhar, Judith, and Qicheng Zhang. 2012. *Ten Thousand Things: Nurturing Life in Contemporary Beijing*. New York, NY: Zone Books.

Goodman, David, ed. 2008. *The New Rich in China*. London and New York, NY: Routledge.

Griffiths, Michael B. 2013. *Consumers and Individuals in China: Standing Out, Fitting In*. Abingdon, Oxon and New York, NY: Routledge.

18 Introduction

Guojia Yuyan Wenzi. 1996. *"Guowuyuan Guanyu Tuiguang Putonghua de Zhishi* (1956-02-06)" ("State Council Directives Concerning the Promotion of *Putonghua* (02-06-1956)"). In *Guojia Yuyan Wenzi Zhengce Fagui Huibian (1949–1995) (Collection of National Policies and Laws on Language and Script)*, edited by Guojia Yuyan Wenzi Gongzuo Weiyuanhui Zhengce Fagui Shi (Office for Policies and Laws under the Committee on National Language and Script), 11–16. Beijing: Yuwen Chubanshe (Philology Publishing House).

Hanser, Amy. 2008. *Service Encounters: Class, Gender, and the Market for Social Distinction in Urban China*. Stanford, CA: Stanford University Press.

Hoffman, Lisa M. 2010. *Patriotic Professionalism in Urban China: Fostering Talent.* Philadelphia, PA: Temple University Press.

Hsu, Carolyn L. 2007. *Creating Market Socialism: How Ordinary People Are Shaping Class and Status in China*. Durham, NC: Duke University Press.

Irvine, Judith, and Susan Gal. 2000. "Language Ideology and Linguistic Differentiation." In *Regimes of Language*, edited by Paul V. Kroskrity, 35–84. Santa Fe, NM: School of American Research Press.

Ji, Fengyuan. 2004. *Linguistic Engineering: Language and Politics in Mao's China.* Honolulu HI: University of Hawai'i Press.

Kemp, Martin. 2012. *Christ to Coke: How Image Becomes Icon*. Oxford and New York, NY: Oxford University Press.

Lee-Wong, Song Mei. 1994. "Address Forms in Modern China: Changing Ideologies and Shifting Semantics." *Linguistics* 32 (2):299–324.

Lewis, M. Paul, Gary F. Simons, and Charles D. Fennig, eds. 2016. *Ethnologue: Languages of the World*. Nineteenth ed. Dallas, TX: SIL International. Online version: www.ethnologue.com.

Leys, Simon. 1977. *Chinese Shadows*. New York, NY: Viking Press.

Li, Chris Wen-Chao. 2004. "Conflicting Notions of Language Purity: The Interplay of Archaising, Ethnographic, Reformist, Elitist and Xenophobic Purism in the Perception of Standard Chinese." *Language & Communication* 24:97–133.

Norman, Jerry. 1988. *Chinese*. Cambridge: Cambridge University Press.

Pun, Ngai. 2005. *Made in China: Women Factory Workers in a Global Workplace*. Durham, NC: Duke University Press.

Qu, Qiubai. 1953 [1932]. *"Dazhong Wenyi de Wenti."* ("The Problem of Popular Literature and Art"). In *Qu Qiubai Wenji (Collected Essays of Qu Qiubai)*, 884–893. Beijing: Zhongguo Wenxue Chubanshe (China Literature Publishing House).

Ramsey, S. Robert. 1987. *The Languages of China*. Princeton, NJ: Princeton University Press.

Ren, Hai. 2013. *The Middle Class in Neoliberal China: Governing Risk, Life-Building, and Themed Spaces*. London and New York, NY: Routledge.

Scotton, Carol Myers, and Wanjin Zhu. 1983. *"Tongzhi* in China: Language Change and Its Conversational Consequences." *Language in Society* 12:477–494.

Scotton, Carol Myers, and Wanjin Zhu. 1984. "The Multiple Meanings of *Shifu*: A Language Change in Progress." *Anthropological Linguistics* 26 (3):326–344.

Shen, Zhongwei. 2015. "Early Mandarin Seen from Ancient Altaic Scripts: The Rise of a New Phonological Standard." In *The Oxford Handbook of Chinese Linguistics*, edited by William S. Y. Wang, and Chaofen Sun, 91–104. Oxford and New York, NY: Oxford University Press.

State Administration for Industry and Commerce. 1998. *"Guanggao Yuyan Wenzi Guanli Zanxing Guiding"* ("Provisional Regulations on the Management of

Language and Characters in Advertisements"). www.saic.gov.cn/ggs/zcfg/200907/t20090727_69358.html. Accessed March 14, 2012.

Sun, Hong Kai. 1999. *"Zhongguo Kongbai Yuyan de Diaocha Yanjiu"* ("Research on the Endangered Languages of China"). In *Zhongguo Yuyan de Xin Tuozhan (New Developments in Chinese Linguistics)*, edited by Feng Shi, and Wuyun Pan, 3–17. Hong Kong: City University of Hong Kong.

Woronov, Terry E. 2016. *Class Work: Vocational Schools and China's Urban Youth.* Stanford, CA: Stanford University Press.

Zhang, Li. 2010. *In Search of Paradise: Middle-Class Living in a Chinese Metropolis.* Ithaca, NY: Cornell University Press.

Zhao, Shouhui, and Richard B. Baldauf Jr. 2008. *Planning Chinese Characters: Reaction, Evolution or Revolution?* New York, NY and London: Springer.

Zhou, Xiaohong, ed. 2004. *Zhongguo Zhongchan Jieceng Diaocha (Survey of the Chinese Middle Classes)*. Beijing: Zhongguo Shehui Kexue Chubanshe (China Social Sciences Press).

Zhou, Minglang, and Hongkai Sun, eds. 2004. *Language Policy in the People's Republic of China: Theory and Practice since 1949.* Boston, MA: Kluwer.

1

SOCIOLINGUISTIC CHANGE, STYLE, AND IDEOLOGY

1.1 Introduction

In this chapter, I discuss the theoretical underpinnings for the examination of Cosmopolitan Mandarin (CM) by proposing a style-based approach to sociolinguistic change. In doing so, this book contributes to recent efforts in developing an enterprise of sociolinguistic change (Androutsopoulos 2014; Coupland 2014a, 2014b, 2016). Specifically, I take an integrative approach to linguistic variation/change and social change, viewing linguistic change as constitutive of social change. I therefore situate the emergence of CM as part of a broader socioeconomic and ideological shift in China. Linguistic innovations, such as CM, are emergent resources articulating and bringing about new social distinctions. Below, I discuss in more detail works in sociolinguistics and linguistic anthropology that I build on in developing a style-based approach to sociolinguistic change.

As Coupland (2014b) points out, the idea of sociolinguistic change—the embedding or integration of linguistic change within social change—is not new. It was planted in the incipient stage of sociolinguistics, in the writings of the field's pioneers (e.g., Gumperz 1964; Hymes 1964, 1974; Labov 1963). Calls for integrating analysis of language change within broader sociopolitical-economic processes have been going on for a long time. For example, Cameron (1990), Fairclough (1992), and many linguistic anthropologists, such as Susan Gal (1989a), Jane Hill (1985, 2006), Judith Irving (1989), and Kathryn Woolard (1985, 1989), have called for incorporating studies of language change (including linguistic innovation and change during language shift and obsolescence) within a broader political economy. As Hill (2006, 334) notes, there is no simple, direct, causal relation between language and sociocultural change, but "the complex mediations between cultural and linguistic systems" must be

Sociolinguistic Change, Style, and Ideology **21**

included in any investigation of linguistic and cultural change that takes the social issue seriously.

Numerous works by linguistic anthropologists, including those cited above, have powerfully illuminated the integral and mutually constitutive nature of language and social change. They examine the use of linguistic elements and their social significance created and construed by social actors as they engage in activities and practices—ranging from the daily mundane to larger projects of modernity and urbanization—in their changing local political economy, which is also often entangled in larger historical and global processes. Language change as examined in such works includes change in the narrower sense of the term at the structural levels of linguistic systems (Gal 1989b; Hill 1985; Hill and Hill 1997; Wong 2005), as well as changes in "discursive practices" more broadly defined (Coupland 2014a, 282), including particular discursive practices, such as changes in business names (Yurchak 2000); writing love letters and a new "development discourse" (Ahearn 2001); variation and change in speech styles (Errington 1988); language shift (Gal 1979; Kulick 1992); the emergence of new registers or styles in the form of named languages, such as "Town Bemba" (Spitulnik 1998), "Urban Wolof" (Swigart 2000) or "Dakar Wolof" (McLaughlin 2001), and "Japanese Women's Language" (Inoue 2006a); and in the form of a "clean" voice invoking a new Christian identity and Christian progress in contemporary South Korea (Harkness 2014).

Much recent discussion on an integrated approach to language and social change—including Coupland's (2014a, 2014b, 2016) proposal for sociolinguistic change—has also come out of critical reflections of the research done in variationist sociolinguistics. Pioneered in the works of William Labov (1966, 1972), this branch of sociolinguistics takes as its primary focus the systematic investigation of language variation and change. It is considered by many sociolinguists, including Coupland (2014b, 68), "the most cohesively and extensively developed paradigm in sociolinguistics." However, the variationist approach, particularly what has become known as the "Labovian Paradigm" (e.g., Gordon 2013, 78) or "First Wave" variationist sociolinguistics (Eckert 2012), has been criticized for prioritizing the discovery of "the most general principles that govern language structure and language change" (Labov 1994, 115) over developing serious social accounts of language variation and change (e.g., Coupland 2007, 9; 2014b, 69; Eckert 2008, 454). Advances in variationist sociolinguistics over the past two decades have thus concentrated on developing more sophisticated accounts of the social meaning of variation and the ways in which linguistic variation and change are involved in emergent and changing social landscapes. Recent work, which is referred to as the "Third Wave" approach to variation (Eckert 2012, 2016), incorporates the social with the linguistic by treating variation as meaning-making resources in the construction of styles. Building on works that integrate linguistic and social change in linguistic anthropology and sociolinguistics, I elaborate on a style-based approach to

22 Sociolinguistic Change, Style, and Ideology

sociolinguistic change in the rest of the chapter. Section 1.2 discusses the crucial theoretical and conceptual tools that inform the investigation of CM, and Section 1.3 explains the methodology that enables such an investigation.

1.2 Style and Ideology in Sociolinguistic Change

As "a pivotal construct in the study of sociolinguistic variation" (Rickford and Eckert 2001, 1), style has been a focal area in the theoretical and methodological development in the sociocultural analysis of language variation and change over the past half century. Style figured prominently in Labov's (1966) foundational work on linguistic variation and change as a methodological and theoretical tool to reveal the orderly heterogeneity of a sociolinguistic structure and "establish the direction and path" of linguistic change in progress (Labov 1994, 158; see also Labov 1972, 2001, 104–105). Two major early approaches known as "attention paid to speech" (Labov 1966, 1972) and "audience design" (Bell 1984, 2001) treat stylistic variation as unidimensional along the axis of formality as a result of varying amount of attention paid to speech, and as accommodation in response to audience types.

More recent advances have been the result of addressing limitations of the earlier approaches; specifically, recent work has explored the multidimensionality of style, integrating it within a wider range of linguistic practices and semiotic resources for making social meaning (Bucholtz 2011; Coupland 2007; Mendoza-Denton 2008). Advances in the sociolinguistic study of style since the 1990s have also paralleled the general trend of taking a more practice-based approach to sociolinguistic variation (Eckert and McConnell-Ginet 1992), examining linguistic variation and variables as meaning-making resources for the construction of social relations, identities, and communities (Bucholtz 2011; Coupland 2007; Eckert 2000; Mendoza-Denton 2008).[1] Studies have thus expanded from a focus on dialectal, particularly phonological, variables because of their role in linguistic change in progress to a wide range of socially significant linguistic resources and their syntagmatic bundling (Auer 2007; Bucholtz 1999a; Chun 2001, 2009; Hernández-Campoy and Cutillas-Espinosa 2012; Moore and Podesva 2009; Podesva 2007; Podesva, Roberts, and Campbell-Kibler 2002; Shankar 2008; Snell 2010; Starr 2015). Style—and indeed styling—has been examined as an agentive, reflexive, and relational process of meaning making whereby language users position themselves vis-à-vis others in their local communities situated within broader sociocultural-historical landscapes (Bucholtz 2011; Bucholtz and Hall 2005; Coupland 2001; Johnstone 1999; Nakassis 2016; Rampton 2011a, 2011b; Schilling-Estes 1998, 2004).

The central goal of this book is to develop a style-based approach to sociolinguistic change that views linguistic change and innovation as emerging stylistic resources for making distinction. My approach enables an analysis of linguistic

Sociolinguistic Change, Style, and Ideology **23**

change and social change as mutually constitutive, embedding linguistic innovation within a broader process of sociopolitical transformation. Ultimately, the book intends to address a crucial issue raised by Coupland (2007, 100): "how 'style' has a particular role to play in effecting change."

1.2.1 Why Style?

As China becomes culturally and economically more diversified under the general shift toward valorizing difference, people are increasingly orienting to "styles," that is, distinctiveness on multiple axes of differentiation, including age, gender, sexuality, and social class, in art, music, fashion, advertising, and so on (Baranovitch 2003; de Kloet 2010; Griffiths 2013; Hanser 2008; Osburg 2013; Otis 2012; Ren 2013; Rofel 1999, 2007; Wang 2008; Yang 1999; Z. Zhang 2000, L. Zhang 2010). Hence, "style" is not just an academic term for the analysts' observation and understanding of the semiotic practices of the people they study. It is also a prevalent experience and a cultural practice that social actors (individuals, institutions, and corporations) engage in their everyday lives. However, diversification of style in the present does not imply that it was irrelevant in the past. Contrary to popular beliefs of pre-reform China, and communist regimes in general, as lacking style (see, e.g., Ewen 1999, 113), style was as pertinent then as it is today. The difference is that the pre-reform socialist style, particularly during the Cultural Revolution, was organized under an oppressive ideology of conformity and homogeneity to effect socialist egalitarianism. The conformity in linguistic expressions during the Cultural Revolution as described in the previous chapter paralleled homogeneity in styles of clothing, music, and art (e.g., Andrews 1994; Benewick 1999; Sullivan 2008). Hence, rather than lacking style, the means and meaning of stylistic distinction were tightly regimented, centered along a highly politicized boundary between "us," "the people" who were loyal to Mao and by extension, the party-state, and "them," the domestic and foreign enemies of the country and the proletarian revolution (e.g., Dutton 2005; Yang 1997). Performing and conforming to the homogeneous style avoided risks of breaking rank with the revolutionary masses (*geming qunzhong*). Thus, the historical-social-political saliency of style in the past and in the present makes it a productive lens to examine the integral relation between linguistic and social change.

In other words, to examine the ways in which linguistic and social change are mutually constitutive, we can examine these styles—the past and the present, and specifically, the ways the present breaks with the past—as embedded in the broader processes of sociopolitical transformation. More specifically, I treat CM as a powerful resource to dismantle the former Maoist stylistic regime organized under the ideology of socialist egalitarianism, hence the subtitle of the book, *Undoing Commonness*. I argue that the rise of CM not only disrupts the linguistic dominance of the "common speech," the conventional

24 Sociolinguistic Change, Style, and Ideology

Beijing-Mandarin-based standard PTH, but more importantly, it is among the emerging stylistic resources that shatter and transform the hegemony of the Maoist stylistic regime by creating meanings that are distinctive from all that "commonness" represents, such as collectivism, ordinariness, "the people"— the proletariat—and uncouthness. Similarly, proletarian plainness and austerity, the overarching principle of the Maoist stylistic regime, served as an instrument of power in overturning the old establishment and maintaining proletarian dominance. Hence, as much today as in the past, style constitutes a "weapon in strategies of distinction" (Bourdieu 1984, 66). It is the link between the configuration and use of meaning-making resources—including linguistic resources—and broader sociopolitical orders and processes.

1.2.2 Style as Ideological Systems of Distinction

Drawing on recent conceptualizations of style (e.g., Coupland 2007; Eckert 2000, 2008; Irvine 2001; Bucholtz 2011), I treat style as an emergent system of distinction (Irvine 2001), constituted by linguistic and other semiotic resources and practices that make distinction meaningful; it is a sociohistorical process, mediated by ideologies of differentiation. This view of style directs attention away from traditional variationist focus on the direction and path of linguistic change and shared norms among members of a speech community.[2] In treating style as a tool to dismantle the Maoist stylistic regime, this book carries the Third Wave variationist approach to style—as a meaning-making resource and process—to a new level: It examines how style, the use and configuration of meaning-making resources, participates in making and changing social and political order.

As an ideological system of distinction, style takes a central place in the representation, (re)production, and contestation of power, negotiation of positions, and the making of social and political order in general (e.g., Ewen 1999; Irvine 2001). This role of style is illuminated by scholars in a variety of disciplines, some of which have inspired Third Wave analysis of the linguistic construction of style: Bourdieu's classic theorization on distinction (1984) and symbolic power (1991), works on youth subcultures in the United Kingdom by the Birmingham School of Cultural Studies (e.g., Hall and Jefferson 1976; Hebdige 1979), James Ferguson's (1999) anthropological analysis of the localist and cosmopolitan style of the mineworkers on the Zambian Copperbelt, Leona Auslander's (1996) historical account of changing furniture styles as a means to produce and maintain the power of the French state in different political regimes, and David Kuchta's (1996) analysis of contesting male fashion styles in England's transition from an aristocratic to bourgeois society.

In all the cases mentioned above, ideology mediates the constitution and organization of styles as systems of distinction. Thus, we can speak of stylistic regimes (Auslander 1996; see also Gal 2012; Kroskrity 2000).[3] The notion of "stylistic regime" highlights that style is imbricated with power and related issues including dominance, hegemony, legitimacy, and contestation. It also emphasizes the role of ideology in the organization and regimentation of the means and meanings of stylistic resources such that contrasting styles in a stylistic regime, similar to linguistic resources in a sociolinguistic regime (Gal 2012), are organized in a certain, often hierarchical, social order. "[H]ierarchical and hierarchizing" (Bourdieu 1991, 152), styles (and their meanings) are shaped by (changes in) the social-political structure, the use of which can position stylistic agents in their social landscape. On the other hand, change in styles and emerging new styles can disrupt an established stylistic regime and consequently constitute and invoke change in an established social order. For example, the drastic shift from diverse artistic styles, and indeed those in all spheres of social life, of pre- and early-socialist China to the homogenized style in the Maoist stylistic regime (Andrews 1994; Chang 1980; Sullivan 2008) was not simply the effect produced by political change but part of the de-eliticization project, aiming to overturn the old social hierarchy by replacing the old elites with the new, proletarian elite.

As beliefs that promote and legitimate the interests of some "socially significant" groups over those of other groups (Eagleton 1991, 29) and in so doing legitimate and maintain the power of such groups, ideology is at the heart of changing stylistic regimes as in the case of China and elsewhere mentioned earlier (e.g., Auslander 1996; Hebdige 1979; Kuchta 1996). Furthermore, as the distinctiveness of a style becomes meaningful only when contrasted with other styles (Ferguson 1999; Irvine 2001), ideology, as "construed practice" (Woolard 1998, 10), shapes people's understanding of socially salient poles of distinction (Ferguson 1999, 95; Irvine 2001, 24); it further shapes the interpretation and evaluation of stylistic elements and practices to create such distinction. For instance, language ideology shapes the construal of linguistic differentiation in the construction of styles between the nobles and griots among Wolof villagers (Irvine 2001), among communities of practice in high schools in the United States and the United Kingdom (Bucholtz 2011; Eckert 2000; Moore and Podesva 2009; Shankar 2008), and between the Norteñas and the Sureñas among gang-affiliated Latinas (Mendoza-Denton 2008). Even the "partially unintelligible" elements and practices that seem to lack a clear "meaning" to an observer and the stylistic agents themselves (if asked explicitly "what does it mean?") take on social significance in a style through a process of construal (Ferguson 1999, 210). Such examples include safety pins and swastikas used by the British punks (Hebdige 1979), the out-of-place and nonsensical English phrases printed on T-shirts and other seemingly unintelligible "noises" that constitute the Zambian Copperbelt's cosmopolitan style (Ferguson 1999), and the "Chinglish" translation of the Chinese advertisement in the previous chapter. Similarly, "indistinction" in the Maoist regime, epitomized in the simple and drab clothing style, and "invidious indistinction" in the sartorial

26 Sociolinguistic Change, Style, and Ideology

style and "inconspicuous consumption" practiced by both aristocratic and middle-class men in late 18th-century and early 19th-century England (Kuchta 1996, 52) took on social significance through ideological construals in their respective systems of distinction, i.e., stylistic regimes. In both cases, indistinction was deployed—more coercively in China—as a strategy of distinction in the struggle for social and political legitimacy and dominance. In China, the proletariat won, which led to the establishment of a socialist regime, whereas in England, the victory of the middle class paved the way to a bourgeois society. Hence, style is as much about distinction as about the struggle over its means and meanings and about the ordering of styles in a stylistic regime.

In the first vignette in the opening chapter, innovative language is used to create new social distinction in a real estate advertisement. However, despite the state-supported overall shift to valorizing difference, the following example attests to the struggle very often involved in the making of distinction through language. From 2007 to 2011, various municipal administrations initiated measures to 'regulate' (*guifan*), 'clean up' (*qingli*), and 'rectify' (*zhengdun*) outdoor advertisements in Beijing and other major cities, including Chongqing, Chengdu, and Zhengzhou (Chinanews 2011). Language use was a major area to be disciplined, particularly by prohibiting "opulent and exaggerating" expressions that "flaunt wealth" (Wu 2007). Such expressions include 'luxury' (*haohua*), 'royal' (*huangjia*), 'supreme' (*zhizun*), 'high class' (*gaodang*), 'unique' (*duyiwuer*), and misleading uses of 'villa' (*bieshu*), and 'luxury residence' (*haozhai*), et cetera (Chinanews 2011; Moore 2011; Wu 2007). They are considered to advocate 'hedonism' (*xianglezhuyi*), 'feudalism and imperialism' (*fengjian diwang*), 'adulation of everything foreign' (*chongyangmeiwai*), 'monarchy and aristocracy' (*tianhuang guizu*) (Beijing Bureau of Industry and Commerce 2011; Chinanews 2011), and "deviating from the traditional Chinese virtue of thrifty and simplicity" and "disruptive of social harmony" (Wu 2007). Hence, despite the state-initiated and -supported valorization of difference, contentions abound in *how* distinctions are, or should be, constructed and expressed. Analysis of CM in Chapter 5 reveals contestation over its meanings vis-à-vis the conventional PTH and their relation in terms of legitimacy and dominance. Further, such struggle and debates over linguistic issues stand in for larger social and political concerns in the transformation of the Maoist stylistic regime and the emergence of a postsocialist regime (see also Cavanaugh 2008; Gramsci 1985, 183–184; Hill 1998; Inoue 2006b). Thus, this book will shed light on how such a regime is coming into being. Foregrounding ideology and power embedded in the notion of stylistic regime, a style-based approach to sociolinguistic change thus enables us to expand the traditional variationist focus on the orderly heterogeneity of sociolinguistic structure to ask deeper and broader questions that incorporate the linguistic with the social: How is the orderliness established and maintained? What does such a sociolinguistic structure—which is indeed a "sociolinguistic regime"—do in terms of organizing and managing linguistic variation and consequently regimenting, positioning, and evaluating language users (Gal 2012)? The goal of asking such questions is to "engage with the political and ideological implications of sociolinguistic variation" and change (Coupland 2007, 83).

Furthermore, an emphasis on ideology, particularly language ideology, entails attention to its multiplicity and contestation (Gal 1998), which falls outside the remit of a model that focuses on the orderliness of sociolinguistic variation manifested in shared norms of evaluation and "uniformity of abstract patterns of variation which are invariant in respect to particular levels of usage" (Labov 1972, 121). Both the shared norms of evaluation and the uniformity of class and stylistic variation found in Labov's pioneering work were cited by Bourdieu as evidence for the linguistic hegemony or the "invisible, silent [symbolic] violence" of the "standard" language (Bourdieu 1991, 52; see also Silverstein 2016). However, as Woolard (1985) and a host of others have argued (e.g., Gal 1998; Haeri 1997; Inoue 2006b; Rampton 2003; Q. Zhang 2005), linguistic hegemony is never complete and invincible. The symbolic power of language, as Bourdieu explains, depends on a language ideology that recognizes (or, in his term, misrecognizes) the legitimacy of a dominant language and its users (1991, 168–170). Consequently, its destruction "depends on *becoming aware* of its arbitrary nature" (Bourdieu 1991, 277 n8; original emphasis). Thus, examining linguistic ideology, specifically, ideological contestations—the focus of Chapter 5—elucidates conflicting construals of linguistic styles regarding their "normativity," "authenticity," and "legitimacy," all of which are arbitrary, ideologically laden essences endowed on particular ways of speaking. Revealing the rising awareness of the arbitrary nature of linguistic hegemony sheds light on another crucial issue, that is, the impetus for sociolinguistic change (see also Milroy 2004).

1.2.3 Style as a Sociohistorical Process

The above discussion further indicates that styles are bound up with the social and political circumstances and exigencies of their particular historical moments. Intertwined with changing ideologies, they condition the possibilities of style. Thus, the proletarian plainness of clothing style and the highly political and formulaic language in the Maoist regime were not only a strategy of distinction but also "a strategy of survival" (Butler 1999, 178) because the performance of style can have "punitive consequences" (ibid.). Hence, in order to survive in the Maoist regime, one had to adopt the style of indistinction and conformity as illustrated in the black-and-white photo in Figure 0.2. Punitive consequences, often experienced by marginalized and minority groups, have been well documented by sociolinguists (Barrett 2006; Baugh 2000; Roth-Gordon 2009), revealing social injustices committed on the basis of ways of speaking. In China, incompetence in using the legitimate linguistic style can

28 Sociolinguistic Change, Style, and Ideology

lead to dire material and symbolic losses for rural migrants living and working in urban cities pursuing upward socioeconomic mobility. Legitimate style varies in the local political economy, for example, speaking "correctly" in Standard PTH among the rural migrant pupils in a Beijing primary school (Dong 2009) and the speaking of Hong Kong Cantonese (but not other varieties of mainland Cantonese) by rural women migrant workers—also known as *dagong-mei* 'working girls'—in a factory owned by Hong Kong capital in Shenzhen, Guangdong Province (Pun 2005, Chapter 4). Thus, as shown later in Chapters 2 and 3, CM without doubt differentiates its users, the Beijing yuppies, from other salient groups, including other wealthy locals and managers working for state-owned enterprises. However, its use is not fully a personal choice and preference. It is, to a certain extent, a strategy of survival, in the sense that CM constitutes the symbolic capital for the Beijing yuppies as viable players in the transnational Chinese and global linguistic markets. This aspect is particularly highlighted in the differential use of CM between the women yuppies and their male counterparts examined in Chapter 3.

Historical conditioning of the possibilities of style, such as political and cultural conformity in the Cultural Revolution and encouragement of differentiation in the postsocialist market economy, is one reason style should be examined as a sociohistorical process. The investigation of style within the particularities of the local historical, political, and economic context addresses the broad question of why a particular style comes to be at a particular historical juncture (see also Inoue 2002).[4] This is a crucial question for developing a style-based approach to sociolinguistic change. To explore the details of the emergence of a style, more specific questions need to be asked, particularly, how do stylistic-linguistic resources take on meaning potential, and where do social meanings come from (see also Coupland 2007, 81)? When and how is the distinctiveness and social significance of a (new) style and its elements recognized, interpreted, made known, and disseminated (Agha 2005)? What social and political work does an emergent style do? The answers to these questions require a sociohistorical perspective on the emergence of a style, its constituents, and their meanings. In what follows, I discuss three conceptual tools that are valuable for treating style as a sociohistorical process: (1) bricolage (Lévi-Strauss 1966), (2) the Bakhtinian notion of dialogism (Bakhtin 1981, 1986), and (3) enregisterment (Agha 2007).

1.2.3.1 Bricolage

Underlying the growing body of scholarship on the sociolinguistic analysis of style is an understanding that style is constructed through the (re)use and (re)combination of linguistic and other semiotic resources. This is a process of "bricolage," originally discussed in Lévi-Strauss (1966), whereby existing semiotic resources are appropriated and combined to create something new. Inspired by the Birmingham School of British cultural studies that adopted the notion in the investigation of youth subcultures in the United Kingdom (e.g., Hall and Jefferson 1976; Hebdige 1979), sociolinguists have applied the concept to examine the linguistic construction of styles (e.g., Bucholtz 2002; Eckert 2000, 2012; Gagné 2008; Hachimi 2012; Tsiplakou and Ioannidou 2012; Wong and Zhang 2000; Q. Zhang 2005). What draws these researchers to the concept of bricolage is the idea of creating something new and distinctive through (re)combining resources. However, two other crucial aspects of the concept also inform the linguistic analysis of style construction: (1) underspecificity and multifunctionality, and (2) semiotic potentials and constraints. As Lévi-Strauss (1966, 17–19) observes, in bricolage, the resources are only specialized to a certain degree but are not specific enough for each one to serve a specific function. In other words, the "bricoleur" or stylistic agent must "make do with whatever is at hand" (1966, 17); the same tool or material may be employed in multiple projects to serve different functions. Hence, the underspecified nature of such existing resources affords them semiotic, meaning-making potential for "indexical mutability" (Eckert 2012, 94; see also Eckert 2016, 70; Jaffe 2016, 89–92).[5] At the same time, the bricoleur does not have unlimited freedom to improvise and manoeuver. According to Lévi-Strauss, the resources come "pre-constrained" (1966, 19; emphasis added):

> ... the possible combinations of which are restricted by the fact that **they are drawn from the language where they already possess a sense which sets a limit on their freedom of manoeuvre.**

What we can see from the above discussion is that bricolage draws attention to not only the agency of stylistic agents but also a sociohistorical process that is inherently dialogic, involving the interconnection between the social history of semiotic resources and their iterations in changing contexts. As the above quote shows, bricolage is readily linked to the Bakhtinian notion of dialogism (Bakhtin 1981, 1986).

1.2.3.2 Dialogism

According to Bakhtin, "a characteristic of all living language is the uninterrupted process of historical becoming" (1981, 288). The dialogic orientation of language rejects the view of language as an abstract, discretely bounded grammatical system that is predetermined and unitary. With this perspective of language as dynamic, emergent, and sociohistorically situated and constituted, words and forms when used by a speaker in a particular sociohistorical environment enter into a dialogic relationship or interrelationship with "alien words, value judgments and accents" (Bakhtin 1981, 276) and with its own uses by other speakers in other sociohistorical contexts. At the same time, they enter an intersubjective relationship, another form of dialogism, with the listener's

30 Sociolinguistic Change, Style, and Ideology

"apperceptive background"—the subjective belief system of "the understanding receiver"—in anticipation of the listener's response (Bakhtin 1981, 282). In Bakhtin's words,

> The living utterance, having taken meaning and shape at a particular historical moment in a socially specific environment, cannot fail to brush up against thousands of living dialogic threads, woven by socio-ideological consciousness around the given object of an utterance. (1981, 276)

> [Thus,] there are no "neutral" words and forms—words and forms that belong to "no one"; language has been completely taken over, shot through with intentions and accents. ... Each word tastes of the context and contexts in which it has lived its socially charged life.... (1981, 293)

A dialogically informed perspective treats style as "a complex and multiplanar phenomenon" (Bakhtin 1986, 92) and emphasizes the sociohistorical embeddedness of its constitution and meanings. It is shaped not only by what we say (the referential, semantic content) and how we say it ("the expressive aspect, ... the speaker's evaluative attitude toward the referentially semantic element in the utterance" (ibid., 90)), but crucially, by the "dialogic overtones" (ibid., 92) imbued in our utterance, linking what we say now (in response) to what has already been said and (in anticipation of) subsequent responses (ibid., 90–94). Such sociohistorical imbuedness of language functions as constraints on the use of stylistic resources and their meaning potentials, and at the same time affords the potential for stylistic distinction (Bakhtin 1981, 275). Thus, a dialogic perspective informs an analysis of style and social meaning as emergent and historically contingent. Consequently, taking into account the "dialogic overtones," or sociocultural associations imbued in linguistic forms or stylistic resources, enables a better understanding of their recontextualizations (Bauman and Briggs 1990)[6] as they move across discursive encounters.[7] As numerous sociolinguistic studies on style have shown, the imbued social significance of linguistic resources conditions how they are used and by whom (e.g., Barrett 1999; Bell 2001, 2007; Bucholtz 1999b; Coupland 2001; Kiesling 1998; Mendoza-Denton 2011; Podesva 2011; Schilling-Estes 2004; Wong and Zhang 2000; Wong 2005; Zhang 2008), their differential availability or accessibility to particular users (e.g., Johnstone 1999; Mendoza-Denton 1996), and who has the right—the legitimacy—to recontextualization/reappropriation (Bauman and Briggs 1990, 76; Bucholtz 2011, Chapter 6; Chun 2004).

In Chapter 3, I explicate in detail the imbued social significance of all the salient linguistic features that constitute the contrast between CM and Beijing-Mandarin-based "common speech." The socially, and indeed politically, charged life of the latter in recent Chinese history was explored in the Introduction. An understanding of what is imbued in the existing linguistic

Sociolinguistic Change, Style, and Ideology **31**

resources informs analyses of their recombination and recontextualization in new style projects.

Treating style as bricolage and taking dialogism into account highlight that the dynamic and emergent construction of styles in the situated, immediate here and now is dialogically linked to other styles (within and without a stylistic regime) in other places and times. Also, it reminds us of the sociohistorically imbued semiotic import in stylistic resources that both potentiate and constrain their recontextualizations. All of these contribute to making the distinctiveness of a style and its elements meaningful. If the distinctiveness of a style is to be socially meaningful and effective, we must ask a further question: How is its distinctiveness recognized and interpreted, not only by the immediate stylistic agents themselves in the production of styles—in the process of bricolage—and by the analyst, but also by a broader range of language users in a given population? To answer this question, we must treat style as a process of enregisterment (Agha 2007, 186; Eckert 2008, 456; Harkness 2014, 234 n12).

1.2.3.3 Enregisterment

Enregisterment is a sociohistorical process whereby particular linguistic (and other semiotic) forms or sets of forms come to be socially recognized, i.e., enregistered, as distinct and are linked to schemes of social meanings or values by a given population of speakers (Agha 2005, 38; 2007, 4, 168). This concept is especially useful in examining the emergence of new styles and stylistic resources, as it provides a tool to examine (a) how linguistic innovation becomes socially meaningful and (b) how it is embedded in the changing social-political life of the community. Particularly, the investigation of the enregisterment of CM addresses the following questions: when and how a new style, including its salient components, becomes recognized; how it comes to be associated with social meanings and cultural values; and what those values are. Furthermore, as the linking of linguistic forms to cultural values is through a reflexive, meta-discursive process of valorization (Agha 2007), a process that is ideologically informed, the enregisterment of CM can reveal patterns of evaluation that shed light on shared and contesting ideologies of language.

The ideological valorizations (and counter-valorizations) reveal the social positioning of groups of speakers and in this way, anchor linguistic innovation and its social significance to particular larger social-political concerns. As Chapter 5 shows, such concerns center on normativity, authenticity, legitimacy, and modernity. Competing definitions of the aforementioned indicate shifting and contested evaluative centers of authority (Blommaert 2007), which further illuminate whose interests are at stake as CM is becoming an alternative, competing supraregional Mandarin style to the conventional Standard PTH. In this way, the book seeks to demonstrate that CM dismantles the Maoist stylistic

32 Sociolinguistic Change, Style, and Ideology

regime in two ways: (1) through its use by particular groups of social actors to produce social distinction, CM participates in the increasing socioeconomic diversification of Chinese society; (2) through its valorizations vis-à-vis the conventional standard language, CM participates in the shaping and configuration of the postsocialist stylistic regime. In the next section, I discuss the methodology that enables an integrated approach to the emergence of CM and how it participates in the "undoing of commonness."

1.3 Methodology

Taking a style-based approach to the emergence of CM entails treating linguistic variation and innovation as emergent meaning-making resources. Hence, this is a project that first, centrally, focuses on meanings of distinction: the semiotic resources for making distinction and the ways in which meanings of distinction are made. Second, by treating style as a sociohistorical process of enregisterment mediated by ideologies of differentiation, this project focuses on the reflexive processes of meaning making—that is, how emergent stylistic resources are recognized as socially salient and come to be linked to typified personae, social attributes, and cultural values via ideological construals. These two major concerns require examination of several types of data and methods of data analysis. Fundamentally, the use of such data and methods of analysis seeks to reveal the "total linguistic fact" that encompasses linguistic forms, their use in context, and the language ideology that mediates the forms and their use (Silverstein 1985). In doing so, this book builds on and combines the strengths of both linguistic anthropology and (variationist) sociolinguistics in the investigation of CM as sociolinguistic change (see also Woolard 2008). In what follows, I explain in detail the types of data and methods of analysis used in this book. I provide the other methodological details—including descriptions of participants and sources of data sets—in Chapters 2 through 5 as different sets of data are presented and analyzed.

The first type of data consists of, for lack of a better term, "production data," that is, linguistic data produced by the speakers under study. All data produced by participants are "production" data, but I use this term specifically to differentiate it from the data discussed later: metalinguistic data. Hence, production data is intended to be understood here as linguistic data produced by speakers where language is not used to explicitly talk about itself and its use.[8] Such data sets are collected from high-quality audio recordings to enable analysis of micro-level linguistic practice, specifically in this book, the use of minute variation in the pronunciation of specific sound features, in addition to the use of the recorded data for content analysis. This type of production data is essential for establishing a clear description of the linguistic components of CM and, consequently, its linguistic differentiation from Beijing-Mandarin-based PTH. In other words, this data helps answer the question: What does CM sound like

Sociolinguistic Change, Style, and Ideology **33**

and how does it sound different from "common speech?" Production data is also indispensable for addressing the question of how and what social meanings are created through the use of linguistic features by social actors in context, including the sound features that do not have denotational meanings in themselves. This question will be discussed in detail below in methods of data analysis. The analyses in Chapters 3 and 4 are primarily conducted on this type of data.

The second type of data is metadiscursive in nature, where language functions as a metasign. In other words, such data consists of language being used to talk about linguistic and other signs, in terms of how they are to be interpreted, evaluated, regimented, and so on (Gal 2016, 114; Lucy 1993). This type of data is required for examining the reflexive processes of meaning making described above; it is particularly needed for revealing the ideological mediation of enregisterment. One set of this kind of data consists of metasemiotic discourse examined in Chapter 4 where language is used to evaluate and regiment stylistic assemblages of consumer products and practices in a TV program on consumption and lifestyle. As the analysis of Chapter 4 shows, metasemiotic discourse mediates the making of distinction by organizing and linking signs—in this case, consumer products and practices—to stylish and cosmopolitan personae and a new urban lifestyle, turning the signs into social indexes (Agha 2011; Inoue 2007). Moreover, the metasemiotic discourse consists not only of the content of talk, which is evaluative and didactic in nature, but equally important, of the form of talk, or *how* the metasemiotic discourse is produced. By examining the form of such metasemiotic talk, i.e., details of the use of linguistic variation at the phonological and lexical level, Chapter 4 reveals that clusters of linguistic features constitutive of CM are used in the metadiscourse that links stylistic configurations to the aforementioned personae and lifestyle. In this way, I am able to show that CM gets indirectly linked to them through co-occurring with other nonlinguistic signs in the stylistic configurations created in the metasemiotic talk. Thus, the co-occurring signs are presented and construed as indexically congruent (Agha ibid., 34), which is based on an ideology of appropriateness. In other words, the linguistic and the nonlinguistic signs are combined and presented as fitting together, looking as well as sounding "appropriate" for the personae enacted in the TV show.

Whereas the metasemiotic discourse examined in Chapter 4 is primarily talk about nonlinguistic signs, the data examined in Chapter 5 is metalinguistic, discourse specifically about language and language use. Metalinguistic discourse, as manifestations of language ideologies, is particularly pivotal in any project on the mutual mediation and constitution of the linguistic and the social (Gal 2016; see also Inoue 2006a, 17–24; Silverstein 1993). It is the primary kind of data needed to examine processes of enregisterment because it reveals the recognition of the distinctiveness of linguistic forms and the interpretations of their social significance (Agha 2007). As shown in Chapter 5, this kind of data enables a more sophisticated analysis of social meaning, by revealing not

34 Sociolinguistic Change, Style, and Ideology

only the fluidity and multiplicity of indexicality but also orders of indexicality motivated by ideologically informed metapragmatics (Silverstein 1998, 2003). In this way, my analysis of metalinguistic data produces a more comprehensive and complex picture of the social meanings of CM than what is revealed in Chapters 3 and 4. Furthermore, examining metalinguistic data can shed light on all five dimensions of sociolinguistic change as outlined in Coupland (2014b; highlighted in the following discussion). As Coupland (ibid., 77) points out, metalinguistic discourse is itself a crucial part of *discursive practices* and where *cultural reflexivity* becomes visible. In other words, by examining metalinguistic discourse, we can reveal the awareness, recognition, and evaluation of the social significance of language change. Furthermore, evaluative discourses about language change reveal changing and contesting *language ideologies*. As shown in Chapter 5, much of the metalinguistic discourse concerns *social normativity*, which is a focal point of ideological contestation as well as part of social change. Indistinction was normative in the Maoist regime but is considered "abnormal" and shunned in today's China. Thus, investigating metalinguistic discourse, itself a regulatory and regimenting practice (Cameron 1990, 92; Gal 2016; Silverstein 1993), can tell us a great deal about how the order of stylistic regimes, including sociolinguistic regimes, is (re)produced, contested, and changing. Finally, metalinguistic discourse is also a pivotal site for investigating the *mediation and mediatization* of sociolinguistic change. Through evaluative discourse on language use and change, linguistic change gets linked to and embedded into "culturally meaningful frameworks" (Coupland 2014b, 79), and mass-mediated, or -mediatized, metalinguistic discourse (see Chapters 4 and 5) plays a pivotal role in the "heightening of sociolinguistic reflexivity" (ibid., 78). This sociolinguistic reflexivity is part of cultural reflexivity—specifically, reflexivity about the sociolinguistic differences between CM and Beijing-Mandarin-based PTH—which can consequently shape the social significance of language change. Thus, based on the above discussion, metalinguistic discourse should be a primary part of any account of sociolinguistic change (Coupland 2014a, 283).

In addition to multiple types of data, a combination of quantitative and qualitative methods of data analysis is needed to achieve an integrated analysis of the emergence of CM. First, this is a project on sociolinguistic variation and change: the use of variable forms of linguistic features that constitute an innovative way of speaking Mandarin. Particularly, it focuses on a few sound features or phonological variables. Although CM also includes new Chinese expressions and Mandarin–English code-mixing, it is the use of these alternative sound features, or phonological variants, that makes it *sound* different from the Beijing-Mandarin-based PTH, which in comparison to CM is referred to in this book as the conventional or conservative PTH. To establish the linguistic differentiation between the conventional Beijing-Mandarin-based PTH and an innovative style of Mandarin, I draw on quantitative methods developed in variationist sociolinguistics. Such quantitative analysis is conducted on production data collected from high-quality audio recordings of sociolinguistic interviews of two groups of native Beijing business professionals. By controlling the dialect background and the profession of the two groups and the topics of the interview, I obtained comparable data sets to enable an analysis of the relation between the use of the linguistic variants and the two professional groups. The results of the quantitative analyses, detailed in Chapter 3, establish a clear correlation between linguistic innovation and the group of the new business elite, the Beijing yuppies. The parallel patterns of variation across all sound features within each professional group offer convincing evidence for the clustering of such features in different linguistic styles. The quantitative analyses thus establish a baseline picture of the stylistic distinction between two professional groups and the basic evidence for the emergence of CM. Additionally, it reveals a robust difference in which the new style is used by women and men in the yuppie group. In this way, the quantitative analysis paints in broad strokes the social significance of CM and its use by one group of leaders in the socioeconomic transformation of China. Simpler quantification in terms of frequency counts of particular linguistic features is performed in Chapter 4, and it provides evidence of how linguistic forms are used to create distinction in interaction.

I conducted qualitative analysis to explain the patterns found in the quantitative analysis and to reveal how CM and its constitutive linguistic features are used in context, that is, how and what meanings are created through their use. Specifically, content analysis of interviews and other ethnographic data collected from fieldwork helps to understand the emergence of CM as part of the emergence of a transnational Chinese linguistic market. The professional biographies of the yuppies shed light on the differential use of CM by men and women in the group. The combined quantitative and qualitative analyses in Chapters 2 and 3 reveal that one area of the indexical field of CM is about a cosmopolitan professionalism—a distinction of which the yuppies are shown to share a keen awareness and that they intend to cultivate. However, the yuppies certainly do not all sound the same nor do they enact such cosmopolitan professionalism in the same way. Discourse analysis of linguistic features used in the yuppies' speech in Chapter 3 further illustrates that it can be enacted in a professional persona that demonstrates profound local cultural expertise or one that highlights meticulous attention to detail.

Attending to both the linguistic details (i.e., form) and the content of talk, my qualitative analysis of production data and metasemiotic discourse in Chapter 4 reveals an expanded range of the linguistic components and social meaning of CM. Discourse analysis of interactions combined with frequency counts of specific linguistic forms clarify how distinction is made through discourse strategies, linguistic contrasts, and other nonlinguistic signs.

More qualitative analysis of the metalinguistic data in Chapter 5 further explores the enregisterment of CM, offering evidence for the recognition of its

36 Sociolinguistic Change, Style, and Ideology

social significance and distinction by a larger population of social actors. Paying attention to the specific linguistic features being commented on in such discourse, the analysis offers supporting evidence for the linguistic makeup of CM revealed through earlier analyses. Drawing on the conceptual tool of indexical order (Silverstein 2003) and the semiotic processes of language ideology (Gal 2016; Irvine and Gal 2000), the qualitative analysis of metalinguistic discourse reveals multiple ways whereby CM takes on indexical values and the contested nature of such values. The analysis sheds light on larger cultural and political issues embedded in the contestation of the social meanings of CM vis-à-vis Beijing-Mandarin-based PTH.

By examining different types of data and using quantitative and qualitative methods of analysis, the investigation undertaken in this book attends to all three dimensions of the "total linguistic fact": form, use, and ideology. In doing so, I offer a linguistically detailed and socially rich analysis of the resources, processes, and ways of meaning making, and I link meaning making at the micro level of linguistic variation to larger changes in the postsocialist stylistic regime of China. The empirical investigation of the rise of CM starts in the next chapter, but it doesn't start with anything linguistic—it starts with style. Specifically, it starts with style as experienced and recognized through (mass-mediated) encounters with stylistic distinction embodied in people and displayed in their social worlds, such as the mural in the shopping mall. Taking a style-based approach thus directs the analyst's and the reader's attention first and foremost to observable stylistic displays and moves of social actors, because linguistic innovation and change are not encountered in isolation.

Notes

1 For recent comprehensive reviews on approaches to variationist sociolinguistic research on style, see Coupland (2007, 32–81), Eckert (2008), Rickford and Eckert (2001), Moore (2012), and Schilling (2013).

2 Traditional variationist analysis of style (as attention paid to speech) finds uniformity in stylistic variation across socioeconomic classes. Such "uniformity of abstract patterns of variation which are invariant in respect to particular levels of usage" constitutes the strongest evidence for shared norms among members of a speech community, despite the lack of "marked agreement in the use of language elements" (Labov 1972, 121).

3 Auslander (1996) uses the term "stylistic regime," without explicitly defining it, in her historical analysis of the relation between style and taste in furniture and the making of the French nation and state. Changes in stylistic regimes (e.g., courtly stylistic regime, bourgeois stylistic regime) go hand in hand with changes in political regimes. "Stylistic system" seems to be an alternative term for stylistic regime (see Auslander 1996, 184). My use of the term stylistic regime, with a focus on analysis of linguistic styles, is more directly inspired by the collected works on regimes of language (Kroskrity 2000) and Susan Gal's (2012) article, "Sociolinguistic Regimes and the Management of 'Diversity'." In all of these works, including Auslander's, "regime" highlights power (and hegemony) and ideology in the systematic organization and management of languages and linguistic resources.

Sociolinguistic Change, Style, and Ideology **37**

4 This question is relevant to the actuation problem in linguistic change. In Labov's words, the actuation problem asks "why [a linguistic change] took place at the particular time and place that it did" (Labov 1972, 283; see also Weinreich, Labov, and Herzog 1968, 102).
5 See also Vološinov's discussion on the multiplicity, or multiaccentuality, and indeterminacy of meaning and meaning potentials (1973, particularly Chapters 2, 3, and 4).
6 Bauman and Briggs (1990) operationalize Bakhtin's notion of dialogism in terms of decontextualization and recontextualization, two aspects or phases of the same transformational process wherein ready-made discourse is extracted from one context, i.e., decontextualization, and fitted into another, i.e., recontextualization (1990, 74–75; Bauman 1996, 301). A decontextualized text, a stretch of discourse made into a unit, is the result of entextualization, "the process of rendering discourse extractable" (Bauman and Briggs 1990, 73).
7 Dialogism has inspired linguistic anthropologists to link and expand analysis of linguistic practice and social meaning in the immediate, local context to broader sociohistorical relations and formations (Goodwin and Duranti 1992; Silverstein and Urban 1996). The terms intertextuality (via Kristeva 1980; see Briggs and Bauman 1992, 146) and, more recently, interdiscursivity (e.g., Bauman 2005; Gal 2007) have been used to highlight the "relational orientation" (Bauman 2004, 4) and interconnectedness among linguistic forms as they circulate temporally and spatially across semiotic encounters (Bauman 2004, 2005; Bauman and Briggs 1990; Briggs and Bauman 1992; Gal 2007; Spitulnik 1996). Interdiscursivity is often used interchangeably with intertextuality. Some scholars, for example, contributors to the *Journal of Linguistic Anthropology* special issue on *interdiscursivity* (2005, Volume 15, Issue 1), consider it a broader term, particularly in dealing with a wide range of discursive phenomena and practices while reserving *intertextuality* for dealing with written texts (Bauman 2005, 146).
8 It is important to keep in mind that an important function of language is metapragmatic. Such function can be performed through metapragmatic discourse about language use even when no explicit comments on language use are present (Lucy 1993; Silverstein 1993). Hence, the so-called production data may well include "matapragmatic-activities-in-talk" (Inoue 2006a, 18) through which the speaker characterizes, evaluates, and regiments (other's) use of language.

References

Agha, Asif. 2005. "Voice, Footing, Enregisterment." *Journal of Linguistic Anthropology* 15 (1):38–59.

Agha, Asif. 2007. *Language and Social Relations*. Cambridge: Cambridge University Press.

Agha, Asif. 2011. "Commodity Registers." *Journal of Linguistic Anthropology* 21 (1):22–53.

Ahearn, Laura M. 2001. *Invitations to Love: Literacy, Love Letters, and Social Change in Nepal*. Ann Arbor, MI: University of Michigan Press.

Andrews, Julia F. 1994. *Painters and Politics in the People's Republic of China, 1949–1979*. Berkeley, CA: University of California Press.

Androutsopoulos, Jannis. 2014. "Mediatization and Sociolinguistic Change. Key Concepts, Research Traditions, Open Issues." In *Mediatization and Sociolinguistic Change*, edited by Jannis Androutsopoulos, 3–48. Berlin; Boston: de Gruyter.

Auer, Peter. 2007. "Introduction." In *Style and Social Identities: Alternative Approaches to Linguistic Heterogeneity*, edited by Peter Auer, 1–21. Berlin: de Gruyter.

38 Sociolinguistic Change, Style, and Ideology

Auslander, Leora. 1996. *Taste and Power: Furnishing Modern France.* Berkeley, CA: University of California Press.

Bakhtin, Mikhail M. 1981. *The Dialogic Imagination: Four Essays.* Translated by Caryl Emerson and Michael Holquist. Edited by Michael Holquist. Austin, TX: University of Texas Press.

Bakhtin, Mikhail M. 1986. *Speech Genres and Other Late Essays.* Translated by Vern McGee. Austin, TX: University of Texas Press.

Baranovitch, Nimrod. 2003. *China's New Voices: Popular Music, Ethnicity, Gender, and Politics, 1978–1997.* Berkeley, CA: University of California Press.

Barrett, Rusty. 1999. "Indexing Polyphonous Identity in the Speech of African American Drag Queens." In *Reinventing Identities: The Gendered Self in Discourse,* edited by Mary Bucholtz, A. C. Liang, and Laurel A. Sutton, 313–331. New York: Oxford University Press.

Barrett, Rusty. 2006. "Language Ideology and Racial Inequality: Competing Functions of Spanish in an Anglo-Owned Mexican Restaurant." *Language in Society* 35 (2):163–204.

Baugh, John. 2000. "Racial Identification by Speech." *American Speech* 75 (4):362–364.

Bauman, Richard. 1996. "Transformations of the Word in the Production of Mexican Festival Drama." In *Natural Histories of Discourse,* edited by Michael Silverstein and Greg Urban, 301–327. Chicago, IL and London: University of Chicago Press.

Bauman, Richard. 2004. *A World of Others' Words: Cross-Cultural Perspectives on Intertextuality.* Malden, MA: Blackwell.

Bauman, Richard. 2005. "Commentary: Indirect Indexicality, Identity, Performance: Dialogic Observations." *Journal of Linguistic Anthropology* 15 (1):145–150.

Bauman, Richard, and Charles L. Briggs. 1990. "Poetics and Performances as Critical Perspectives on Language and Social Life." *Annual Review of Anthropology* 19 (1):59–88.

Beijing Bureau of Industry and Commerce. 2011. *"Beijing Shi Gongshang Xingzheng Guanliju guanyu Kaizhan Huwai Guanggao Qingli Zhengdun Gongzuo de Gonggao"* ("City of Beijing Bureau of Industry and Commerce Announcement on Initiating Cleaning-up and Rectifying Outdoor Advertisements"). www.baic.gov.cn/zwgk/xzgg/201103/t20110317_465602.htm. Accessed April 10, 2011.

Bell, Allan. 1984. "Language Style as Audience Design." *Language in Society* 13 (2):145–204.

Bell, Allan. 2001. "Back in Style: Re-Working Audience Design." In *Style and Sociolinguistic Variation,* edited by Penelope Eckert, and John R. Rickford, 139–169. Cambridge and New York: Cambridge University Press.

Bell, Allan. 2007. "Style in Dialogue: Bakhtin and Sociolinguistic Theory." In *Sociolinguistic Variation: Theories, Methods and Applications,* edited by Robert Bayley, and Ceil Lucas, 90–109. New York and Cambridge: Cambridge University Press.

Benewick, Robert. 1999. "Icons of Power: Mao Zedong and the Cultural Revolution." In *Picturing Power in the People's Republic of China: Posters of the Cultural Revolution,* edited by Harriet Evans, and Stephanie Donald, 123–138. Lanham, MD: Rowman & Littlefield.

Blommaert, Jan. 2007. "Sociolinguistics and Discourse Analysis: Orders of Indexicality and Polycentricity." *Journal of Multicultural Discourses* 2 (2):115–130.

Bourdieu, Pierre. 1984. *Distinction: A Social Critique of the Judgment of Taste.* Translated by Richard Nice. Cambridge, MA: Harvard University Press.

Bourdieu, Pierre. 1991. *Language and Symbolic Power.* Translated by Gino Raymond, and Matthew Adamson. Cambridge, MA: Harvard University Press.

Briggs, Charles L., and Richard Bauman. 1992. "Genre, Intertextuality, and Social Power." *Journal of Linguistic Anthropology* 2 (2):131–172.

Bucholtz, Mary. 1999a. "'Why Be Normal?' Language and Identity Practices in a Community of Nerd Girls." *Language in Society* 28 (2):203–223.

Bucholtz, Mary. 1999b. "You Da Man: Narrating the Racial Other in the Production of White Masculinity." *Journal of Sociolinguistics* 3 (4):443–460.

Bucholtz, Mary. 2002. "Youth and Cultural Practice." *Annual Review of Anthropology* 31:525–552.

Bucholtz, Mary. 2011. *White Kids: Language, Race, and Styles of Youth Identity*. Cambridge: Cambridge University Press.

Bucholtz, Mary, and Kira Hall. 2005. "Identity and Interaction: A Sociocultural Linguistic Approach." *Discourse Studies* 7 (4–5):585–614.

Butler, Judith. 1999. *Gender Trouble: Feminism and the Subversion of Identity*. 10th Anniversary Edition. New York: Routledge.

Cameron, Deborah. 1990. "Demythologizing Sociolinguistics: Why Language Does Not Reflect Society." In *Ideologies of Language*, edited by John E. Joseph, and Talbot J. Taylor, 79–93. London and New York: Routledge.

Cavanaugh, Jillian R. 2008. "A Modern Questione Della Lingua: The Incomplete Standardization of Italian in a Northern Italian Town." *The Journal of the Society for the Anthropology of Europe* 8 (1):18–31.

Chang, Arnold. 1980. *Painting in the People's Republic of China: The Politics of Style*. Boulder, CO: Westview Press.

Chinanews. 2011. "*Chengdu Guifan Fangdichan Guifan Yingxiao Guanggao Jin Luanyong 'Bieshu'*" ("Chengdu Rectifies Real Estate Marketing Prohibiting Indiscriminate Use of 'Villa' in Advertisements"). www.chinanews.com/estate/2011/05-26/3068921.shtml. Accessed May 30, 2011.

Chun, Elaine W. 2001. "The Construction of White, Black, and Korean American Identities through African American Vernacular English." *Journal of Linguistic Anthropology* 11 (1):52–64.

Chun, Elaine W. 2004. "Ideologies of Legitimate Mockery: Margaret Cho's Revoicing of Mock Asian." *Pragmatics* 14 (2/3):263–289.

Chun, Elaine. 2009. "Speaking Like Asian Immigrants: Intersections of Accommodation and Mocking at a U.S. High School." *Pragmatics* 19 (1):17–38.

Coupland, Nikolas. 2001. "Dialect Stylization in Radio Talk." *Language in Society* 30 (3):345–375.

Coupland, Nikolas. 2007. *Style: Language Variation and Identity*. Cambridge: Cambridge University Press.

Coupland, Nikolas. 2014a. "Language Change, Social Change, Sociolinguistic Change: A Meta-Commentary." *Journal of Sociolinguistics* 18 (2):277–286.

Coupland, Nikolas. 2014b. "Sociolinguistic Change, Vernacularization and Broadcast British Media." In *Mediatization and Sociolinguistic Change*, edited by Jannis Androutsopoulos, 67–96. Berlin and Boston: de Gruyter.

Coupland, Nikolas. 2016. "Five Ms for Sociolinguistic Change." In *Sociolinguistics: Theoretical Debates*, edited by Nikolas Coupland, 433–454. Cambridge: Cambridge University Press.

Dong, Jie. 2009. "'Isn't It Enough to Be a Chinese Speaker': Language Ideology and Migrant Identity Construction in a Public Primary School in Beijing." *Language & Communication* 29 (2):115–126.

Dutton, Michael. 2005. *Policing Chinese Politics*. Durham, NC: Duke University Press.

40 Sociolinguistic Change, Style, and Ideology

Eagleton, Terry. 1991. *Ideology: An Introduction.* New York and London: Verso.

Eckert, Penelope. 2000. *Linguistic Variation as Social Practice: The Linguistic Construction of Identity in Belten High.* Oxford: Blackwell.

Eckert, Penelope. 2008. "Variation and the Indexical Field." *Journal of Sociolinguistics* 12 (4):453–476.

Eckert, Penelope. 2012. "Three Waves of Variation Study: The Emergence of Meaning in the Study of Sociolinguistic Variation." *Annual Review of Anthropology* 41:87–100.

Eckert, Penelope. 2016. "Variation, Meaning and Social Change." In *Sociolinguistics: Theoretical Debates*, edited by Nikolas Coupland, 68–85. Cambridge: Cambridge University Press.

Eckert, Penelope, and Sally McConnell-Ginet. 1992. "Think Practically and Look Locally: Language and Gender as Community-Based Practice." *Annual Review of Anthropology* (21):461–490.

Errington, Joseph. 1988. *Structure and Style in Javanese: A Semiotic View of Linguistic Etiquette.* Philadelphia, PA: University of Pennsylvania Press.

Evans, Harriet, and Stephanie Donald, eds. 1999. *Picturing Power in the People's Republic of China: Posters of the Cultural Revolution.* Lanham, MD: Rowman & Littlefield.

Ewen, Stuart. 1999. *All Consuming Images: The Politics of Style in Contemporary Culture.* Revised edition. New York: Basic Books.

Fairclough, Norman. 1992. *Discourse and Social Change.* Cambridge, MA and Cambridge: Polity Press.

Ferguson, James. 1999. *Expectations of Modernity: Myths and Meanings of Urban Life on the Zambian Copperbelt.* Berkeley, CA: University of California Press.

Gagné, Isaac 2008. "Urban Princesses: Performance and "Women's Language" in Japan's Gothic/Lolita Subculture." *Journal of Linguistic Anthropology* 18 (1):130–150.

Gal, Susan. 1979. *Language Shift: Social Determinants of Linguistic Change in Bilingual Austria.* New York: Academic Press.

Gal, Susan. 1989a. "Language and Political Economy." *Annual Review of Anthropology* 18 (1):345–367.

Gal, Susan. 1989b. "Lexical Innovation and Loss: The Use and Value of Restricted Hungarian." In *Investigating Obsolescence: Studies in Language Contraction and Death*, edited by Nancy C. Dorian, 313–332. Cambridge: Cambridge University Press.

Gal, Susan. 1998. "Multiplicity and Contention among Language Ideologies: A Commentary." In *Language Ideologies: Theory and Practice*, edited by Bambi B. Schieffelin, Kathryn A. Woolard, and Paul V. Kroskrity, 317–331. New York and Oxford: Oxford University Press.

Gal, Susan. 2007. "Circulation in the 'New' Economy: Clasps and Copies." Paper presented at The 106th Meeting of the American Anthropological Association. Washington, D.C.

Gal, Susan. 2012. "Sociolinguistic Regimes and the Management of 'Diversity'." In *Language in Late Capitalism: Pride and Profit*, edited by Alexandre Duchêne, and Monica Heller, 22–42. New York: Routledge.

Gal, Susan. 2016. "Sociolinguistic Differentiation." In *Sociolinguistics: Theoretical Debates*, edited by Nikolas Coupland, 113–136. Cambridge: Cambridge University Press.

Goodwin, Charles, and Alessandro Duranti. 1992. "Rethinking Context: An Introduction." In *Rethinking Context: Language as an Interactive Phenomenon*, edited by Alessandro Duranti, and Charles Goodwin, 1–42. Cambridge: Cambridge University Press.

Gordon, Matthew J. 2013. *Labov: A Guide for the Perplexed.* London and New York: Bloomsbury Academic.

Sociolinguistic Change, Style, and Ideology **41**

Gramsci, Antonio. 1985. *Selections from Cultural Writings*. Translated by William Boelhower. Edited by David Forgacs, and Geoffrey Nowell-Smith. London: Lawrence and Wishart.

Griffiths, Michael B. 2013. *Consumers and Individuals in China: Standing Out, Fitting In*. Abingdon, Oxon and New York: Routledge.

Gumperz, John J. 1964. "Linguistic and Social Interaction in Two Communities." In *The Ethnography of Communication*, edited by John J. Gumperz, and Dell Hymes, 137–153. Washington, D.C.: American Anthropological Association.

Hachimi, Atiqa. 2012. "The Urban and the Urbane: Identities, Language Ideologies, and Arabic Dialects in Morocco." *Language in Society* 41 (3):321–341.

Haeri, Niloofar. 1997. "The Reproduction of Symbolic Capital: Language, State, and Class in Egypt." *Current Anthropology* 38 (5):795–816.

Hall, Stuart, and Tony Jefferson, eds. 1976. *Resistance through Rituals: Youth Subcultures in Post-War Britain*. New York: Hutchinson.

Hanser, Amy. 2008. *Service Encounters: Class, Gender, and the Market for Social Distinction in Urban China*. Stanford, CA: Stanford University Press.

Harkness, Nicholas. 2014. *Songs of Seoul: An Ethnography of Voice and Voicing in Christian South Korea*. Berkeley, CA: University of California Press.

Hebdige, Dick. 1979. *Subculture: The Meaning of Style*. London: Methuen.

Hernández-Campoy, Juan Manuel, and Juan Antonio Cutillas-Espinosa, eds. 2012. *Style-Shifting in Public: New Perspectives on Stylistic Variation*. Amsterdam and Philadelphia, PA: John Benjamins.

Hill, Jane H. 1985. "The Grammar of Consciousness and the Consciousness of Grammar." *American Ethnologist* 12 (4):725–737.

Hill, Jane H. 1998. "'Today There Is No Respect': Nostalgia, 'Respect,' and Oppositional Discourse in Mexicano (Nahuatl) Language Ideology." In *Language Ideologies: Practice and Theory*, edited by Bambi B. Schieffelin, Kathryn A. Woolard, and Paul V. Kroskrity, 51–67. New York and Oxford: Oxford University Press.

Hill, Jane H. 2006. "Language Change and Cultural Change." In *Encyclopedia of Language & Linguistics*, edited by Keith Brown, 332–339. Oxford: Elsevier.

Hill, Jane H., and Kenneth C. Hill. 1997. "Culture Influencing Language: Plurals of Hopi Kin Terms in Comparative Uto-Aztecan Perspective." *Journal of Linguistic Anthropology* 7 (2):166–180.

Hymes, Dell. 1964. "Introduction: Towards Ethnographies of Communication." In *The Ethnography of Communication*, edited by John J. Gumperz, and Dell Hymes, 1–34. Washington, D.C.: American Anthropological Association.

Hymes, Dell. 1974. "The Scope of Sociolinguistics." In *Foundations in Sociolinguistics: An Ethnographic Approach*, 193–209. Philadelphia, PA: University of Pennsylvania Press.

Inoue, Miyako. 2002. "Gender, Language, and Modernity: Toward an Effective History of Japanese Women's Language." *American Ethnologist* 29 (2):392–422.

Inoue, Miyako. 2006a. *Vicarious Language*. Berkeley, CA: University of California Press.

Inoue, Miyako. 2006b. "Standardization." In *Encyclopedia of Language & Linguistics*, edited by Keith Brown, 121–127. Oxford: Elsevier.

Inoue, Miyako. 2007. "Things That Speak: Peirce, Benjamin, and the Kinesthestics of Commodity Advertisement in Japanese Woman's Magazines, 1900 to the 1930s." *Public Culture* 15 (3):511–552.

Irvine, Judith T. 1989. "When Talk Isn't Cheap: Language and Political Economy." *American Ethnologist* 16 (2):248–267.

Irvine, Judith. 2001. "'Style' as Distinctiveness: The Culture and Ideology of Linguistic Differentiation." In *Style and Sociolinguistic Variation*, edited by Penelope Eckert, and John R. Rickford, 21–43. Cambridge: Cambridge University Press.

42 Sociolinguistic Change, Style, and Ideology

Irvine, Judith, and Susan Gal. 2000. "Language Ideology and Linguistic Differentiation." In *Regimes of Language*, edited by Paul V. Kroskrity, 35–84. Santa Fe, NM: School of American Research Press.

Jaffe, Alexandra. 2016. "Indexicality, Stance and Fields in Sociolinguistics." In *Sociolinguistics: Theoretical Debates*, edited by Nikolas Coupland, 86–112. Cambridge: Cambridge University Press.

Johnstone, Barbara. 1999. "Uses of Southern-Sounding Speech by Contemporary Texas Women." *Journal of Sociolinguistics* 3 (4):505–522.

Kiesling, Scott Fabius. 1998. "Men's Identities and Sociolinguistic Variation: The Case of Fraternity Men." *Journal of Sociolinguistics* 2 (1):69–99.

de Kloet, Jeroen. 2010. *China with a Cut: Globalisation, Urban Youth and Popular Music*. Amsterdam: Amsterdam University Press.

Kristeva, Julia. 1980. *Desire in Language: A Semiotic Approach to Literature and Art*. New York: Columbia University Press.

Kroskrity, Paul V. 2000. "Regimenting Languages: Language Ideological Perspectives." In *Regimes of Language: Ideologies, Polities, and Identities*, edited by Paul V. Kroskrity, 1–34. Santa Fe, NM: School of American Research Press.

Kuchta, David. 1996. "The Making of the Self-Made Man: Class, Clothing, and English Masculinity, 1688–1832." In *The Sex of Things: Gender and Consumption in Historical Perspective*, edited by Ellen Furlough, and Victoria De Grazia. Berkeley, CA: University of California Press.

Kulick, Don. 1992. *Language Shift and Cultural Reproduction: Socialization, Self, and Syncretism in a Papua New Guinean Village*. Cambridge: Cambridge University Press.

Labov, William. 1963. "The Social Motivation of a Sound Change." *Word* 19:273–309.

Labov, William. 1966. The Social Stratification of English in New York City. Washington, D.C.: Center for Applied Linguistics.

Labov, William. 1972. Sociolinguistic Patterns. Philadelphia, PA: University of Pennsylvania Press.

Labov, William. 1994. *Principles of Linguistic Change. Volume 1: Internal Factors*. Oxford and Cambridge, MA: Blackwell.

Labov, William. 2001. *Principles of Linguistic Change. Vol.2: Social Factors*. Oxford: Blackwell Publishers.

Lévi-Strauss, Claude. 1966. *The Savage Mind*. Chicago, IL: The University of Chicago Press.

Lucy, John A. 1993. "Reflexive Language and Human Disciplines." In *Reflexive Language: Reported Speech and Metapragmatics*, edited by John A. Lucy, 1–32. New York: Cambridge University Press.

McLaughlin, Fiona. 2001. "Dakar Wolof and the Configuration of an Urban Identity." *Journal of African Cultural Studies* 14 (2):153–172.

Mendoza-Denton, Norma. 1996. "Pregnant Pauses: Silence and Authority in the Anita Hill-Clarence Thomas Hearings." In *Gender Articulated*, edited by Kira Hall, and Mary Bucholtz, 51–66. New York and London: Routledge.

Mendoza-Denton, Norma. 2008. *Homegirls: Language and Cultural Practice among Latina Youth Gangs*. Malden, MA: Blackwell.

Mendoza-Denton, Norma. 2011. "The Semiotic Hitchhiker's Guide to Creaky Voice: Circulation and Gendered Hardcore in a Chicana/o Gang Persona." *Journal of Linguistic Anthropology* 21 (2):261–280.

Milroy, Lesley. 2004. "Language Ideologies and Linguistic Change." In *Sociolinguistic Variation: Critical Reflections*, edited by Ronald K. S. Macaulay, and Carmen Fought, 161–177. Oxford and New York: Oxford University Press.

Moore, Emma. 2012. "The Social Life of Style." *Language and Literature* 21 (1):66–83.

Moore, Emma, and Robert Podesva. 2009. "Style, Indexicality, and the Social Meaning of Tag Questions." *Language in Society* 38 (04):447–485.

Moore, Malcolm. 2011. "China Bans Luxury Advertising in Beijing." www.telegraph. co.uk/news/worldnews/asia/china/8398097/China-bans-luxury-advertising-in-Beijing.html. Accessed April 8, 2011.

Nakassis, Constantine V. 2016. *Doing Style: Youth and Mass Mediation in South India*. Chicago, IL: University of Chicago Press.

Osburg, John. 2013. *Anxious Wealth: Money and Morality among China's New Rich*. Stanford, CA: Stanford University Press.

Otis, Eileen M. 2012. *Markets and Bodies: Women, Service Work, and the Making of Inequality in China*. Palo Alto, CA: Stanford University Press.

Podesva, Robert J. 2007. "Phonation Type as a Stylistic Variable: The Use of Falsetto in Constructing a Persona." *Journal of Sociolinguistics* 11 (4):478–504.

Podesva, Robert J. 2011. "The California Vowel Shift and Gay Identity." *American Speech* 86 (1):32–51.

Podesva, Robert J., Sarah J. Roberts, and Kathryn Campbell-Kibler. 2002. "Sharing Resources and Indexing Meanings in the Production of Gay Styles." In *Language and Sexuality: Contesting Meaning in Theory and Practice*, edited by Kathryn Campbell-Kibler, Robert J. Podesva, Sarah J. Roberts, and Andrew Wong, 175–189. Stanford, CA: CSLI Press.

Pun, Ngai. 2005. *Made in China: Women Factory Workers in a Global Workplace*. Durham, NC: Duke University Press.

Rampton, Ben. 2003. "Hegemony, Social Class and Stylization." *Pragmatics* 13 (1):49–83.

Rampton, Ben. 2011a. "From 'Multi-Ethnic Adolescent Heteroglossia' to 'Contemporary Urban Vernaculars'." *Language & Communication* 31 (4):276–294.

Rampton, Ben. 2011b. "Style Contrasts, Migration and Social Class." *Journal of Pragmatics* 43 (5):1236–1250.

Ren, Hai. 2013. *The Middle Class in Neoliberal China: Governing Risk, Life-Building, and Themed Spaces*. London and New York: Routledge.

Rickford, John R., and Penelope Eckert. 2001. "Introduction." In *Style and Sociolinguistic Variation*, edited by Penelope Eckert, and John R. Rickford, 1–18. Cambridge: Cambridge University Press.

Rofel, Lisa. 1999. *Other Modernities: Gendered Yearnings in China after Socialism*. Berkeley, CA: University of California Press.

Rofel, Lisa. 2007. *Desiring China: Experiments in Neoliberalism, Sexuality, and Public Culture*. Durham, NC: Duke University Press.

Roth-Gordon, Jennifer. 2009. "The Language That Came Down the Hill: Slang, Crime, and Citizenship in Rio De Janeiro." *American Anthropologist* 111 (1):57–68.

Schilling, Natalie. 2013. "Investigating Stylistic Variation." In *Handbook of Language Variation and Change*, edited by J. K. Chambers, and Natalie Schilling, 2nd ed., 327–349. Hoboken, NJ: Wiley-Blackwell.

Schilling-Estes, Natalie. 1998. Investigating "Self-Conscious" Speech: The Performance Register in Ocracoke English. *Language in Society* 27 (1):53–83.

Schilling-Estes, Natalie. 2004. "Constructing Ethnicity in Interaction." *Journal of Sociolinguistics* 8 (2):163–195.

Shankar, Shalini. 2008. "Speaking Like a Model Minority: 'Fob' Styles, Gender, and Racial Meanings among Desi Teens in Silicon Valley." *Journal of Linguistic Anthropology* 18 (2):268–289.

44 Sociolinguistic Change, Style, and Ideology

Silverstein, Michael. 1985. "Language and the Culture of Gender: At the Intersection of Structure, Usage and Ideology." In *Semiotic Mediation*, edited by Elizabeth Mertz, and Richard J. Parmentier, 219–259. Orlando, FL: Academic Press.

Silverstein, Michael. 1993. "Metapragmatic Discourse and Metapragmatic Function." In *Reflexive Language: Reported Speech and Metapragmatics*, edited by John Lucy, 33–58. New York: Cambridge University Press.

Silverstein, Michael. 1998. "The Uses and Utility of Ideology: A Commentary." In *Language Ideologies: Practice and Theory*, edited by Bambi B. Schieffelin, Kathryn A. Woolard, and Paul V. Kroskrity, 123–145. New York and Oxford: Oxford University Press.

Silverstein, Michael. 2003. "Indexical Order and the Dialectics of Sociolinguistic Life." *Language & Communication* 23 (3–4):193–229.

Silverstein, Michael. 2016. "The 'Push' of Lautgesetze, the 'Pull' of Enregisterment." In *Sociolinguistics: Theoretical Debates*, edited by Nikolas Coupland, 37–67. Cambridge: Cambridge University Press.

Silverstein, Michael, and Greg Urban. 1996. "The Natural History of Discourse." In *Natural Histories of Discourse*, edited by Michael Silverstein, and Greg Urban, 1–17. Chicago, IL and London: University of Chicago Press.

Snell, Julia. 2010. "From Sociolinguistic Variation to Socially Strategic Stylisation." *Journal of Sociolinguistics* 14 (5):630–656.

Spitulnik, Debra A. 1996. "Social Circulation of Media Discourse and the Mediation of Communities." *Journal of Linguistic Anthropology* 6 (2):161–187.

Spitulnik, Debra A. 1998. "The Language of the City: Town Bemba as Urban Hybridity." *Journal of Linguistic Anthropology* 8 (1):30–59.

Starr, Rebecca L. 2015. "Sweet Voice: The Role of Voice Quality in a Japanese Feminine Style." *Language in Society* 44 (01):1–34.

Sullivan, Michael. 2008. *The Arts of China*. 5th. ed. Berkeley, CA: University of California Press.

Swigart, Leigh. 2000. "The Limits of Legitimacy: Language Ideology and Shift in Contemporary Senegal." *Journal of Linguistic Anthropology* 10 (1):90–130.

Tsiplakou, Stavroula, and Elena Ioannidou. 2012. "Stylizing Stylization: The Case of Aigia Fuxia." *Multilingua* 31 (2/3):277–299.

Vološinov, V. N. 1973. *Marxism and the Philosophy of Language*. Translated by Ladislav Matejka, and I. R. Titunik. Boston, MA: Harvard University Press.

Wang, Jing. 2008. *Brand New China: Advertising, Media, and Commercial Culture*. Cambridge, MA: Harvard University Press.

Weinreich, Uriel, William Labov, and Marvin I. Herzog. 1968. "Empirical Foundations for a Theory of Language Change." In *Directions for Historical Linguistics*, edited by Winfred P. Lehman, and Yakov Malkiel, 97–195. Austin, TX: University of Texas Press.

Wong, Andrew D. 2005. "The Reappropriation of *Tongzhi*." *Language in Society* 34 (6):763–793.

Wong, Andrew, and Qing Zhang. 2000. "The Linguistic Construction of the *Tongzhi* Community." *Journal of Linguistic Anthropology* 10 (2):248–278.

Woolard, Kathryn A. 1985. "Language Variation and Cultural Hegemony: Towards an Integration of Sociolinguistic and Social Theory." *American Ethnologist* 12 (4):738–748.

Woolard, Kathryn A. 1989. "Language Convergence and Language Death as Social Processes." In *Investigating Obsolescence: Studies in Language Contraction and Death*, edited by Nancy C. Dorian, 355–367. Cambridge: Cambridge University Press.

Woolard, Kathryn A. 1998. "Introduction: Language Ideology as a Field of Inquiry." In *Language Ideologies: Practice and Theory*, edited by Bambi B. Schieffelin, Kathryn A. Woolard, and Paul Kroskrity, 3–47. New York: Oxford University Press.

Woolard, Kathryn A. 2008. "Why Dat Now?: Linguistic-Anthropological Contributions to the Explanation of Sociolinguistic Icons and Change." *Journal of Sociolinguistics* 12 (4):432–452.

Wu, Qingcai. 2007. *"Beijing Quanshi Kaicha 'Xuanfu' Guanggao Yaoqiu Yinling Dazhong Lixing Xiaofei"* ("Beijing City-Wide Investigation of 'Wealth-Flaunting' Advertisements Requirements on Leading the Masses' Rational Consumption"). www.chinanews.com/gn/news/2007/05-18/938066.shtml. Accessed April 8, 2011.

Yang, Mayfair Mei-hui. 1997. "Mass Media and Transnational Subjectivity in Shanghai: Notes on (Re)Cosmopolitanism in a Chinese Metropolis." In *Ungrounded Empires: The Cultural Politics of Modern Chinese Transnationalism*, edited by Aihwa Ong, and Donald M. Nonini, 287–319. New York and London: Routledge.

Yang, Mayfair Mei-hui. 1999. "From Gender Erasure to Gender Difference: State Feminism, Consumer Sexuality, and Women's Public Sphere in China." In *Spaces of Their Own: Women's Public Sphere in Transnational China*, edited by Mayfair Mei-hui Yang, 35–67. Minneapolis, MN: University of Minnesota Press.

Yurchak, Alexei. 2000. "Privatize Your Name: Symbolic Work in a Post-Soviet Linguistic Market." *Journal of Sociolinguistics* 4 (3):406–434.

Zhang, Qing. 2005. "A Chinese Yuppie in Beijing: Phonological Variation and the Construction of a New Professional Identity." *Language in Society* 34 (3):431–466.

Zhang, Qing 2008. "Rhotacization and the 'Beijing Smooth Operator': The Social Meaning of a Linguistic Variable." *Journal of Sociolinguistics* 12 (2):201–222.

Zhang, Li. 2010. *In Search of Paradise: Middle-Class Living in a Chinese Metropolis*. Ithaca, NY: Cornell University Press.

Zhang, Zhen. 2000. "Mediating Time: The 'Rice Bowl of Youth' in Fin De Siecle Urban China." *Public Culture* 12 (1):93–113.

2

BEIJING YUPPIES

The New Business Elite

"White collar" is a new group in the metropolis of the 20th century. When this term is mentioned in today's China, what emerges in people's imagination is usually the figure of those *waiqi* 'foreign enterprise' professionals. **Their image is always connected with youthfulness, business, high salaries, modern office buildings, comfortable homes, and an avant-garde style of consumption and entertainment.**

— *"Shanghai 'white-collar' image sketch" Zheng [2001, 19]*

2.1 Introduction

On a scorchingly hot summer afternoon in early July 1997, I sat on a sofa in the air-conditioned lobby of the five-star Kempinsky Hotel in the Landmark (*Liangma*) business district of Beijing, waiting to meet with Mr. Wang Jun, the chief representative of a European bank in Beijing. We had confirmed our meeting over the phone the night before while, he apologized, he was cooling down on his treadmill at home, a rare piece of exercise equipment to have in one's house in the late 1990s. I focused on the young men wearing business suits entering the hotel, so it took me by surprise when a man in a casual summer outfit came sauntering up to me, asking, "Are you Zhang Qing?" Indeed, it was Mr. Wang, wearing a creamy white canvas cap, an oversized sandy-yellow t-shirt, olive-green shorts, and light brown suede loafers with no socks and carrying a sandy-yellow suede backpack on one shoulder. His whole earth-tone outfit had an air of ease and nonchalance, the complete opposite of the well-groomed conservative business suit of a banking professional. However, I could tell that his clothing was not the kind found in the cheap street markets. The only thing about him that met my expectation was his cell phone, a ubiquitous symbol among business people. But he was the first person I had seen wearing a headset on that trip.

Through Mr. Wang and other friends of mine, I came to know 25 Chinese managerial professionals working for foreign businesses in Beijing. Their companies were either *du-zi qiye* 'wholly foreign-owned enterprises' or *daibiao chu* 'representative offices'. Such businesses are commonly called *waiqi* 'foreign enterprises', an umbrella term that also refers to white-collar employees of these businesses. In contrast to *waiqi*, state-owned enterprises are known as *guoqi*. A majority of the *waiqi* professionals worked for North American and European companies; a few were employed by Hong Kong and Japanese companies. They are part of the top echelon of a new breed of business professionals created by the influx of foreign investments since the late 1970s. Many of these people joined the foreign business sector in the early and mid-1980s as the first generation of local Chinese employees of foreign companies. All of the 25 had bachelor's degrees, and 4 had Master's degrees. Two had worked for companies in the United States before taking up their positions in Beijing. Among those willing to disclose information about their income, monthly salaries ranged from about 6,000 renminbi (herein after RMB) ($720) to 40,000 RMB ($4,800). The highest monthly salary (40,000 yuan, $4,800) was that of a manager in an American multinational manufacturing company; it was about 24 times the average monthly salary of a state employee in 1997 (based on data from *Beijing Statistical Yearbook* 1998). The status of their companies and their positions, their high education, and their income confer on them considerable prestige (Pearson 1997). As one of the major beneficiaries of economic reform, this group has become part of the emerging Chinese middle and upper-middle class that constitutes the new urban elite in China (Goodman and Zang 2008; Lu 2002; Pearson 1997; Yan 2002; Zhang 2000). The professionals I talked with for this study are part of what Pearson (1997) referred to as the core of the business elite in the foreign sector, due to the status of their Western companies.

The *waiqi* business elite—and white-collar workers in foreign companies in general—have attracted attention from the popular media. They are perceived not only as a group that epitomizes China's increasing participation in the global market but also as trendsetters in a modern, cosmopolitan lifestyle characterized by Western-influenced practices of consumption and leisure. Commercial magazines and marketers are zealous promoters of this lifestyle (e.g., Fang and Omestad 2006, Lakshmanan 1997). For example, a 1997 issue of *Zhongguo Duiwai Fuwu 'China Foreign Service'*, a glossy magazine catering to *waiqi* professionals, features Caucasian models[1] and articles on horse racing in Hong Kong and Macau; golf; go-kart racing; modern interior decoration; legal issues in purchasing a house or a piece of land; and luxury brands, such as Ralph Lauren clothing, Cartier glasses, and new and classic models of Mercedes-Benz cars. It also introduces readers to art collecting and participation in auctions, described as *gaoyade xiuxian aihao* 'a refined hobby of leisure' (*China Foreign Service* 1997, 95), and Western elite institutions of higher education, featuring Columbia University in the 1997 issue. All section and article titles are in both

48 Beijing Yuppies

Chinese and English, and special terms in English are provided with Chinese translations, for instance, golf terms such as 'caddy/caddie,' 'birdie,' and 'eagle'.

The young, upwardly mobile white-collar professionals are called Chinese yuppies, or *yapishi* (e.g., Miao-er and Yan 1995; Pringle 1994; Rosen 2004). Western media also call them "chuppies," Chinese yuppies (e.g., Fang and Omestad 2006). The first two syllables of the Chinese term are the transliteration of 'yuppie,' and the third syllable/character, *shi*, is a deference marker. The character of the first syllable, *ya*, means 'elegant, refined, cultured'. Hence *yapishi* explicitly conveys elegance and respectability. In addition to being associated with *ya*, they are perceived to be *yang*; as a popular saying about professionals in the foreign sector goes: "They wear *yang* clothes, they speak *yang* language, eat *yang* food, and deal with *yang* people." Originally meaning 'foreign' or 'Western,' *yang* is now a general descriptor of what is considered cosmopolitan, modern, stylish, and progressive. As Yan (1997, 50) observes, "Eating foreign food, and consuming foreign goods, has become an important way for these Chinese yuppies to define themselves as middle-class professionals." Market research finds that *waiqi* professionals are major consumers of foreign luxury goods (Ernst & Young 2005, 2).

The popular media participate in the glamorization and sensationalization of the new professional group. For example, the 2010 box office hit *Du Lala Shengzhi Ji 'Go Lala Go!'* is the story of a young woman's rise from secretary to director of human resources at DB, a fictional American Fortune 500 company.[2] The Chinese cast is made up of young, beautiful actors from the mainland, Hong Kong, and Taiwan, and they wear stylish and fashionable costumes designed by Patricia Field from *Sex and the City*. The *waiqi* professionals in my study do not display a flashy style like the characters in *Go Lala Go!* However, the film does reflect the milieu of the *waiqi* professionals to a certain extent, particularly their sociolinguistic environment. With the major characters speaking Mainland *Putonghua*, Hong Kong Mandarin, Taiwan Mandarin, and English, the world of DB epitomizes what I call the "transnational Chinese linguistic market" (discussed in more detail in Section 3.5.2) where Mainland Standard PTH is but one of several forms of linguistic capital.

In addition, the film accentuates a stark contrast between *waiqi* and *guoqi* 'state businesses' that I visited in my fieldwork: the decorative use of women in *waiqi*, particularly at the front end of the corporation, which was not seen in *guoqi* in the late 1990s, as I discuss below. The actresses in the film all wear stylish, bright, and figure-flattering costumes. They create what is in Chinese *liangli de fengjing xian* 'beautiful scenery' for the public face of the Western corporation. They are also emblematic of the glamorous label and image made popular by the media for *waiqi* professional women, called *bai-ling liren* 'white-collar beauty' (e.g., Lou 2003, 5):

> Busily going in and out of the metropolis' office buildings and the ever-growing foreign-funded enterprises are the graceful figures of

Beijing Yuppies **49**

white-collar beauties. Living a high life, they have a youthful face, high education credential, and considerable income, enjoy a comfortable work environment, and have a fast-paced work style.

2.2 *Waiqi* and *Guoqi*: The Different Dynamics of Gender

The different gender dynamics of the foreign companies and state businesses became palpable the moment I entered a foreign company. As I examine in Chapter 3, these differences are also played out linguistically. The decorative use of women was more prevalent and conspicuous in the foreign than in the state companies. Every time I visited a foreign company or a representative office, I was greeted by a friendly, polite, and pleasant "face," and this face was feminine. The public face of the company typically included a reception area decorated with floral arrangements, a young, attractive female Chinese receptionist or secretary, and her polite and soft greetings in Standard Mandarin or in both Mandarin and English if on the phone. It seemed to be the trend in the summer of 1997 that many of these women wore long, flowing, flowery skirts with fitted white or solid-colored blouses; the managers wore more formal business attire. The pleasant feminine front resembles "the pretty package" in Kanter's description of American corporations (1993, 76). It is part of the aesthetic labor performed by employees, particularly in service work and front-end positions in general, through deportment, appearance, and styles of speaking that embody the identity and style of the corporation and cater to the customers' class and cultural expectations (Warhurst et al. 2000; Witz, Warhurst, and Nixon 2003). Although the professionals were not doing typical interactive service work, there was clearly an effort to "look good and sound right" (Williams and Connell 2010, 350) in my encounters with the professionals in *waiqi,* particularly the women.[3] The pleasant feminine front was absent in most of the state companies I visited, and these state companies also had no clearly defined front area. I went directly to the manager's office, if I had been told of its location beforehand, or I had to ask the first person I encountered after I had entered the building. In several cases, right after the interview, the manager introduced me to other employees either personally or by calling in a (subordinate) colleague or a secretary. In several companies, the secretary was a man.

The less overt display of gender differences and women's less engagement in aesthetic labor in the state companies can be viewed as a result of the lingering influence of state feminism in the state sector. State feminism, or gender equality mandated by the state, was part of the greater endeavor to eliminate social inequality when the CCP established the PRC (Barlow 1994). In the three decades after 1949, women's liberation disrupted the traditional patriarchy and propelled women into the public sphere of social production. However, because gender equality was treated as part of demolishing social inequalities, the CCP tried to abolish gender inequality through erasing (feminine) gender difference so that women became the same as men (e.g., women taking up jobs

50 Beijing Yuppies

traditionally held by men and wearing androgynous clothing) (e.g., Barlow 1994; Dai 1995; J. Yang 2007). State feminism thus diminished the salience of gender as a site of identity production (Rofel 1999; M. Yang 1999).

Related to the feminine front of *waiqi* is a clustering of women in front-end visible positions, a consequence of their gendered-recruitment practice. Among the state professionals I interviewed, the majority (who graduated from college in the 1980s) were *assigned* to a state enterprise through the traditional system: work opportunities were controlled and allocated to college graduates by the government, theoretically regardless of gender. Although blatant gender discrimination exists in the state assignment system (e.g., Hoffman 2010; Hooper 1984; Z. Wang 2003), none of the women in the state group was recruited for a position that did not match her major but mainly served the public face of the corporation. The government played a central role in the job allocation of state professionals, but among the *waiqi* the market assigned jobs. Gender as well as language skills were found to be crucial in how the *waiqi* professionals were recruited.

Despite their current comparable positions, *waiqi* women and men had arrived at them through different career trajectories—women, through front-end work and men through work more directly related to doing business. Furthermore, although many of the professionals capitalized on their language skills, language played different roles in their career paths. When foreign companies come to China, they have an office with all the necessary equipment and some managerial staff from their headquarters. What they need immediately is someone who can speak their language so they can communicate with their Chinese partners, clients, and the bureaucracy. They also need a secretary. Hence, a lot of women are recruited as secretaries and assistants to upper management for both their decorative value and assumed superiority in (foreign) language skills. Front-line jobs demanded aesthetic labor: appearance, deportment, and, most importantly, style of speaking, to project the image of the corporation.

Although my sample was small (25 *waiqi* professionals), the gendered character of recruitment and career trajectory is likely to be a common part of the foreign business sector (see also a similar observation in Duthie's [2005] study of *waiqi* professionals in Shanghai). In the same issue of *China Foreign Service* noted earlier, there was a section called "photo collection of the white-collar" (1997, 40), where pictures and short biographies of professionals were published. Four women were featured in that issue. Despite differences in their current positions, the women were all foreign-language majors: three in English and one in Japanese.

The gendered character of recruitment is further supported by some of the advertisements collected at a job fair for foreign businesses and Sino-foreign joint ventures (August 29–30, 1997, Beijing). When gender was part of the requirement of the position, women were preferred for the front-end positions: secretaries, administrative assistants, and receptionists.[4] Jobs that recruited only men included sales engineers, sales assistants, project managers, technical engineers, and international trade market representatives. Although I could not find an official record of the sex ratio of professionals in foreign businesses, a survey of white-collar jobs in Beijing in 1997 found that secretarial work in foreign corporations was rapidly becoming feminized (Yao 1998).

Among the women *waiqi* participants in this study, regardless of their college degrees and work experiences, all but one started in a secretarial position. As Catherine recalled in her interview:

> Although I majored in International Finance, I was recruited by my first company as a secretary in '87 mainly because I could speak and write English well. In fact I thought I was overqualified for the position, but I had to get started from working as a secretary. I could see that with my finance knowledge and previous experiences, I could do a better job than my supervisor, an American lady. But I had to take orders from her, because she was directly appointed by headquarters.

Later, some women were promoted to managerial positions, but they moved up along the margins of the market. By contrast, most of the men started their careers in the foreign businesses by doing "real" business work, such as marketing and sales. The career trajectories of Jenny, Michael, and Sheldon provide a good example. I met Michael and Sheldon through their mutual friend, Jenny. All three had majored in German in college and had been friends since they served as Chinese-German interpreters for the government. When I interviewed them, Jenny and Sheldon were both chief representatives of the Beijing offices of German companies, and Michael was the product manager of a German manufacturing firm. Although their German background was a major factor in their recruitment, Jenny started as an assistant to a German chief representative and worked her way up to her current position; her two male friends started their *waiqi* careers in sales.

Some women, even after being promoted to a higher position, still had to fulfill secretarial and administrative responsibilities. This was the case with Jane, who was hired a year after she received her bachelor's degree in English. At the time of the interview, she was a vice president of marketing in a French company. She said:

> Originally, I was the secretary to the chief representative [who was from France]. I worked as a secretary for two years. Later, in the beginning of my third year, I asked to work in the marketing department. Then, at the end of the third year—it took a year—I was transferred to the marketing department where I am now. But I am not completely separate from secretarial work. So, I still do most of the secretary's work plus <u>sales</u> and <u>administrative</u> work also.

52 Beijing Yuppies

2.3 Making Distinctions: Cultured Cosmopolitans

The professionals I interviewed are far from the flashy, glamorous, and fashionable characters in *Go Lala Go!* On the contrary, they are best described as cosmopolitan conservative. Their Western-influenced, conventional corporate style originated in the style of the foreign parent company and is reflected in the employees' conservative appearance; the arrangement of office space and décor; and the use of conventional style of business communications, such as formulaic telephone conversations by receptionists and operators and the use of memos and minutes. I found less variation in this corporate style among the *waiqi* professionals and their offices than among their counterparts in the state sector. The best description of such a cosmopolitan conservative style is given to me by Catherine, a 35-year-old assistant chief representative of a European multinational financial group whose Beijing office focuses on real estate development. Graduating with a bachelor's degree in international finance in 1986, she joined her first foreign company after a one-year stint at a state company because she could no longer endure the "*jieji douzheng*" 'class struggle', by which she meant company politics. Her current company, where she has worked since 1995, is her third foreign employer. She considers it appropriate for a *waiqi* professional to be "professional" and "conservative" and to project an image of "honesty and trustworthiness." Outside the workplace, she prefers "very simple styles" that do not have excessive decorations, which she thinks are "redundant gild-the-lily kind of stuff." She likes her clothes to be "not too trendy."

Catherine personifies this conservative style at her interview. She wears a well-fitting black jacket over a white silk blouse and a black pencil skirt hitting at the knee, a pair of black leather low-heeled pumps; her hair is neatly tied into a short ponytail with a black band. She wears glasses with a thick, dark brown plastic angular frame, not the thin, metal-rimmed glasses that are in fashion. Many professionals I spoke with agree with the importance of a conservative image, which in a Chinese context contains both conventional and innovative elements: Such a style conforms to the style in the world of international corporations and is hence "conservative," but this clean-cut, well-dressed corporate style is new and considered *yang* in China. To a lot of mainland Chinese who do not work in the foreign sector, this conservative style is perceived as modern and new, and the *waiqi* professionals are in this sense trendsetters in today's corporate world in China.

The cosmopolitan professional style consists of not only Western business attire but also, for many, Western brands, which are much more expensive than domestic brands. At their interviews, I asked each person for his or her preferred brands of clothes, shoes, and accessories. Many wore Western brand names that are expensive for ordinary wage earners. Terry, 41, the chief representative of a North American bank, gave me the most comprehensive list of his preferred brands: Valentino and (Alfred) Dunhill work clothes, Burberry casual clothes, Bally shoes, Dunhill accessories, and Calvin Klein underwear. Although many could not name the specific brands they were wearing at the interview, most did prefer Western brands for their style, design, and quality. Many also liked to buy their clothes on business trips abroad since the same brand cost much less overseas.

The topic of brand names often led to discussions about consumption and lifestyle. Most of them emphasized that, although they could afford expensive brands, they did not buy them just to show off their status, and they expressed contempt toward those who did. To not flaunt their status through consumption—that is, to express disdain for conspicuous consumption—is a strategy of distinction (Bourdieu 1984) used by the Beijing yuppies to present themselves as cultured cosmopolitans.

Terry's comments represent the view of many yuppies. Talking about the importance of image, he first pointed out that people have always paid attention to self-image and have used clothing to show differences. What has changed is how the distinction is made. In the past, when choices were limited, "people wore new clothes to look good and clean, and not to look scruffy [*lata*]." Now, differentiation is made through the choice of style, brand, and, importantly, the brand's price. He distinguishes himself from "many rich young guys wearing designer brands like Dunhill from head to toe" to "flaunt their status." In his opinion, real rich people do not need expensive clothes to prove their status; instead, clothes get their value from the economic status of the wearer. On the contrary, for "someone with a butt-load of debt," even if he wears famous brands, "others would say they are fake." For Terry, his preference for imported brands is due to their "superior texture, style, and design." He views "the booming fake designer brand market" as the result of increasing demand from people who want to *xuanyao* 'show off'. "People like us, even when we wear genuine designer brands, we don't show off." To further illustrate his disdain for conspicuous consumption, Terry explains to me his choice of a car, a Toyota Camry. For him, a Camry is practical and suitable for his position at a medium-sized company. It is also a conscious decision to avoid "appearing ostentatious by driving a more expensive brand, such as Mercedes and BMW," two of the brands associated with rich Chinese in media reports. He considers those brands "too frivolous and restless." He further emphasizes the practicality of his choice by saying, "I don't do those, what's called *la feng* in Taiwan speech, or what's called *zhaoyao* 'ostentatious' things in Beijing speech, but more practical things."

As in Terry's comments, younger people and lower-level professionals are one type from whom the managerial group that Terry is a part of distinguish themselves. They are portrayed as inappropriate consumers because they engage in the ostentatious consumption of brand names that do not fit their income level. As people who are not wealthy enough but aspire to the lives of the rich, their showy behavior is interpreted as a reflection of immaturity and superficiality. In addition, many participants disassociate themselves from rich Chinese,

54 Beijing Yuppies

who are called *baofahu* (or *baofahur* with a Beijing accent), 'parvenu' or 'upstart', a derogatory term for a person who becomes rich in a short period of time (by chance or suspicious means). In contrast to the deference-indicating *-shi* in *yapishi*, *-hu* in *baofahu* is often used in other pejorative terms, such as *poluohu* 'impoverished person or family', and *kunnanhu* 'a person or family in distress'. The character of *baofahu* is typically associated with private entrepreneurs, another newly rich group created by economic reform. Some of its members are notorious for a lavish, materialistic lifestyle and conspicuous consumption (e.g., Gold 1990; S. Wang 1995; G. Wang 2000). Despite the variety of private business owners, their popular images throughout the 1980s and even in 1997 were largely negative; they were considered uneducated, greedy, and uncultured (Carrillo 2008; Goodman 1996; Hsu 2006).

A common stereotype of a *baofahu* was described by Sarah, 27, an assistant manager of marketing at a European building products company. In her discussion of the importance of image for *waiqi* professionals, she pointed out that the professional image had more to do with "qualities that are not displayable through glamorous clothing." Such qualities were *qizhi* 'refined disposition' and *neihan* (*neizai de hanyang*, literally, 'inner-meaning'), which refers to the inner ability of self-control or, more generally, being cultured. Work experiences and social connections also affect one's image. She then gave an example of the sumptuous but "superficial people," the opposite of those with *qizhi* and *neihan*.

Excerpt 2.1 Sarah: "You can immediately spot those superficial people"
Even if dressed in very pretty clothes, you can immediately spot those superficial people. We've all had this kind of experience. Walking in the street, **you see [one] wearing very nice, designer brands from head to toe, wearing a big gold watch, that [person], as soon as you see, is *nong*- not to say [s/he's a] peasant. I don't look down upon peasants. [They] are also [known as] the *baofahur*. You can immediately recognize [them].** ... I feel like, what people wear, you have to know what suits you.

Using "you" as a generic pronoun and the inclusive "we" (*zanmen*), Sarah described a presumably common experience of spotting the so-called *baofahu*. She first associated such people with peasants, or *nongmin*, but as she caught herself after the first syllable, "*nong*-," she quickly clarified that she did not have a prejudice against peasants. What she meant to say was that these peasants were also known as *baofahu*. Sarah's self-correction and clarification reveal another common association with *baofahu*: they are assumed to be from a rural background, which is further associated with a rustic style and taste that reflects a lack of *qizhi* and *neihan*.

Whereas Sarah's account of the "designer-brand-big-gold-watch-wearing" upstarts focuses only on the lavish but unrefined appearance of the stereotype, Terry's example below explicitly portrays the *baofahu* as people of a low class, *dangci di*. *Dangci di* does not merely describe a person's socioeconomic status but also an inferiority in the person's overall quality, including appearance, deportment, demeanor, taste, and even moral standing. The following excerpt is in response to my question about his leisure activities. I was surprised when Terry said he was a member of the Chang'an Club. I had been told that it was the most exclusive social club in Beijing at the time. Terry paid an initiation fee of about $9,000 as well as annual membership dues. When asked why he had joined the club, he said he had thought it would offer a nice environment where he and his family could do several things at the same place, such as dining, exercising (e.g., swimming, squash, tennis), and relaxing (sauna). Another perhaps more important reason was that the club would provide an opportunity to make business connections, which would be beneficial when he started his own company in the near future. However, he was disappointed by his experience. As it turned out, some members' behavior, in his view, were not appropriate to such an exclusive club:

Excerpt 2.2

Terry: **Not all members are like us. Some are** *baofahur.* **The main reason for them to join the club is to show off their wealth and status. Their class [***dangci***] is pretty low.** Sometimes when we go to the club to consume, if we're not satisfied with some service, we'll say to the service people, "It doesn't matter. Let it go, let it go." Then the service person can't help saying, "Ah yah, wouldn't it be great if all members were like you [polite form]!"

QZ: Hmm.

Terry: Then that shows that some members are not like this, right? **They don't care about public morality [***gong-de***]. For example, littering the floor with cigarette butts. Or, say, making the place of consumption very dirty, chaotic.** There is also this kind of people.

Terry distanced himself from the *baofahur,* who joined the club to flaunt their wealth and status. He described them as *dangci di* 'low class', which made them unsuitable for a supposedly high-class club. The first example was how to deal with unsatisfactory service. By saying "It doesn't matter. Let it go, let it go," Terry projected himself and members like him as handling the situation calmly, without making a big fuss. Handling a situation without displaying strong emotions is called *youhanyang*, 'having the ability to exercise self-control in adverse situations'. This ability and quality of self-control is what Sarah referred to as *neihan* earlier. The contrast between people like him and those

56 Beijing Yuppies

without *hanyang* was reiterated through the constructed speech of the service person who lamented that not all members were like Terry, implying that some members made a big fuss if they were not satisfied. Although the rhetorical question of the service person implied that not all members were like him, he emphasized the difference again by saying "some members are not like this." He further distanced himself from those members by describing them as lacking *gong-de* 'public morality'. His examples were stereotypical: "littering the floor with cigarette butts" and "making the place of consumption very dirty, chaotic." In this way, he made a distinction between himself and others like him as the cultured, responsible, and morally upright citizen-consumers of the club and the *baofahus*, who were rich but inferior in culture and morality.

A more general distinction between the yuppies and the new rich can be seen in Catherine's discussion on the composition of the "yuppies." She suggests they consist of three groups: people who studied overseas and who also brought back a Western lifestyle, the top professionals in *waiqi* like herself, and owners of private businesses. In the last group, she explicitly excludes "*neixie tu laoban*": **"those uncouth/rustic private proprietors who have money but can't afford to be rich. As soon as they have money, they'll (spend it on) eating-drinking-whoring-gambling."** *Tu*, the character for 'dirt' and 'soil', is used here as an adjective with a set of derogatory meanings associated with someone who is rustic, lacks urban sophistication, is uncouth and without taste in appearance (e.g., coordination of colors and styles in clothing and accessories) and conduct (including "improper" ways of speaking) and exhibits inappropriate, "uncivilized" public behavior (see also Griffiths, Chapman, and Christiansen 2010). *Tu* is the arch-opposite of *ya* and *yang*, two of the perceived characteristics of the yuppies. Catherine uses the Chinese idiom "*chi-he-piao-du*" 'eat-drink-whore-gamble' to describe the dissipating and debauched materialistic lifestyle of "uncouth private proprietors." In contrast, she believes the yuppies to be people who "have money but keep on **xiu-shen-yang-xing** and **raise one's own class [dangci]**." The idiom *xiu-shen-yang-xing*, reminiscent of Confucianism, means to develop one's moral character and cultivate one's temperament, a way of life that refrains from the trappings of extravagance and materialism. Such a lifestyle produces a person who has *xiuyang* and is cultivated and cultured. Hence, according to Catherine, the yuppies are affluent cosmopolitans who live a cultured lifestyle. They do consume more than ordinary wage earners, but they do it in a different style from that of the rustic private proprietors. In her view, the uncouth private proprietors do not have the appropriate *xiuyang*—the quality of being cultured and cultivated—to match their wealth. Hence, she suggests, "They can't afford to be rich."

Not only do the yuppies refrain from excessive markers of consumerism, but some also use items associated with tradition and ordinariness to place such elements in a cosmopolitan ensemble, as in the case of Ling, 38, the chief representative of a North American multinational financial management and investment firm. Returning from the United States with an MBA and experience at an American multinational financial company, Ling fits into the first subgroup of Catherine's yuppies and is among the most desirable people hotly sought after by foreign firms for operations in China. Back in China, he first worked at what he called a semi-government office, providing research and consulting services on the security market of China. He was hired by his current company in 1996. At the interview in his office, he offered me a Diet Coke while he drank from a white extra-large, traditional enamel cup, a *tangci gangzi*. The large cup looked out of place on his sleek desk. Like the other professionals in foreign companies, his business card had one side in English and the other in Chinese, but the Chinese was printed vertically, in the traditional printing style. Talking about the issue of image among *waiqi* professionals, he commented on the "disease" of "competitive consumption" of designer brands among some younger professionals as a sign of immaturity. When asked what brands he was wearing, he could not remember the brand of his suit but said that he probably bought it on his business trip to Hong Kong or the United States, a Brooks Brothers shirt, a Rado watch, and Italian shoes. He quickly pointed out that they "<u>happened to be</u> foreign products" and that he also often wore domestic brands. He then explained how clothes and brands had become less and less important for him, because "what is important are your abilities, refined disposition [*qizhi*], and your <u>interpersonal skills</u>. I don't need clothes to prop myself up. For those who do, it's a sign of lacking confidence." Feeling that he was doing fine, he would sometimes "intentionally wear something like the 'old man's shoes'." These shoes, *laotorxie*, are inexpensive traditional style black cotton shoes.

Sarah's example of the excessively bedizened *baofahu*, Terry's examples of the designer-brand-clad young men and ostentatious upstarts who disregard public morality, and Catherine's example of "uncouth private proprietors" who live a life of "eating-drinking-whoring-gambling" contribute to the image of affluent consumers who use symbols of excess to show off their new wealth. Such negative descriptions position the yuppies as having superior taste, different from that displayed by the "naive exhibitionism of 'conspicuous consumption,' which seeks distinction in the crude display of ill-mastered luxury" (Bourdieu 1984, 31). The upstarts are portrayed as not only low-class with inferior taste but also as lacking in morality (wastefulness) and self-possession and disregarding the public good. The *baofahu*'s (and other rich but uncouth Chinese) provide the foil against which the Beijing yuppies define themselves as appropriate and cultured cosmopolitans, refraining from expressive markers of excess, non-flashy and conforming to traditional Chinese virtues such as self-possession and an adherence to public morality.

2.4 Conclusion

This chapter described the ways through which the *waiqi* Beijing yuppies presented themselves as cultured cosmopolitans: their Western-influenced professional style and their views on consumption and taste. They differentiated

58 Beijing Yuppies

themselves from other types of people through metadiscourse, that is, *talk about* differentiation—even though the yuppies and their related others share many of the practices and signs that index what is widely called the new Chinese middle classes, for example consuming (often high-end) foreign brands, going to health clubs, traveling abroad for work and leisure, or owning cars and private residences.

In the next chapter, I focus on their use of language beyond explicit metadiscourse about differentiation. In a similar way to their drawing on nonlinguistic signs from various sources to assert their distinction, such as foreign-brand business suits with traditional local style shoes, they combine, or bricolage, regional and supraregional linguistic material to create a new linguistic style. This innovative linguistic style constitutes a core semiotic resource and plays a unique role in the styling of distinction among the Beijing yuppies when their other cultural practices, such as consumption and others mentioned above, overlap with those of other groups.

Notes

1 All the models in the magazine were Caucasian except for featured Chinese celebrities.
2 The film is based on a bestseller of the same title by Li Ke (2007), which has also inspired a popular television series and two sequels. The books have sold over 500 million copies (Chang 2012).
3 Hanser (2008, Chapter 4) and Otis (2012, Chapter 3) provide excellent examples where the development and manipulation of embodied aesthetic labor is formally established through employee training in an upscale department store in Harbin and a luxury hotel in Beijing.
4 Two companies were hiring front-desk receptionists. Although no gender was specified in the job description, the appellation *xiaojie*, 'Miss', in the Chinese job title *qiantai jiedai xiaojie*, 'Miss front-desk reception', makes it exclusively female.

References

Barlow, Tani E. 1994. "Politics and the Protocols of Funü." In *Engendering China: Women, Culture, and the State*, edited by Christina K. Gilmartin, Gail Hershatter, Lisa Rofel, and Tyrene White, 339–359. Cambridge, MA: Harvard University Press.
Beijing Statistical Yearbook. 1998. Beijing: China Statistical Publishing House.
Bourdieu, Pierre. 1984. *Distinction: A Social Critique of the Judgment of Taste*. Translated by Richard Nice. Cambridge, MA: Harvard University Press.
Carrillo, Beatriz. 2008. "From Coal Black to Hospital White: New Welfare Entrepreneurs and the Pursuit of a Cleaner Status." In *The New Rich in China: Future Rulers, Present Lives*, edited by David S. G. Goodman, 99–111. London: Routledge.
Chang, Leslie T. 2012. "Working Titles: What Do the Most Industrious People on Earth Read for Fun?" Letter from China. *New Yorker*, February 6, 2012. www.newyorker.com/reporting/2012/02/06/120206fa_fact_chang?printable=true&current Page=6. Accessed August 15, 2012.
China Foreign Service. 1997. Issue 4. Beijing: Zhongguo Duiwai Fuwu Zazhi She (*China Foreign Service* Magazine Office).

Dai, Jinhua. 1995. "Invisible Women: Contemporary Chinese Cinema and Women's Film." Translated by Mayfair Mei-hui Yang. *Positions* 3 (1):255–280.

Duthie, Laurie. 2005. "White Collars with Chinese Characteristics: Global Capitalism and the Formation of a Social Identity."*Anthropology of Work Review* 24:1–12.

Ernst & Young. 2005. "China: The New Lap of Luxury." www.ey.com/global/download.nsf/China_E/050914_Report_E/$file/China-The%20New%20Lap%20of%20Luxury_Eng%20(Final).pdf. Accessed October 10, 2005.

Fang, Bay, and Thomas Omestad. 2006. "Spending Spree: They're Young, They Have Money to Burn, and the Race is on to Win Them as Customers." *U.S. News & World Report* 140 (16):42–48, 50.

Gold, Thomas B. 1990. "Urban Private Business and Social Change." In *Chinese Society on the Eve of Tiananmen: The Impact of Reform*, edited by Deborah Davis, and Ezra F. Vogel, 56–78. Cambridge, MA: Council on East Asian Studies/Harvard University.

Goodman, David S.G. 1996. "The People's Republic of China: The Party-State, Capitalist Revolution and New Entrepreneurs." In *The New Rich in Asia: Mobile Phones, McDonald's, and Middle Class Revolution*, edited by R. Robison, and D.S.G. Goodman, 225–242. London: Routledge.

Goodman, David S. G., and Xiaowei Zang. 2008. "The New Rich in China: The Dimensions of Social Change." In *The New Rich in China*, edited by David S. G. Goodman, 1–20. London: Routledge.

Griffiths, Michael B., Malcolm Chapman, and Flemming Christiansen. 2010. "Chinese Consumers: The Romantic Reappraisal." *Ethnography* 11:331–357.

Hanser, Amy. 2008. *Service Encounters: Class, Gender, and the Market for Social Distinction in Urban China*. Stanford, CA: Stanford University Press.

Hoffman, Lisa M. 2010. *Patriotic Professionalism in Urban China: Fostering Talent*. Philadelphia, PA: Temple University Press.

Hooper, Beverley. 1984. "China's Modernization: Are Young Women Going to Lose Out?" *Modern China* 10 (3):317–343.

Hsu, Carolyn. 2006. "*Cadres, Getihu*, and Good Business People: Making Sense of Entrepreneurs in Early Post-Socialist China." *Urban Anthropology and Studies of Cultural Systems and World Economic Development* 35 (1):1–38.

Kanter, Rosabeth Moss. 1993. *Men and Women of the Corporation*. New York, NY: Basic Books.

Lakshmanan, Indira A. R. 1997. "China's Chuppie Revolution: The Name of the Game is to Woo the Upwardly Mobile Consumer—and the State Condones It." *Boston Globe*, April 29, D1.

Li, Ke. 2007. *Du Lala Shengzhi Ji (Diary of Du Lala's Promotion)*. Xi'an, China: Shanxi Shifan Daxue Chubanshe (Shanxi Normal University Publishing House).

Lou, Chen. 2003. "*Bailing Liren: Dianya zhong de Shishang*" ("White-Collar Beauty: Fashion in Elegance"). *Yiyao yu Baojian (Medicine and Healthcare)* 11:5.

Lu, Xueyi, ed. 2002. *Dangdai Zhongguo Shehui Jieceng Yanjiu Baogao (Report on the Study of Social Strata in Contemporary China)*. Beijing: China Social Sciences Academic Press.

Miao-er, and Li Yan. 1995. "*Zhongguo Yapishi*" ("Chinese Yuppies"). *Xinwen Chuban Jiaoliu (News Publication Exchange)* 6:36.

Otis, Eileen M. 2012. *Markets and Bodies: Women, Service Work, and the Making of Inequality in China*. Palo Alto, CA: Stanford University Press.

Pearson, Margaret M. 1997. *China's New Business Elite: The Political Consequences of Economic Reform*. Berkeley: University of California Press.

60 Beijing Yuppies

Pringle, James. 1994. "Peking Yuppies Turn Blind Eye to Images of Revolution." *The Times*, April 19, n.p.

Rofel, Lisa. 1999. *Other Modernities: Gendered Yearnings in China After Socialism*. Berkeley: University of California Press.

Rosen, Stanley. 2004. "The Victory of Materialism: Aspirations to Join China's Urban Moneyed Classes and the Commercialization of Education." *China Journal* 51:27–51.

Wang, Gan. 2000. "Cultivating Friendship Through Bowling in Shenzhen." In *The Consumer Revolution in Urban China*, edited by Deborah S. Davis, 250–67. Berkeley, CA: University of California Press.

Wang, Shaoguang. 1995. "The Politics of Private Time." In *Urban Spaces in Contemporary China: The Potential for Autonomy and Community in Post-Mao China*, edited by Deborah S. Davis, Richard Kraus, Barry Naughton, and Elizabeth J. Perry, 149–172. Cambridge: Woodrow Wilson Center Press and Cambridge University Press.

Wang, Zheng. 2003. "Gender, Employment and Women's Resistance." In *Chinese Society: Change, Conflict and Resistance*, edited by Elizabeth J. Perry, and Mark Selden, 2nd ed., 158–182. London: Routledge Curzon.

Warhurst, Chris, Dennis Nickson, Anne Witz, and Anne Marie Cullen. 2000. "Aesthetic Labour in Interactive Service Work: Some Case Study Evidence from the 'New' Glasgow." *Service Industries Journal* 20:1–18.

Williams, Christine L., and Catherine Connell. 2010. "'Looking Good and Sounding Right': Aesthetic Labor and Social Inequality in the Retail Industry." *Work and Occupations* 37:349–377.

Witz, Anne, Chris Warhurst, and Dennis Nickson. 2003. "The Labour of Aesthetics and the Aesthetics of Organization." *Organization* 10:33–54.

Yan, Yunxiang. 1997. "McDonald's in Beijing." In *Golden Arches East: McDonald's in East Asia*, edited by James L. Watson, 39–76. Stanford, CA: Stanford University Press.

Yan, Yunxiang. 2002. "Managed Globalization: State Power and Cultural Transition in China." In *Many Globalizations: Cultural Diversity in the Contemporary World*, edited by Peter L. Berger, and Samuel P. Huntington, 19–47. Oxford: Oxford University Press.

Yang, Jie. 2007. "'Re-Employment Stars': Language, Gender and Neoliberal Restructuring in China." In *Words, Worlds, and Material Girls: Language, Gender, Globalization*, edited by Bonnie S. McElhinny, 73–102. Berlin and New York, NY: de Gruyter.

Yang, Mayfair Mei-hui. 1999. "From Gender Erasure to Gender Difference: State Feminism, Consumer Sexuality, and Women's Public Sphere in China." In *Spaces of Their Own: Women's Public Sphere in Transnational China*, edited by Mayfair Mei-hui Yang, 35–67. Minneapolis, MN: University of Minnesota Press.

Yao, Fuyou. 1998. "*Bailing Liren Zhiye Toushi*" ("Seeing through the Occupation of White-Collar Beauty"). *Zhongguo Renli Ziyuan Kaifa* (*China Human Resources Development*) 8:35–36.

Zhang, Wei-Wei. 2000. *Transforming China: Economic Reform and its Political Implications*. New York, NY: St. Martin's Press.

Zheng, Kailai. 2001. "*Shanghai 'Bailing' Sumiao*" ("Sketch of Shanghai 'White Collar"). *Shehui (Society)* 5:19.

3

COSMOPOLITAN MANDARIN IN THE MAKING OF BEIJING YUPPIES

Those who frequent office buildings of foreign corporations and Sino-foreign joint ventures would find themselves appearing rustic and stupid without understanding English, even when communicating with local employees. This is because when local employees talk, they always like to add some trendy **hybrid Chinese**. … The phenomenon of hybrid Chinese has caused distress and anguish among linguists who call for standardization of Mandarin Chinese. But as more and more people join such hybrid entities—working in joint ventures, eating hybrid Chinese-style fast food—it's inevitable that they regurgitate this kind of hybrid language.

("Hybrid Chinese," X. Chen 1997, 9)

The **white-collar accent** in office buildings seems to be carved out of the same mold: The intonation is soft and rustling, no tongue-curling, nor rhotacization, packaging professional restraint and formulaic politeness; occasional use of the most trendy business jargon … and often some fluent English sentences. All these come to be markers of them keeping up with the times.

("White-Collar Beauty: Fashion in Elegance," Lou 2003, 5)

3.1 Linguistic Styling of Beijing Yuppies

This chapter focuses on the construction of social distinction through linguistic styling. As an integral part of the project of distinction making, linguistic styling refers to the construction of a style through bricolage, that is, (re)using and combining linguistic resources. The analysis presented in the rest of the chapter shows that the Beijing yuppies combine a clustering of linguistic

62 Cosmopolitan Mandarin in the Making of Beijing Yuppies

resources to create their cosmopolitan identity in relation to other groups, particularly state professionals and other wealthy locals. The linguistic styling of distinction is achieved through the use of an innovative Mandarin style that is distinctive from the local Beijing Mandarin (BM) as well as the supraregional Standard PTH.

Not only are the yuppies recognized as a new social group, such recognition is often accompanied by their perceived linguistic traits. As shown in the two quotations above, their speech is described as something new and fashionable, and most importantly, different from PTH. The description of "hybrid Chinese" in the first excerpt emphasizes their use of English and expressions from Cantonese (not shown in the excerpt); such a "hybrid" linguistic style is viewed as cosmopolitan, trendy, and iconic of their hybrid lifestyle. The "white-collar accent" described in the second excerpt specifically depicts the speech characteristics of *waiqi* women, or "white-collar beauties" (*bai-ling liren*). In addition to the use of English and business jargon, the "white-collar accent" is defined by the lack of, or avoidance of, two features emblematic of Standard PTH and BM: retroflex onsets (commonly known as *juan-she yin* 'tongue-curling sounds') and rhotacization (commonly known as *er-hua*). Portrayed as "soft" and "rustling" (presumably due to the replacement of retroflex onsets with dental sibilants), the accent is one of the components that constitute a "fashionable and elegant lifestyle" of the "white-collar beauties" (Lou 2003, 5).

As expected, the media reports, such as X. Chen (1997) and Lou (2003), overgeneralize linguistic features used by the new professionals and present their linguistic style as a discrete "accent" that is a reflection of their professional category membership and a cosmopolitan lifestyle, rather than focusing on usage patterns of the features identified in the reports. Based on the speech data collected from the Beijing yuppies, for example, none of them was found to replace the retroflex onsets with dental sibilants, and all used rhotacization but at a much lower frequency than *guoqi* professionals. However, despite such overgeneralizations, the reports do point to a few salient linguistic resources used by the Beijing yuppies found in my study, particularly, the use of English expressions and technical terms; above all, the media coverage highlights that Beijing yuppies' linguistic style is indeed distinctively different from Standard PTH, which is based on the phonology of their native dialect.

The following analysis shows that the linguistic styling of distinction is created through patterning of linguistic variation, analyzed quantitatively, as well as the use of linguistic features in the discourse even when the talk is not explicitly about distinction. As I described in Chapter 1, quantitative analysis of linguistic variation is crucial to reveal broad patterns of inter- and intragroup variation, providing a general picture of the yuppies' linguistic style and its positioning in relation to that of another relevant group in the sociolinguistic landscape. Furthermore, my analysis of the linguistic forms used in discourse reveals how the composition of style is done in context and what specific

Cosmopolitan Mandarin in the Making of Beijing Yuppies **63**

meanings emerge when speakers employ linguistic resources to create differentiation and alignment. Section 3.2 describes the four sociolinguistic variables and explores their cultural saliency; Section 3.3 presents my quantitative analyses of them. Section 3.4 highlights the yuppie–state-professional intergroup differences as contrasted between two styles of Mandarin: The yuppies create an innovative Cosmopolitan Mandarin style to differentiate themselves from the state professionals, who speak a local style of Mainland Standard Mandarin. Section 3.5 further examines the rise of Cosmopolitan Mandarin in the context of China's economic transformation, which gives rise to a new transnational Chinese Linguistic Market. Section 3.6 focuses on the relation between gender and sociolinguistic variation, taking into account a multitude of factors that interact with the ways through which women and men in the yuppie group style their cosmopolitan professional identity. Section 3.7 offers a more nuanced analysis of linguistic variation used in discourse as stylistic resources for making distinctions. Section 3.8 concludes the chapter.

3.2 "Beijing Smooth Operator," "Alley Saunterer," and the "Cosmopolitan Chinese": Linguistic Variables and Their Imbued Cultural Saliency

Quantitative analysis of the linguistic style of the *waiqi* professionals focuses mainly on their use of four phonological variables and is based on data collected from high-quality audio recordings of sociolinguistic interviews with 14 of the 25 *waiqi* professionals (7 women and 7 men). These participants were selected based on a combination of factors, mainly including the linguistic background of the speaker, the sound quality of the interview, and the smaller number of women managerial level professionals that I was able to find and interview. All 14 speakers were born in and grew up in Beijing. In addition, they had not lived an extended period of time outside of Beijing. They all had undergraduate level education and had gone through all of their schooling (from primary school to undergraduate studies) in Beijing. For purposes of comparison, the same number of professionals working in state-owned companies with comparable linguistic and educational background was interviewed. The age of the 28 speakers ranged from 28 to 41. All interviews were conducted at the speaker's workplace. The interview focused on two general topics: professional experiences and Beijing society and culture. Having the participants talk about their job-related experiences in their own workplace created a context in which their professional identity became relevant and salient. The second topic was designed to elicit conversations about BM, as well as local culture and history, including locally salient social characters and groups.

As mentioned in the Introduction to this book, Standard PTH shares a phonetic inventory with BM. Thus, in terms of pronunciation, BM speakers can be said to be native speakers of PTH with varying degrees of localness

64 Cosmopolitan Mandarin in the Making of Beijing Yuppies

in their accents. Within BM, phonological variation has been found among speakers of different age groups and between urban and suburban speakers (Linguistics Group 1995, 7–8 fn. 12). Many local accent features and expressions are not incorporated into Standard PTH. The difference between BM and Standard PTH is best described as a continuum of the sort sociolinguists have generally relied on: The fewer the local BM features, the closer the speech is to Standard PTH. The extreme local end of the continuum is known as *Beijing tuhua* or *Jing pian-zi* 'Beijing vernacular'. In the same way that Northern Mandarin speakers have difficulty understanding speakers of Southern varieties, such as Wu (e.g., Shanghai *hua*) and Cantonese (e.g. Guangdong *hua*), nonlocals often complain that they have a hard time understanding Beijing vernacular.

Furthermore, unlike earlier variationist sociolinguistic studies that focused on linguistic variables involved in linguistic change, particularly sound change, the four variables in this study are *stable* in the sense that they are not involved in sound change in their respective phonological systems. However, as I show in this chapter, the nonlocal variants of these variables are combined, together with other resources, to create a *new* ensemble, an innovative Mandarin style. This is a process of "bricolage" discussed in Chapter 1, whereby existing semiotic elements are combined to create something new. Also, recall from Chapter 1 that bricolage is inherently dialogic in the sense that the bricoleur or stylistic agent reuses and combines semiotic resources that are imbued with semiotic significance. Hence, treating linguistic variables as stylistic resources requires the examination of imbued cultural significance of the linguistic variables. The purpose of such an examination is to inform the analysis of their reuse by the yuppies in their current project of distinction making. Indeed, all four phonological variables investigated in this study are locally salient in the sense that they are recognized to varying degrees and linked to culturally salient character types. In other words, as shown below they are *enregistered* sociolinguistic variables (see Section 1.2.3.3)—that is, they are recognized as associated with culturally salient character types (Agha 2007). As the degree of awareness of variables and their variants differs, the researcher's linguistic insights are indispensable in figuring out which feature(s) are associated with a particular character type when the participants' description is vague. Thus, the following discussion of the linguistic variables combines technical description with folk metalinguistic portrayals.

I start the description of the linguistic variables with a general introduction to the historical and cultural significance of BM. Similar to culturally salient and well-known regional dialects in other parts of the world, such as New York English and Cockney, BM or Beijing *hua* is one of the best-known dialects in the Chinese-speaking world. The term *dialect* used here refers to the folk conception and perception of a culturally distinctive way of speaking (similar to Agha's [2003] definition of the folk term *accent*). From a sociolinguistic perspective, however, Beijing *hua* does not refer to a single local variety. Rather, it is a general term that encompasses a variety of local ways of speaking. In this sense, it is similar to "London English" as a cover term for a range of dialectal variation, including the Cockney dialect of the East End of London, the dialect of the polite/upper-class society that serves as the basis for Received Pronunciation, and more recently Multicultural London English (Cheshire et al. 2011). In addition to *Jing pian-zi*, folk terms referring to "authentic" Beijing speech include *Jing qiangr* 'Beijing accent'; *Jing diaor* 'Beijing tone or tune'; and the more general *Jing weir* 'Beijing flavor' that can refer to anything authentically Beijing from speech to food to literary style. Unlike New York English and Cockney, which enjoy local pride but are stigmatized "accents" more generally, *Jing qiangr* has sustained a special national status with which few other regional varieties can compete. Although since the 1980s the status of certain Southern varieties, such as Shanghai *hua* and Cantonese, has risen due to the rapid economic development of the two regions (e.g., Erbaugh 1995), their heightened prestige is considered by some as a fad. For instance, the popularization of Cantonese in the 80s and 90s was called *Yueyu re* 'Cantonese fever' (e.g., Songlin Chen 1991).

What gives Beijing speech its special national status is its tremendous cultural prominence. One source of its cultural prominence lies in its being the dialect of the capital city. Beijing has been the capital of China since the Yuan Dynasty (1271–1368), and since the 1920s a conservative variety of this dialect has been designated the phonological basis for the national language. Furthermore, a long tradition of literary writing in the Beijing vernacular has given this local dialect a rich cultural heritage and prestige (L. Zhang 1994). Many earlier *baihua* 'vernacular' literary masterpieces, such as Cao Xueqin's *Hong Lou Meng* 'Dream of the Red Chamber' (c. 1765) and Wen Kang's *Ernü Yingxiong Zhuan* 'The Gallant Maid' (1878), were written in Beijing colloquial style (Jin and Bai 1993; Lü 1994). Modern and contemporary writers continue the tradition and contribute to what is called *Jing wei wenxue* 'Beijing flavor literature' or *Jing wei xiaoshuo* 'Beijing flavor novels' in which Beijing vernacular features are used to depict cultural characters of Beijingers, their lives, living environments, and folk customs (Lü 1994; L. Zhang 1994; Y. Zhao 1991; D. Zhao 1996). Many Beijing flavor literature writers are eminent nationally, including Lao She (1899–1966), Zhang Henshui (1895–1967), Deng Youmei (1931–), Liu Xinwu (1942–), and Wang Shuo (1958–). These authors also often write about BM itself. For example, Lao She's *Zheng Hong Qi Xia* 'Under the Red Banner' portrays the handsome and suave protagonist, Fuhai, speaking "such beautiful Beijing speech that others think he must be the creator of this noble language" (Lao 1984 [1979], 208).

Beijing-flavor literary works are reproduced as plays, films, and television drama series. Such creations constitute a crucial metadiscursive genre through which the link between local linguistic features and social images and character

66 Cosmopolitan Mandarin in the Making of Beijing Yuppies

types are reproduced, reified, and brought into wider recirculation through mass media (Agha 2007). In this way, particularly salient Beijing linguistic features and stereotypes have come to be nationally and even internationally well known. Two of the most famous Beijinger character types are *Jing youzi* 'Beijing smooth operator' and *hutong chuanzi* 'alley saunterer', and they are associated with three of the linguistic variables in this study.

In the following description of the linguistic variables, they are grouped into two categories, three local variables, and one cosmopolitan variable. Such categorization is based on linguistic considerations and in accordance with the established semiotic saliency of these linguistic features in the local language ideology. Two of the local variables (rhotacization and lenition) are linked to the most famous Beijing cultural icon *Jing youzi* 'Beijing smooth operator'. The third local variable (interdental realization of (ts)) is associated with the *hutong chuanzi* 'alley saunterer'. The cosmopolitan variable (a tone variable) represents a case of linguistic innovation in Northern Mandarin that has become socially salient as a result of contact between Standard PTH and non-mainland Mandarin varieties, particularly Hong Kong Cantonese and Taiwan Mandarin. In the following discussion, I introduce the character type first, followed by a description of the linguistic variable(s) to which the character type is linked.

3.2.1 The "Beijing Smooth Operator" Variables: Rhotacization and Lenition

Few local stereotypes are as well known as *Jing youzi*, the Beijing smooth operator. *Jing* in *Jing youzi*, refers to 'Beijing'. *You*, the Mandarin word for 'oil' means *youhua* 'oily' or 'slippery'. When used to describe a personality, *you* connotes smoothness and being worldly-wise. With the nominalization suffix -*zi*, *youzi* refers to someone who is versed in the ways of the world. It is the only local stereotype that receives an entry in the *Modern Chinese Dictionary*, defined as "a longtime resident of Beijing who is worldly and slick" (*Xiandai Hanyu Cidian* 1998, 663). Beijing-flavor literature offers many vivid examples of various kinds of Beijing smooth operator characters who are expert at wheeling and dealing their way through particularly difficult times in the country's capital city.

A famous example of the Beijing smooth operator is portrayed in Lao She's novel *Zheng Hong Qi Xia* '*Beneath the Red Banner*' (1984 [1979]; written in the late 1950s), a masterpiece of Beijing flavor literature. The protagonist, Fuhai, is the son of a large Manchurian noble family that has lost its fortune with the decline of the Qing Dynasty. A descendent of the Manchu nobility, he is accomplished with both the pen and the sword and is well versed in both Manchurian and Han culture. He is regarded as the most popular

Cosmopolitan Mandarin in the Making of Beijing Yuppies **67**

character among his relatives and friends. *"Piaoliang you laocheng,"* 'handsome and experienced', he is the epitome of impeccably "beautiful" manners: "He greets people beautifully, sits beautifully, walks beautifully, rides on horseback beautifully" (Lao 1984, 207). This handsome and suave character, who speaks "beautiful Beijing accent" (1984, 208) and "has the gift of gab" (1984, 292), is often asked to help his family and friends deal with difficult situations. Fuhai is an example of the "cultured" Beijing smooth operator type who comes from a privileged background. But as demonstrated in Lihang Zhang's (1994) survey of literary instantiations of this stock character, the "Beijing smooth operator" comes from all walks of life, including businessmen, fallen Manchurian noble descendants, entertainers and artists, politicians, and intellectuals. However, despite their diverse socioeconomic and professional backgrounds, they share a set of characterological attributes centering on worldly wisdom, street smarts, slickness, remarkable urban versatility, and *savoir-faire*. Furthermore, it is worth noting that the literary Beijing smooth operators in L. Zhang's survey are all **urban male characters**. This gendered attribute is also corroborated by the participants in my sociolinguistic interviews: **The archetype of a Beijing smooth operator is always a man.** As I demonstrate later in the linguistic analysis, the association of "smoothness" with a male character sheds light on the gendered distribution of the two "Beijing smooth operator" variables.

In addition to the smoothness of the Beijing smooth operator, there is a widely shared belief that Beijing speech is smooth. As demonstrated by numerous examples in my earlier study (Q. Zhang 2008), a process of iconization (Irvine and Gal 2000, 37), or rhematization (Gal 2016, 122), is at work, whereby the smoothness of Beijing speech is interpreted as a reflection of the inherent nature of the Beijing smooth operator and of Beijingers in general. For example, Lü (1994), in her analysis of Beijing speech as a rich stylistic resource for Beijing-flavor novels, naturalizes a causal relation between Beijingers' cultural character of being "well versed in the ways of the world" and the smoothness of their speech (1994, 155–156; emphasis added):

> [*Jing qiang*] sounds mellow, familiar, formed over a long history of being the residents of the capital. ... As such, **Beijingers are well versed in the ways of the world. This makes their speech sound smooth and mellow....**

She further attributes the smoothness of Beijing speech to the result of **"extensive use of 'rhotacization,' which smoothes out the edges and corners of speech** ... [makes it] sound smooth and mellow, and engenders a feeling of warmth and intimacy" (1994, 156; emphasis added).

As shown in the quote above, rhotacization, or *er-hua,* is one of the linguistic features associated with the Beijing smooth operator and the smooth quality

68 Cosmopolitan Mandarin in the Making of Beijing Yuppies

of Beijing speech. A similar case of iconization is illustrated in the following excerpt from my interview:

Excerpt 3.1 Liu (38, male, chief representative of a foreign bank)

1 *Qishi, shuo Beijing ren you,*
   In fact, Beijingers are said to be smooth,
2 *suowei Jing youzi ma,*
   the so-called Beijing smooth operator,
3 *zhuyao shi yinwei Beijing hua you haoduo er-hua yin.*
   mainly because Beijing speech has a lot of rhotacization.
4 *Beijing ren benlai jiu neng shuo,*
   Beijingers are naturally gifted with gab,
5 *zai jiashang er yin zhong,*
   and with **heavy r-sounding,**
6 *na jiu xiande youhua.*
   then [Beijingers] appear to be **smooth.**
7 *Ni ting shei shuo guo Guangdong ren youqiangr* **[+R]** *huadiaor* **[+R]** *a.*
   Have you heard anybody saying the Cantonese have 'oily accent **[+R]** slippery tone **[+R]**'.
8 *Na shi yinwei tamen shetou bu hui dawar* **[+R]**.
   That's because their tongues can't curl **[+R]**.

In the above excerpt, a mutually causal relation is construed between the smooth characteristic of the stereotypical Beijinger and the linguistic feature of rhotacization and the so-called 'heavy r-sound' (line 5). Using a familiar idiom of 'oily accent slippery tone' (line 7), another smoothness-related characterization of Beijing speech, the speaker contrasts the smooth-tongued Beijinger against a salient southern group, the Cantonese, who are thought to be unable to curl their tongues. The "oily" and "slippery" sound and quality of Beijing speech is instantiated through the speaker's use of rhotacization (represented by word-final *r* in boldface) in the pronunciation of the key expressions: "oily accent **[+R]**, slippery tone **[+R]**" in line 7 and the verb "curl **[+R]**" in line 8. The comment on (the ability of) "tongue curling" to produce rhotacization, while seemingly an insignificant layperson's perception of Beijing speech in this example, turns out to be a focal point of ideological contestation over the legitimacy of Beijing-Mandarin-based PTH, which I will discuss in Chapter 5.

Considered the most telltale feature of BM, rhotacization is commonly known among Chinese speakers and many learners of Chinese as *er-hua*. It involves the addition of a subsyllabic retroflex −*r* [ɻ] to the final, causing the final to take on *r*-coloring and becoming rhotacized (Chao 1968; Lu 1995). Other common terms include *er-hua yun* 'rhotacized rhyme' and *er-hua yin* 'rhotacized sound'. This feature is shared among many Northern Mandarin and Southwestern Mandarin varieties and is especially prominent in BM (ibid.). Rhotacization is represented in *piyin* as "r" and in Chinese character as 儿 *er* [ɚ],

Cosmopolitan Mandarin in the Making of Beijing Yuppies **69**

literally meaning 'son'. In the following examples, the IPA transcriptions of the non-rhotacized forms are followed by their rhotacized counterparts.

(1) 'upstart' *bao4fa1hu4* [paufahu], *bao4fa1hur4* [paufahuɻ]
(2) 'famous brand' *ming2pai2* [miŋpʰai], *ming2par2* [miŋpʰaɻ][1]

The tokens of rhotacization in this study exclude cases in which the addition of -*r* changes the semantic meaning or the part of speech of the word, as in the following examples:

(3) *Qian2Men2* as a proper noun, referring to the *Zhengyang Men* 'Zhengyang Gate' in the historic city wall of Beijing vs. *qian2mer2*, 'front door' of a building or a vehicle
(4) *xin4* 'letter' vs. *xir4* 'information'
(5) *gai4* 'cover' (verb) vs. *gar4* 'lid, cover' (noun)

Historically, the present subsyllabic /ɻ/ was a diminutive suffix, a syllabic retroflex vowel /ɚ/, meaning 'son' in classical Chinese (Li and Thompson 1981; Lu 1995; Norman 1988; Wang 1958). Its use is found as early as the Tang Dynasty (618–907) (Norman 1988; Wang 1958), but it occurred only after animated nouns and the suffixation added the meaning of junior and being young. Later, its use extended to nouns in general but the specific meaning of being young was lost. In modern BM, it has lost much of its morphological significance and semantic content in that the occurrence of the retroflex ending does not categorically add a diminutive meaning to the root morpheme. For example, rhotacization of *men2 feng4* 'crack of the door' as *men2 fengr4* does not always distinguish the difference between a large and a small crack of the door. It can occur after certain verbs (e.g., *war2* 'play', and *huor3* 'to be angry'); measure words or classifiers (e.g., *ber3* 'classifier for books, albums', and *piar4* 'piece, flake'); some temporal adverbs, such as *jir1* 'today', and *mingr2* 'tomorrow'; and certain locative particles, such as *zher4* 'here' and *nar4* 'there'; and locative particles with the suffixes −*bian* and −*mian*, for instance, *li3-biar* 'inside', *wai4-biar* 'outside', and *qian-miar* 'in front of'.[2] However, because historically -*r* developed from a nominal diminutive suffix, one of the pragmatic functions of rhotacization in modern Beijing (and Standard) Mandarin is to express diminutive connotations. For example, BM speakers may use rhotacization in *xiao3 cha2 hur2* when referring to a small and elegantly made teapot; a rhotacized *xiao3 gui1nür* 'little girl' may express affection; and a rhotacized *xiao3tour1* 'thief' may express contempt. It is important to note that rhotacization is a feature characteristic of colloquial speech. This is why it is rarely used and heard in formal speech such as broadcast news reports.

Another variable associated with the Beijing smooth operator, albeit at a lower degree of awareness, is lenition of retroflex obstruent initials *sh* /ʂ/, *zh* /tʂ/, and *ch* /tʂʰ/. In BM, these retroflex initials sometimes are lenited, or

70 Cosmopolitan Mandarin in the Making of Beijing Yuppies

weakened, and realized as the approximant retroflex [ɻ] (Chao 1968). Both rhotacization and lenition contribute to the perception of Beijing speech as "heavy *r*-sounding." Lenition can occur word medially in a multisyllabic word and across word boundaries. It is briefly mentioned in Chao (1968) and Norman (1988), both claiming lenition to be a feature of weakly stressed (i.e., neutral tone) syllables. In my data, however, lenition also occurs in stressed (i.e., tonal) syllables. In this study, the retroflex obstruent initials are represented by the fricative (ʂ). The tokens used in the statistical analysis are word-medial occurrences, as shown in the following two examples. In (6), the second syllable of *xuesheng* 'student' has a neutral tone. In (7), the second syllable of *huasheng* 'peanut' has a high-level tone.

(6) 'student' *xue2sheng* [ɕyɛʂəŋ], *xue2reng* [ɕyɛɻəŋ]
(7) 'peanut' *hua1sheng1* [huaʂəŋ], *hua1reng1* [huaɻəŋ]

The participants' awareness of this variable is not as strong as that of rhotacization. No participant uses the technical term *ruo-hua* to refer to lenition. However, their examples make it clear that they do associate this feature with "heavy *r*-sounding." In the following quote, the speaker uses two examples to illustrate what he means by "heavy *r*-sound."

(8)
1   *Beijing ren shuohua eryin zhong, ai da dulu,*
    Beijingers talk with heavy r-sound, like to trill,
2   *Haoxiang zuili hanle kuair* [**+R**] *rede kao hongshu.*
    as if holding a piece [**+R**] of hot baked sweet potato in their mouth.
3   *Xiang ba tongzhi shuocheng tongri* [**+lenition**],
    Such as comrade [tʰuŋtʂ]³ is pronounced as comrade [tʰuŋɻ]⁴ [**+lenition**],
4   *paichusuo, pairsuor* [**+lenition, +R**].
    police station [pʰaitʂʰusuo] as police station [pʰaiɻusuoɻ] [**+lenition, +R**].

The first example for "heavy *r*-sounding" is a case of lenition (line 3) in which the syllable initial retroflex [tʂ] in *tongzhi* 'comrade' is lenited. In the 'police station' example in line 4, both lenition and rhotacization occurred so that [pʰaitʂʰusuo] was realized as [pʰaiɻusuoɻ].

Some participants describe lenition as a "swallowing sound," as shown in the next example.

(9)
1   *Beijing ren ai shuo "xiang maoru'i* [**+lenition**] *baoreng* [**+lenition**]"
    (([ɕiaŋ·mau·ɻu·i·pau·ɻəŋ])).
    Beijingers like to say "promise [**+lenition**] to Chairman [**+lenition**] Mao".

Cosmopolitan Mandarin in the Making of Beijing Yuppies 71

2 *Nikan xiang-mao-zhu-xi-bao-zheng*
(([ɕiaŋ·mau·tʂu·ɕi·pau·tʂəŋ])),
Look, promise-to-Chair-man-Mao,

3 *liuge zir* [+R] *biancheng xiang maoru'i* [+lenition] *baoreng* [+lenition]
(([ɕiaŋ·mau·ɹu·i·pau·ɹəŋ])).
six words [+R] are changed to promise [+lenition] to Chairman
[+lenition] Mao.

4 *Ji ge? Sa zir* [+R] *le.*
How many? Three words [+R].

5 *Beijing ren nengshuo, shuohua kuai, ai tun yin.*
Beijingers are glib, talk fast, like to swallow sounds.

6 *Jiu xiande bijiao yuanhua.*
Hence [they] appear to be smooth.

In the expression "promise to Chairman Mao" in line 2, /tʂ/ in both "chairman" and "promise" is lenited, and the initial/onset in the second syllable of /tʂu·ɕi/ is deleted. Although the number of syllables remains the same, the speaker perceives the result of "swallowing sounds" as a reduction in words, or more precisely, syllables. In lines 5 and 6, the speaker also links Beijingers' speech characteristics of "being glib, talking fast, swallowing sounds" to smoothness.

3.2.2 The "Alley Saunterer" Variable: Interdental Realization of (ts)

The second local stereotype is called *hutong chuanzi* 'alley saunterer', as shown in the following excerpt from my interview:

Excerpt 3.2 Tian (36, assistant manager at a national bank)
Real Beijingers are those old Manchurians, like the grandmother of our colleague, Zhao Hao. Or those *hutong chuanzi*, **born in** *hutong*, **growing up in** *hutong*, **wandering around in** *hutong* **if they have nothing else to do.** Some of my middle-school classmates were like that.

Hutong is the local term for narrow streets or alleys. Traditionally, no private residence was built on the side of a main street, or *dai jie*, so *hutong* was the corridor connecting the main street to residential neighborhoods. Nowadays, *hutongs* are being replaced by thoroughfares as traditional one-story houses give way to high-rise apartment complexes. *Chuanzi* is a person who saunters around without a destination, and *hutong chuanzi* 'alley saunterer' is a stereotypical Beijing male character: a man who is feckless and walks about in the alleys, waiting for something to happen. D. Yang (1994, 257) suggests that this term originated during the Cultural Revolution (1966–1976) when children of privileged high-ranking communist carders, or the *da yuan* 'big compound' youth

72 Cosmopolitan Mandarin in the Making of Beijing Yuppies

as they were called, staged fights in streets or alleys against opposing groups. Because alley fights were considered common among *hutong* youth, the privileged youth used the label as a stigmatized term to refer to the *hutong* children. Lihang Zhang (1994, 54) makes the same distinction between "alley saunterers" and "big compound" youth of the political and military elite who had higher social status and who were considered more educated and culturally refined. Thus, according to such accounts, *hutong chuanzi* is a more recently created term than *Jing youzi*. An alley saunterer is a stigmatized stereotype whose essential characteristics include lack of education, fecklessness, inclination toward troublemaking, and exclusively local. Although they are residents of the capital city, the national cultural and political center, their world is constrained to the grids of *hutongs*. They are among what Beijing-flavor writer Liu Xinwu calls the "indigenous" people of the metropolis. In his novel *Zhong Gu Lou 'Bell Drum Tower'*, Liu (1985, 122) describes the "indigenous" Beijingers as those having lived in the city for more than three generations. They share the characteristics of having low socioeconomic status and education, working in the service industry or blue-collar jobs, living in the alleys (*hutong*) in the inner city, and being less mobile than other Beijingers (ibid.).

One memorable literary figure of *hutong chuanzi* is Song Baoqi in Liu Xinwu's short story *"Ban Zhuren"* 'The Class Headteacher' (see L. Zhang 1994, 49). He is a high school adolescent, rebellious against the school, and a delinquent. Yao Xiangdong is another alley saunterer in *Bell Drum Tower* by the same author. He is an unemployed hooligan with little education, idling away his time in the alleys. These Beijing locals are the main characters in Liu's (1997) collection of short stories entitled *Hutong Chuanzi 'Alley Saunterers'*. The following are some of the activities of literary characters of alley saunterers: hanging about at the doorway watching people pass by, bullying kids, drawing graffiti, and committing vandalism and petty theft (see also L. Zhang 1994, 49–52). Although misbehavior and delinquency are often associated with alley saunterer characters, they are at the same time portrayed as kindhearted and willing to help others. However, because of their low education and low economic and occupational status they live on the margins of society.

The main difference between the two Beijing local character types is that the smooth operator applies to many types, whereas the alley saunterer calls forth a stereotypical lower-class male image (D. Yang 1994). The smooth operator is a resourceful wheeler and dealer well versed in the circumstances of Beijing as the national cultural and political center whereas the alley saunterer is restricted to the grids of alleys (Liu 1997). Unlike the Beijing smooth operator who is willing to work the system to his own advantage, the alley saunterer seems to be non-participatory, at ease with his position on the margin and the bottom of society, occasionally engaging in small acts of non-conformity.

The speech feature associated with the alley saunterer is the interdental realization of the dental sibilants *s* /s/, *z* /ts/, and *c* /ts^h/ as [θ], [tθ], and [tθ^h],

Cosmopolitan Mandarin in the Making of Beijing Yuppies **73**

respectively.[5] In this study, they are represented by /ts/. In the following examples, the realizations in PTH are presented first, followed by the interdental "alley saunterer" variant:

(10) 'alley saunterer' *hu2tong4 chuan4zi* [hut^{h}uŋ tʂ^{h}uantʂ], *hu2tong4 chuan4thi* [hut^{h}uŋ tʂ^{h}uantθ]

(11) 'now' *xian4zai4* [ɕiantsai], xian4thai4 [ɕiantθai]

In the following excerpt, this feature is used to characterize the "authentic" BM of alley saunterers in the words "saunter" (line 2) and "cabbage" (line 4):

Excerpt 3.3 Chang (35, North American law firm)

1   Mine is not the real Beijing Mandarin,
2   because I'm not one of those alley **saunters** (((tʂ^{h}uantθ])).
3   They speak the authentic Beijing speech.
4   They say 'big **cabbage**' (((ta paits^{h}ai])) as (((ta paitθ^{h}ai])).

In Tian's comments below, he further characterizes their speech feature as "big-tongued":

Excerpt 3.4 Tian (36, assistant manager at a national bank)

Tian: Those *hutong chuanzi*, ... they are big-tongued.
QZ: What do you mean by big-tongued?
Tian: Like, we say little four's mother (((ɕiau sɚ t^{h}a ma])). They say little **four**'s mother (((ɕiau-θɚ t^{h}a ma])), and kid (((haitʂ])), they say kid (((haitθ])). Big-tongued, [they] bite their tongue when talking.

3.2.3 The "Cosmopolitan" Variable: Full-Tone Realization of a Neutral Tone

In contrast to the previous two locally based Beijing characters, the third character type is the "cosmopolitan Chinese" who transcends the territorial boundary of mainland China. Brought about by particularly mass-mediated encounters with characters and personalities from Hong Kong and Taiwan (jointly referred to in PTH as *Gang-Tai*) popular culture products that dominated the mainland market in the 1980s and 1990s (e.g., Barmé 1993; Baranovitch 2003; Gold 1993), the cosmopolitan Chinese is a trendy modern urbanite whose identity is not confined by geopolitical boundaries but rather is defined by a blurring or transcendence of such boundaries. Hong Kong and Taiwan film and television drama characters and show business celebrities, particularly pop music stars, are among the early exemplars of the cosmopolitan Chinese for the mainlanders. With *Gang-Tai* popular culture dominating the mainland market, Hong Kong Cantonese and

74 Cosmopolitan Mandarin in the Making of Beijing Yuppies

Taiwan Mandarin have exerted an influence on PTH, particularly in the lexicon and phonology (e.g., Songlin Chen 1991; Shuixian Chen 2006; Tang 2001). The new pop cultural icons play a vital role in the spread of non-mainland Mandarin features, which are associated with the cachet of the cosmopolitan Chinese (Erbaugh 1995). One such feature is the use of full tone instead of a neutral tone in a weakly stressed syllable. It is well known among Chinese mainlanders, particularly Northern Mandarin speakers, as evidence of the so-called *Gang-Tai qiang* 'Hong Kong-Taiwan accent' (see more discussion on this "accent" in Section 5.2.2). It even catches the attention of the government. *The Implementation Guidelines for the Putonghua Proficiency Test* specifies that (PSCSG 2004, 41)

> mastery of words with a neutral tone is a basic requirement for learning *Putonghua*. One of the major reasons for the so-called speech with a *"Gang-Tai qiang"* is failure to master the pronunciation of neutral-tone words.

The realization of a neutral tone as a full tone in a weakly stressed syllable is the fourth variable in this study, and I refer to it as the "cosmopolitan" variable. In the following examples, the neutral tone realization in *pinyin* and IPA is followed by the full-tone variant with the tone mark in boldface:

(12) 'understand' *ming2bai0* [mɪŋpaɪ], *ming2bai2_* [mɪŋpaɪ]
(13) 'student' *xue2sheng0* [ɕyɛʂəŋ], *xue2sheng1* [ɕyɛʂəŋ]

In BM and other Northern Mandarin dialects, every stressed syllable has a full tone with a fixed pitch value. In other words, each stressed syllable has one of the four Mandarin tones. When a syllable is weakly stressed, it has a neutral tone (Chao 1968). Unlike the four basic tones, a neutral-tone syllable does not have a distinguishing pitch value. Its pitch is determined by that of its preceding syllable (Norman 1988; Shen 1990). Although neutral tone is a common feature of the Northern Mandarin varieties, it is particularly prominent in BM (Chao 1968). In contrast, most of the Southern varieties, including Shanghai *hua*, Cantonese, and Min (including Southern Min, also known as Taiwanese) have very limited or almost no use of neutral tone (e.g., Chao 1968; Qian 1995; Ramsey 1987). BM neutral-tone syllables are significantly weaker than those in other Northern Mandarin dialects, and they are particularly short in duration and articulated with less intensity (Lu 1995). Their special pitch and rhythmic features contribute to the perceived "rhythmic and melodious" characteristic of *Jingqiang* and *Jingdiao*, the 'Beijing tune'. In my interviews, many participants shared the view that *Jing qiang* is rhythmic and melodious. The use of full tone in its place transforms the rhythmic Beijing style into what Kubler (1985) describes as a staccato effect, and hence it can be immediately identified by Beijingers as nonlocal and non-mainland.

Variation in the use of the three local variables discussed earlier indicates differential degrees of local accent, which can be located along the BM–Standard-PTH continuum. The tone variable is different from the previous

Cosmopolitan Mandarin in the Making of Beijing Yuppies **75**

three variables in that the use of a full tone instead of a neutral tone **among BM speakers** (and more generally Northern Mandarin speakers) cannot be described simply in terms of the BM–Standard-PTH continuum. In other words, the use of the full-tone variant by BM speakers indicates not only less local Beijing/Northern Mandarin accent (moving away from the local dialect) but also **"deviating" from the norm of Beijing-Mandarin-based PTH**. This tonal variation is stable between Northern Mandarin and Southern varieties and commonly found in local-accented PTH of southern Mandarin speakers. Although the full-tone variant is a telltale feature of southern mainland PTH speakers and non-mainland Mandarin speakers from Hong Kong, Taiwan, and other parts of the world,[6] its use in the PTH of Northern Mandarin speakers for **stylistic purposes** is a new phenomenon. In this sense the use of the full-tone variant by BM and Northern Mandarin speakers is linguistically innovative.

An important point to bear in mind is that the recent increasing use of the full-tone variant among Northern Mandarin speakers is not simply the result of contact between Standard PTH and Southern varieties, as such contact has been there all along (although increased internal migration has intensified such contact). In other words, what gives the tonal variable social significance is not linguistic contact *within* the mainland—rather, it is contact *between* the mainland Beijing-Mandarin-based Standard PTH and non-mainland varieties, particularly Hong Kong Cantonese and Taiwan Mandarin, since the installation of the opening-up policy in the late 1970s. Integral to this linguistic contact is, of course, a contact of differences—that is, different ways and ideologies of being urban, modern Chinese (Ong 1997; M. Yang 1997). Thus, such contact affords the full-tone variant a higher order of indexicality (Silverstein 2003) in addition to indexing the location of the "South" and Hong Kong and Taiwan. As the following analysis shows, it has become a potential resource at any bricoleur's disposal to index personae and attributes that are associated with the "cosmopolitan Chinese." Its social meaning is then further specified by the stylistic ensemble of which it is a component.

The above discussion of the four variables highlights the point that the variables are more than linguistic forms available to speakers: They are semiotic resources whose imbued cultural values afford them with both meaning-making potentials and constraints on their reuse. At the fundamental level, they are 1st-order indexicals that presuppose the geographical-based identity of the speaker (Silverstein 2003). That is, the local variant of each variable (rhotacization, lention of (*sh*), interdental realization of (*ts*), and neutral tone) indexes the pre-established geographical origin of the speaker as Beijing among the professionals in this chapter. At the same time, the association between the variables and their respective character type reveals that these dialectal variables are endowed with beliefs about Beijing, Beijingers, locals, and the "cosmopolitan Chinese." Thus, the use of these linguistic forms as resources has to come into dialogue with their imbued cultural significance in the process of bricolage. Table 3.1 summarizes the linguistic variables and the cultural characters with which they are associated.

76 Cosmopolitan Mandarin in the Making of Beijing Yuppies

TABLE 3.1 Summary of Linguistic Variables

Linguistic variable	Example	Associated character type
Rhotacization (r)	'famous brand' *ming2pai2* [miŋpʰai], *ming2pair2* [miŋpʰaɻ]	Beijing smooth operator
Lenition of (sh)	'student' *xuesheng* [ɕyɛʂəŋ], *xuereng* [ɕyɛɻəŋ]	Beijing smooth operator
Interdental realization of (ts)	'now' *xianzai* [ɕiantsai], *xianthai* [ɕiantθai]	Alley saunterer
Full-tone realization of a neutral tone	'understand' *ming2bai0* [miŋpai], *ming2bai2* [mingpai]	Cosmopolitan Chinese

3.3 Patterns of Variation

In this section, I present the results of quantitative analysis of the four variables. The data were coded and analyzed for linguistic and social constraints. Statistical analyses were conducted using GoldVarb 2.0 (Rand and Sankoff 1990), a stepwise multiple regression program designed specifically for analysis of linguistic variation, or VARBRUL. In what follows I focus on the effects of three social constraints on patterns of variation, namely, professional group, gender, and topic (for analysis of internal constraints, see Q. Zhang 2001). Table 3.2 presents the results of the initial analysis, in which all linguistic and social factor groups were included. Across all four variables, the most robust differentiation is found between the two professional groups. Gender also has a strong effect but is less robust than the professional group. The effect of topic is significant on all but rhotacization.

Two prominent patterns emerged after the initial analysis in which the three social constraints were treated as independent, as shown in Table 3.2. First, there was a sharp contrast between the two professional groups across all four variables: The yuppies used all of the local variants significantly less than the state professionals did. Specifically, the two "smooth operator" variables—rhotacization and lenition—patterned similarly: Professional group was the most significant factor group, and gender was secondary. The "alley saunterer" variant was almost categorically associated with male speakers, with the state professionals strongly favoring it; only three tokens of the interdental variant were produced by a total of two female speakers, both state professionals. The state professionals did not use the innovative "cosmopolitan" full-tone variant at all.

The second prominent pattern from the initial analysis was that women used local variants less than men did. In addition to the sharp contrast in terms of professional group and gender, topic—although a significant factor group for all variables except rhotacization—did not have as much of a prominent effect as the other two factor groups. Full tone was the only variant that demonstrated a robust shift depending on topic: It was used significantly more often by the yuppies in Topic 1 (VARBRUL value = 0.608) when discussing job-related experiences.

Cosmopolitan Mandarin in the Making of Beijing Yuppies **77**

TABLE 3.2 Effects of Professional Group, Gender, and Topic on Variation[a7]

Variable	Prof. group		Gender		Topic		Input	Sig.
	Yuppie	State	Women	Men	Topic1	Topic2		
Rhotacization	0.246	0.733	0.346	0.644	Not significant		0.710	0.003
Lenition	0.348	0.660	0.387	0.616	0.438	0.571	0.447	0.000
Interdental[b]	0.332	0.664	(1%)	(27%)	0.406	0.574	0.224	0.000
Full tone[c]	(21%)	(0%)	0.655	0.320	0.608	0.408	0.183	0.000

a Additional factor groups included in the runs: internal constraints.
b Only three tokens of interdental realization of /ts/ were produced by two women in the state group. The VARBRUL results for this variable are for men only.
c As state professionals did not produce any full-tone realization of a neutral tone, the VARBRUL results for the full-tone realization of a neutral tone are for yuppies only.

TABLE 3.3 Effects of Gender and Topic in Yuppie Group

Variable	Gender		Topic		Input	Sig.
	Female	Male	Topic 1	Topic 2		
Rhotacization	0.263	0.708	0.423	0.568	0.433	0.044
Lenition	0.309	0.708	0.376	0.636	0.267	0.000
Interdental	(0%)	(15%)	Not significant		0.119	0.000
Full tone	0.655	0.320	0.601	0.408	0.183	0.000

Additional factor groups included in the runs: internal constraints.

TABLE 3.4 Effects of Gender and Topic in State Professional Group

Variable	Gender		Topic		Input	Sig.
	Women	Men	Topic 1	Topic 2		
Rhotacization	Not significant		Not significant		0.864	0.009
Lenition	0.453	0.545	Not significant		0.613	0.005
Interdental	(1%)	(40%)	0.326	0.656	0.369	0.000
Full tone	(0%)	(0%)	(0%)	(0%)		

Additional factor groups included in the runs: internal constraints.

Further analyses were carried out to examine the effects of gender and topic within each professional group. The VARBRUL results are presented in Tables 3.3 and 3.4. The two groups showed different patterns of variation with regard to both gender and topic. The results in percentages are presented graphically in Figure 3.1 (gender variation) and Figure 3.2 (topic variation).

Except for the "alley saunterer" variant, which was overwhelmingly favored by male speakers in both groups, gender variation was mild to insignificant in the state group (Table 3.4) but dramatic among the yuppies (Table 3.3). In the former group, differences in the use of rhotacization and full tone were insignificant (Table 3.4). Variation was moderate in the use of lenition, with male state professionals slightly favoring it at 0.545, or merely 6% more than female speakers.

In contrast, across all four variables, female yuppies overwhelmingly favored the nonlocal variants. Hence, the observation from the initial analysis, that is, that female speakers disfavored the nonlocal variants (see Table 3.2), is inaccurate when we compare the professional groups. Female speakers in the state group used the two "smooth operator" variants much more frequently than male yuppies (see Figure 3.1). Women's appearing to be conservative in the initial analysis (Table 3.2) was primarily the result of female yuppies' extremely limited use of the local features, which resulted in the overall lower rate of women's use of local features than men.

Similar to gender variation, the state group demonstrated slight topic variation, whereas topic had a significant effect on all but one variable in the yuppie group. Only one feature—the "alley saunterer" variant—was used significantly more often in Topic 2 by the state professionals. It may be that their lower use of the interdental variant in Topic 1 is related to the stigmatized nature of the "alley saunterer" image and the negative qualities associated with it—fecklessness and lack of education. The overall rate of the male yuppies' use of this feature was much lower, and it did not show a significant topic shift among them when examined together with internal constraints (preceding segment and tone; see Table 3.3). However, when topic was examined by itself, the VAR-BRUL weightings were Topic 1, 0.434; Topic 2, 0.596; significance, 0.0125. In

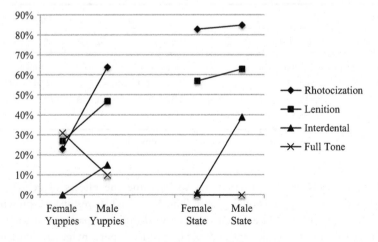

FIGURE 3.1 Gender Variation in Each Professional Group

Cosmopolitan Mandarin in the Making of Beijing Yuppies 79

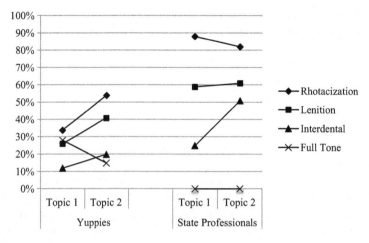

FIGURE 3.2 Topic Variation in Each Professional Group

addition, a chi-square test on the frequencies of the interdental variant in the two topics showed that the p value was less than or equal to 0.025, which indicated that the difference in topic was significant. The nonlocal variants of the other three variables were all used significantly more often when the yuppies discussed their work-related experiences.

3.4 Contrasting Styles: Cosmopolitan vs. Local

The most striking difference between the state professionals and the yuppies is found in their use of the "cosmopolitan" full-tone variant, with the female yuppies using it most frequently. The other three variables show similar, although less dramatic, patterning, with the state professionals favoring the local variants. As mentioned earlier, the full-tone variant is evidence of influence from non-mainland Mandarin varieties. The state professionals' lower use of the full-tone variant seem to indicate that they are less affected by this influence than the yuppies are.

One potential factor directly related to this difference in the use of the full tone is the extent of direct contact with non-mainland Mandarin varieties and their speakers. That is, because of the nature of their work, professionals in foreign businesses have more opportunities to interact with non-mainland Mandarin speakers, who tend to use the full-tone variant. Hence, their use of the full tone is almost surely related to their greater exposure to this feature. Although exposure is a condition for speakers to recognize an innovative linguistic form, it does not entail consequent uptake. Furthermore, Table 3.3 shows that within the yuppie group, there is significant gender variation in the use of full tone. Thus, exposure alone cannot explain why female yuppies use

80 Cosmopolitan Mandarin in the Making of Beijing Yuppies

the full-tone variant more often than male yuppies, since it can be assumed that they have similar exposure to this feature. I explore why this is the case in Section 3.6.

Rather than treating the full-tone variable in isolation as a marker of "yuppieness" or as indexing an aspiration to being a Hong Konger or a Taiwanese,[8] explanations for its variable use should be sought in relation to variation in the three local variables from the perspective of contrast in the styles of the two professional groups. As shown in Figure 3.3, for each variable, the state professionals use the local variant more often than the yuppies. Hence, in terms of the degree of localness, the speech style of the state professionals is prominently Beijing, whereas the style of the yuppies is overwhelmingly nonlocal. Furthermore, the linguistic difference between the two professional groups cannot simply be described along a linear dimension from vernacular to standard. In other words, the lesser degree of localness in the style of the yuppies does not contribute to a more "standard" PTH accent. A "more standard PTH accent" masks the complexity of the yuppies' linguistic practice. Adoption of the full-tone variant in combination with the preference for the other nonlocal features expands the range of linguistic variation among the yuppies *beyond* Mainland Standard *Putonghua* (here in after MSP). In contrast, the absence of this variant from the state professionals and their greater use of Beijing variants locate their range of linguistic variation *within* MSP. The yuppies are constructing an innovative, supraregional linguistic style that is distinct from the conventional Beijing-Mandarin-based Standard PTH. In this sense, their linguistic style is *cosmopolitan* in that it orients away from the established norms of Mainland Standard Mandarin, which itself is a regional variety based on BM phonology. I refer to this new style as "**Cosmopolitan Mandarin.**" Linguistic components of Cosmopolitan Mandarin are not limited to the use of the full tone, limited rhotacization, and other nonlocal sound features as shown above. Lexical items, such as expressions from Cantonese and Taiwan Mandarin, as well as Mandarin-English code-mixing, can also give Mandarin discourse a non-local cosmopolitan flavor. Thus, Cosmopolitan Mandarin (here in after CM) is a supraregional linguistic style consisting of a fluid set of linguistic features, the combination of which is distinctive from the Beijing-Mandarin-based Standard PTH, or MSP.

In the following analysis of the different patterns of linguistic variation between the yuppies and state professionals, I first discuss that explanations based on professional group difference cannot adequately account for the sharp intergroup variation. I then draw on Bourdieu's (1977, 1991) notion of linguistic market to examine the changing symbolic value of Standard Mandarin, specifically, the rise of the transnational Chinese linguistic market and the symbolic value of CM in that market as a form of linguistic capital for the yuppies and as a stylistic resource that gives meaning to an emergent cosmopolitan professional identity.

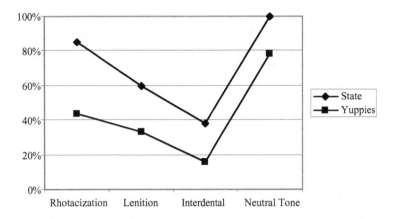

FIGURE 3.3 Contrast in Styles

3.5 Cosmopolitan Mandarin: Changing Economy, Changing Markets

Because the social variables in this study—geographical origin, level of education, and professional ranking—were controlled so that they would not exert considerable effect on the use of the linguistic variables, the sharp intergroup variation seems to reflect the differences between the two professional groups: working in state-owned vs. foreign businesses. In other words, to say that the linguistic variation reflects professional category difference is to assume that the less frequent use of the local features reflects the part of the yuppies' work that deals with non-mainland Chinese. However, such an assumption is implausible if we consider the fact that, as employees of the mainland China (Beijing) branches of international businesses, their work involves interactions with people from both Chinese domestic and international businesses.

Despite the differences among the companies they work for (Chinese versus foreign), we would predict more similarity in the linguistic practice of the two groups. For instance, because many sociolinguistic studies have shown that standard language is expected in formal (and by extension, corporate) settings, we should expect the two groups to demonstrate a high degree of similarity in their use of nonlocal features. Particularly, we would expect that the state professionals would show significant intraspeaker (in this study, topic-dependent) variation in their use of variables. However, the results show significant topic variation in only one variable in the state group. The businesses that the state professionals work for, although based in Beijing, are all large enterprises with nationwide operations. The majority of their clients are from other parts of the country. This fact represents another aspect of similarity between state professionals and those in the foreign sector who also conduct business at a nonlocal level and often interact with non-Beijing clients. Moreover, in both national

82 Cosmopolitan Mandarin in the Making of Beijing Yuppies

and foreign enterprises, native Beijingers make up only a small portion of the total number of employees. Thus, in both groups, most of their colleagues are non-BM speakers. The above discussion shows that the assumption that intergroup variation reflects professional group difference fails to explain why state professionals do not show significant topic-dependent variation, or why the yuppies use a cosmopolitan style that does not strictly conform to the norms of MSP. In what follows, I argue that the intergroup variation is the result of the professionals' participation in two different linguistic markets and of the differences in the symbolic value of MSP and Cosmopolitan Mandarin on each market. I show that the state professionals participate in a Mainland Standard *Putonghua* linguistic market, whereas the yuppies participate in a transnational Chinese linguistic market.[9] Although both are supralocal language markets, the symbolic value of Mandarin on each is different.

3.5.1 The Mainland Standard Putonghua Linguistic Market

PTH, the officially designated common medium of communication in China, is used in large national enterprises and other national and government organizations headquartered in the capital city. National corporations, educational institutions, the media, and other cultural institutions constitute the sites of the standard linguistic market in Beijing. However, the standard linguistic market in China is very different from what Bourdieu (1977, 1991) describes. He argues that competence in the legitimate language constitutes the most valuable linguistic capital on the standard linguistic market. Possession of this kind of linguistic capital helps one become a viable participant in the standard linguistic market. Six decades after the establishment of PTH as the national standard language, the standard linguistic market of China is far from being unified. Scholars over the decades have made similar observations that Standard PTH has not become an emblem of social prestige or a symbolic asset necessary for access to elite status in mainland China (Blum 2004; Chao 1976 [1961], 73; Duanmu 2000, 5; Guo 1990; Harrell 1993; Zhu and Chen 1991). Competence in written Standard Chinese, however, is required for access to elite status (e.g., Harrell 1993, 100–101). Although the government has established mechanisms to promote the use of Standard PTH, such as the *Common Language Law* and the *Putonghua* Proficiency Test required for state employees in the government, education, and the media, speaking PTH without a local accent has not become an index of social prestige sought after by the majority of mainland Chinese. As Blum (2005, 150) notes, "In China there is no inevitable social advantage to possession of the standard in the same way as has become familiar in Anglo-European societies" and "ideas of the standard are limited, circumscribed, and not especially powerful" (ibid, 152). Most Chinese on the mainland are content to speak a localized variety of PTH (e.g., as demonstrated in Blum's [2004] study of speakers in the southwestern metropolis of Kunming).

My interviews with state professionals confirm other scholars' observation about the symbolic value of Standard PTH. Most of them did acknowledge its importance in their work, but for them its value lies in the instrumental function of facilitating communication; Standard PTH was not viewed as a prime indicator of educational level or cultural refinement. A possible explanation is that BM is the phonological standard for PTH; hence, native Beijingers are, in a sense, native speakers of PTH, or more precisely, native speakers of a local variety of the standard language. Hence, unlike many speakers of other Chinese varieties, Beijingers do not have to learn the spoken standard language at school. As Bourdieu (1984, 86) argues, the encouragement of the acquisition of a specific competence can be achieved only when the market promises or guarantees profit for this competence. The Beijing state professionals in the MSP linguistic market are "endowed" with the linguistic capital, the officially established common medium for communication. As there is not much anticipation of reward for speaking Standard PTH, the state professionals do not have to strive to speak PTH without a Beijing accent. Hence, the high frequency in their use of the two best-known Beijing features and little style shifting is not surprising.

3.5.2 The Transnational Chinese Linguistic Market

While the professionals in *guoqi* participate in the MSP linguistic market, the yuppies in the international sector are engaged in a different linguistic market. China's participation in the global economy has given rise to a new job market. In this market, the traditionally dominant system of state-controlled job assignment has become obsolete (Hoffman 2010). Individuals become competitors and commodities in the market. Job applicants have to sell themselves. The selling process starts with the job interview, a totally new experience to job seekers when first introduced by foreign companies. Making a good self-presentation at the job interview—packaging and comporting oneself appropriately according to the rules of the game in the new market—has become a crucial practice for anyone who wants to enter the international business sector, a stepping-stone to a new cosmopolitan lifestyle.

To become a commodity in demand in the new market, one has to acquire the kinds of symbolic capital that are valued in that market. On the employer's side, specific language skills alongside educational credentials, specialized skills, and other requirements are expected of job seekers. These include the ability to speak Standard Mandarin without a local accent and proficiency in one or more foreign languages. English is unquestionably the most valued foreign language; others include Japanese, German, and French. Very often, requirements of appearance,[10] age, and gender also appear explicitly in job descriptions.

In consequence, the establishment of the international business sector has given rise to a new linguistic market that creates linguistic values different

84 Cosmopolitan Mandarin in the Making of Beijing Yuppies

from those in the MSP linguistic market. In the latter, the BM phonological system is the standard, and PTH is valuable as a lingua franca. In contrast, the ability to speak Mandarin without a local accent has become profit-generating linguistic capital in the new linguistic market. Working for international businesses engages the yuppies in a market in which MSP is only one of the varieties of Mandarin—others include Taiwan Mandarin, Hong Kong Mandarin, Singapore Mandarin, and so on. The following comment from Mr. Wang, my contact person, displays a keen awareness among these professionals of the fact that they are members of a market in which Beijing-Mandarin-based PTH is not the single standard variety:

> In fact, Beijingers in the whole <u>business world</u>, are not a <u>majority</u>, so, that is to say, speaking of Beijing, in the <u>business world</u>, when you reach a certain level, you'll find, that is to say, a Greater China <u>integration</u>. When speaking in <u>Mandarin</u>, you'll meet Taiwanese, Hong Kongers, Singaporeans, and Shanghainese....

It is worth noting that Wang uses the English word **Mandarin** rather than its Chinese equivalent, *Putonghua*. This indicates that he is using a term that can refer to multiple varieties of Mandarin: *Putonghua* in the mainland; *Guoyu,* the standard Mandarin variety in Taiwan; and *Huayu,* the standard Mandarin variety in Singapore.

I call the new linguistic market the "transnational Chinese linguistic market." Recall the movie *Go! Lala Go!* mentioned in Chapter 2. The fictional world of DB—whose employees speak BM, Hong Kong Mandarin, Taiwan Mandarin, and English—is a microcosm of the transnational Chinese linguistic market. The yuppies' use of CM shows that they do not conform to the norms of Mainland Standard Mandarin, which are based on BM. Indeed, the value of CM extends far beyond facilitating communication. During their interviews, the yuppies emphasized speaking Mandarin without a local accent as an important aspect of building their professional and corporate image. For them, therefore, CM is no longer an object of need—a common medium for communication—but rather a resource for distinction. The yuppies use CM to distinguish themselves from those in the MSP linguistic market. Its use not only distinguishes them from their state counterparts but also helps create and perpetuate the sanctions of the new linguistic market. The effects of the market sanctions on linguistic behavior are elaborated by Bourdieu (1977, 654):

> Agents continuously subjected to the sanctions of the linguistic market, functioning as a system of positive or negative reinforcements, acquire durable dispositions which are the basis of their perception and appreciation of the state of the linguistic market and consequently of their strategies for expression.

Cosmopolitan Mandarin in the Making of Beijing Yuppies **85**

Hence, the linguistic market requires that to present oneself as a competent business professional in the international sector, yuppies use CM as part of their cosmopolitan style to produce symbolic profit and, ultimately, economic profit. Thus, it is not completely a matter of personal choice whether to speak Mandarin in an innovative style that does not strictly conform to Standard PTH, as failure or inability to use it would be detrimental to one's image as a competent professional. The fact that senior professionals sometimes go so far as assuming the responsibility of norm reinforcement indicates that the yuppies are aware of the sanctions of the market. It is in this sense that CM constitutes "a strategy of survival" (Butler 1999, 178) for these yuppies (see Section 1.2.3). In the following example, the speaker, David, is a deputy representative of a European bank:

> Working in a foreign business, it's inappropriate to speak to clients with a heavy Beijing accent. Once, I heard my secretary talking to a client on the phone, she said *"tei wan la"* ['too late']. *"Tei"* is Beijing vernacular. I had to tell her to get rid of it.

The yuppies also exercise self-censorship to reduce local accent in their speech. Another participant, Ning, acknowledges that he sometimes speaks *chunzheng* 'pure' PTH with many people at work. When I asked him if *chunzheng* means reducing Beijing flavor in PTH, he confirms:

> Yes. I sometimes talk like this [reducing Beijing accent]. Of course there are (people like this). <u>The reason</u> is that, like this. One, if one talks with a strong Beijing flavor, others may not understand them well. This is one (reason). Of course this is not the most important (reason). **The most important is that if your Beijing flavor is too strong, others will feel you're rustic. They'll have this impression. (They) will feel you are totally out of place**. I myself am like this. Others are also like this. Or they may not be conscious about it. Yes, there is situation like this.

For Ning, PTH with a strong Beijing accent creates an impression of being *tu* 'rustic', a quality from which yuppies seek to disassociate themselves (see Chapter 2). Furthermore, a strong Beijing accent is considered not matching up to the professional image, as shown when he uses the colloquial expression *ni man bushi zheme huishir*, which means 'you are totally not what you thought you were'. Here the expression means that the local accent would make the speaker appear to be out of place in the context of *waiqi*.

3.6 Gender and Linguistic Styling

Although both the censoring examples come from the metalinguistic comments of two men, as the quantitative results clearly show, the *waiqi* women lead

86 Cosmopolitan Mandarin in the Making of Beijing Yuppies

their male counterparts in the use of all nonlocal variants. Not only does their speech have less Beijing features, but it also sounds more cosmopolitan due to more frequent use of the full-tone variant. In contrast to the *waiqi* professionals, gender does not play so significant a role in the use of variables among the state professionals except for the "alley saunterer" variable. The interdental variant is almost exclusively used by men in both professional groups albeit in a much lower frequency than the other local features. The association between the local variant and the "alley saunterer" character as elaborated earlier sheds light on the women's extremely limited use of this feature. A man who saunters around aimlessly in alleys waiting for something to happen may appear to be feckless and lazy, but the same conduct of a woman would be not only considered inappropriate but also suspected of having loose morals. Thus, the association with the image of an alley saunterer is likely to be more damaging to a woman's image than that of a man.

In Q. Zhang (2007), I suggest that to explain the different effects of gender in the two professional groups, we need to historicize the relation between gender and work and gender as a site for the discursive construction and production of professional—and more generally social—identities. As discussed in the previous chapter, due to the lingering influence of state feminism in the state sector, the professional women in the state companies in this study did not appear to engage in the kind of aesthetic labor as did the *waiqi* women. Thus, gender was less salient in both the corporate image and the linguistic style of the professionals in *guoqi*.

In the following, I focus on gender variation in the *waiqi* group and show that in contrast to the *guoqi* professionals, gender difference was salient in the yuppie group. The heavier use of local features makes the men's speech style exhibit more of the stereotypical quality of being "smooth" and "rhythmic/melodious," but at the same time their speech may also sound "muddled" as a result of rhotacization and lenition such that they may sound like "holding a piece of hot baked sweet potato in their mouth" (example 8) or "talking with hot tofu in their mouth" (Xi 1995, 5). The use of more local variants also makes their speech sounds more casual and relaxed than that of the women. In contrast, the less frequent use of local variants and the more frequent use of the full tone make the women's speech more enunciated and staccato. The contrast between the comparatively "smooth" and casual style of the male yuppies and the enunciated and staccato style of the women reminds us of the unhurried steps of Mr. Wang as he strolls into the Kimpinsky Hotel in his loafers and casual earthy-tone outfit versus the crisp clicking sounds from Catherine's heels while wearing her formal business suit (see Chapter 2).

My friend with whom I was sharing an apartment during my fieldwork captured the women's speech style in a vivid way. I played for her an excerpt of my interview with Rebecca, who was one of the least frequent users of local features. Her impression of Rebecca's speech was: "She sounds like a China world/overseas [*duiwai*] broadcaster talking, international *Putonghua*, has *yang* flavor, words [she] used weren't like the daily words of ordinary folks, a bit literary [meaning formal]."[11] It is not surprising that the choice of words made her speech sound formal, as Rebecca was discussing her work in investment banking. What is interesting, however, is that her Mandarin was characterized as "international *Putonghua*," resembling that of a radio announcer broadcasting to an overseas audience. Regardless of my friend's familiarity with the broadcasting style of China Radio International, she differentiated Rebecca's speech from Standard PTH, linking the so-called "international PTH" to a speech style that appeals to a transnational audience rather than a domestic, mainland Chinese audience. This exogenous association is construed as *yang*, which is, as explained earlier, a descriptor for being Western, modern, stylish, and extralocal.

The quantitative results show that the *waiqi* women make stricter or greater use of Cosmopolitan Mandarin than their male colleagues. In what follows, I examine gender variation in the *waiqi* group by taking into account two crucial issues: (1) the historical condition of the emergence of the new professional group, which contributes to the different career trajectories of the men and women in the foreign businesses (see Chapter 2) and (2) the imbued cultural significance of the linguistic variables, which affects their reuse by the yuppies.

Regarding the first issue, the different career paths of men and women contribute to gendered sociolinguistic biographies and the differential significance of language skills in their work. In Chapter 2, I explained that most of the female yuppies in this study started their professional career from front-end positions, capitalizing on their linguistic skills. As most of the *waiqi* professionals in my study were among the first generation of Chinese employees in foreign businesses, working in a foreign company was a new experience for them. Although some of them had previous work experience when they joined their first foreign company, they still had to learn how to be professionals in the international business sector. Because the female professionals started in front-end positions that demanded the performance of aesthetic labor, a large part of their learning and their job involved "looking good and sounding right" to project the public face of their corporations, whereas their male colleagues' learning focused more on doing business. Dong, a chief representative, described her learning experience when she first started as a secretary: "I learned for the first time in my life what a company secretary means... I had to learn everything from scratch, even had to learn how to answer phone calls." As a large number of women were hired for their decorative value and as "language technicians" (Sankoff and Laberge 1978) in the early years of foreign businesses, women constitute part of the symbolic capital of their corporations from the very beginning of their career. The important symbolic capital of language itself became the cornerstone of their

88 Cosmopolitan Mandarin in the Making of Beijing Yuppies

future success in the business world. Although most of the *waiqi* professionals emphasized the importance of presenting the corporate image of their companies through speaking and dress style, women shouldered more responsibilities in presenting the face of their company in everyday work than their male colleagues. Thus, work imposes greater constraints on female yuppies to make stricter use of Cosmopolitan Mandarin, whereas male yuppies have a greater leeway in their use of the linguistic features.[12] Linguistic competences in foreign languages and a Mandarin style that does not invoke strong local associations are crucial assets that the female yuppies capitalize on to become "translators and framers" (Ong 2008, 194) of foreign interests for the Chinese domestic market.

While the career trajectories help to explain the contrast between the women's and the men's linguistic practice in broad terms, a more nuanced understanding of the gendered patterns of linguistic variation requires taking into account the imbued cultural significance of the linguistic variables elaborated in Section 3.2. In other words, as all the variables have lived a socially charged life and are saturated with others' voices (Bakhtin 1981), their semiotic baggage affects the ways in which they are recontextualized by the yuppies. Although the male yuppies used all the local variants more often than their female counterparts, the biggest difference is in the use of rhotacization and lenition, the two variables associated with the "Beijing smooth operator," the most well-known local character type. And between the two, rhotacization—the variant with the highest level of metapragmatic awareness as the emblem of the character type—shows a wider range of variation between the *waiqi* women and men. As explained in Section 3.2.1, rhotacization's enregistered association with the smooth operator—an urban male character—and his "smooth" qualities makes the feature less compatible with the women's cosmopolitan professional image; further, the deeply locally rooted street-smartness (that is, local knowledge), urban versatility, and resourcefulness complement the men's professional persona. The casualness and ease of a "Beijing smooth operator" would jeopardize the women's credibility and authority as a *waiqi* professional. Their less frequent use of rhotacization (and lenition) thus disassociates the women from the "smooth operator" image.

In addition, the women's less frequent use of lenition, "the swallowing sound" feature in which three retroflex obstruent initials merge to [ɻ], also makes them sound precise. As several studies have shown, precise enunciation is a strategy used to express learnedness and intelligence (Benor 2001; Bucholtz 2001; Podesva, Roberts, and Campbell-Kibler 2002). Their clear enunciation, combined with less use of rhotacization and less variation in rhythm (partly due to their higher use of the full-tone variant), makes the women's speech impersonal and detached, typical of academic and formal business style. It is the extreme opposite of the "smooth," "rhythmic," and "melodious" colloquial Beijing style. The women yuppies use this style to create an intelligent, impersonal, diligent, and meticulous feminine business persona, the hallmark of which is its cosmopolitan outlook. Such an image of a businesswoman challenges the stereotypical feminine image, that is, emotional and personal, adding a human touch to the impersonal corporation—an image that works against women in the managerial level of the corporation.

The use of the local and nonlocal variants in the following excerpts from Rebecca and David exemplifies the subtle differences in the self-styling of their professional personae. Working for the same bank, Rebecca, 28, is the chief representative, and David, a veteran *waiqi* professional and 12 years her senior, is a deputy representative. The youngest chief representative in the group, Rebecca's career in *waiqi*, from 1994 to 1998 when I interviewed her, is shorter than most of the other professionals, but she moved up the ranks the fastest. After graduating with a bachelor's degree in international business in 1992, Rebecca was hired by the then largest state-owned investment company in China. A year later she was recruited by another state-owned credit rating agency, working in "capital markets consulting" (underlining indicates English words used by Rebecca). She worked on launching the stocks of numerous Chinese companies in Hong Kong and international stock markets. "Feeling limited by doing only consulting work at the company and hoping to work for a bank in the real investment bank business," she joined one of the four largest Japanese securities companies. Two years later, in 1996, she accepted a position as the chief representative of a joint venture between a North American bank and a Hong Kong financial group. Her current bank, which had contacted her a year earlier, started heavily recruiting her a month after she had taken up the new position. Considering that the bank "just started targeting China as their primary market," she thought that "it was the right moment to join the company," and it was beneficial to her career development. In her own words:

> There will be more **opportunities** (*ji1hui4* [T4]) to give full play to my talents and more **learning opportunities** (*ji1hui4* [T4]). So I came over. I've been **here** (*zhe4li3* [-R, T3]) for about two years.

Through the concise summary of her professional history, Rebecca presents herself as one of a minority of professional local Chinese with appropriate credentials, expert knowledge, professional skills, and experiences who are highly sought after by foreign companies to work in the China market. Her persona of an accomplished banking professional is presented through Cosmopolitan Mandarin and technical terms in English (underlined). In the short quote above, she pronounced 'opportunities' twice as *ji1hui4* with a full tone (T4) instead of a neutral tone. For the word 'here', instead of the rhotacized expression *zher4* commonly used by BM speakers, she used *zhe4li3* 'here', a non-rhotacizable word and with a full tone (T3) on the second syllable, which is usually

90 Cosmopolitan Mandarin in the Making of Beijing Yuppies

pronounced with a neutral tone. Many technical terms in English were used, for instance <u>marketing</u>, <u>placement</u>, <u>(A, B, H) shares</u>, <u>securities</u>, <u>roadshow</u>, <u>presentation</u>, and <u>proposal</u>. Also note that she sees the work at the new company as offering valuable **learning opportunities**, a point she emphasized again in Excerpt 3.5 below.

In the following excerpt, she views learning as an important part of being a *waiqi* professional. In the interview leading up to the excerpt below, Rebecca complains that some of her junior colleagues with college degrees are not willing to do "small things," such as typing up a proposal and preparing presentations and brochures. In her view, such "small things" are important learning opportunities, as she herself has moved up the ranks through doing small things.

Excerpt 3.5 Rebecca: "One should start from doing small things"

1   *Suoyi wo shi juede* **[T2]**
   So I think **[T2]**

2   *ren jiu yinggai cong xiao shiqing* **[T2]** *zuoqi.*
   one should start with doing small things [T2].

3   *Yinwei wo ziji yeri* **[+lenition]** *cong zui xiao de shiqing* **[T2]** *zuoqi.*
   Because I myself also [+lenition] started from doing the smallest things [T2].

4   *Yeshi* **[−lenition]** *zuo le zheme* **[T0]** *duo nian,*
   Also **[−lenition]** have done so for so **[T0]** many years,

5   *manman* **[−R, T4]** *lian chulai de.*
   slowly **[−R, T4]** become experienced.

6   *Danshi* **[−lenition]** *wo xianzai* **[-interdental]** *bu neng shuo*
   But **[−lenition]** I can't say now **[-interdental]**

7   *wo ziji duo, bi biren qiang.*
   I myself am much, better than others.

8   *Zhishao* **[−lenition]** *jiushi* **[−lenition]** *shuo*
   At least **[−lenition]** that is **[−lenition]** to say

9   *wo bi neixie gang-gang gang qibu de ren hui qiang.*
   I'm better than those who just-just just started.

10 *Yinwei wo juede* **[T2]** *zhei ren de xintai hen zhongyao.*
   Because I think **[−lenition]** one's attitude is very important.

11 *Ni bu neng jiuri* **[+lenition]** *shuo,*
   You can't that's **[+lenition]** to say,

12 *xiao shiqing* **[T2]** *bu zuo.*
   not do small things **[T2]**.

13 *Qishi* **[−lenition]** *xiao shiqing* **[T2]** *zuo de shihou* **[T4]**
   in fact[−lenition], when [T4] doing small things [T2]

14 *doushi xuexi de shihou* **[T4]**.
   [they're] all times [T4] for learning.

Cosmopolitan Mandarin in the Making of Beijing Yuppies **91**

In the above excerpt, Rebecca presents another aspect of her professional image. *Cong xiao shiqing zuoqi* 'to start from doing small things' (line 3) is a hackneyed Chinese saying about great achievements being accomplished by doing small things. This phrase is recontextualized here to emphasize her view that success is not solely built on having the desirable educational credentials and professional experiences but is achieved through learning from and doing small things. Despite her fast career advancement, she presents herself in the above excerpt as a hard-working, diligent professional. This diligent professional image is again projected through the use of CM with minimal local features. The key expression of this excerpt, *xiao3 shi4qing0* 'small things', which has a neutral tone in the second syllable of *shi4qing0*, is pronounced with a full tone (T2) in all four occurrences (in lines 2, 3, 12, and 13).

When comparing *waiqi* with state professionals, she thinks that those in state-run work units "do not have sufficient pressure ... with respect to competition" and that "they aren't diligent enough." In contrast, her own workday typically starts around eight in the morning and does not end till eight or nine at night. She sees foreign companies having "stricter requirements on every aspect [of the job] starting with the most basic dress code." As a result, *waiqi* employees "may feel a bit **[-R]** more professional." However, she quickly points out that "there is still some distance between one's feelings about her/ himself and one's real ability":

Excerpt 3.6 Rebecca: "One has to admit incompetence"

1 Rebecca: *Ta keneng xiang de xiang de*
           S/he may think think
2   *ziji ge:ng geng gao le yidian* **[-R]**.
           a bit **[-R]** too too highly about her/himself.
3 QZ: Hm hm.
4 Rebecca: *Qishi* **[−lenition]** *wo juede* **[T2]**,
           In fact **[−lenition]** I think **[T2]**,
5   *Beijing hua jiuri* **[+lenition]** *shuo,*
           a Beijing saying that's **[+lenition]** to say,
6   *zhe ren dei ren SONG.*
           one has to admit INCOMPETENCE.
7   *Jiuri* **[+lenition]** *shuo,*
           That's **[+lenition]** to say,
8   *ni bu xing jiuri* **[+lenition]** *bu xing.*
           if you're incompetent [then you] really are **[+lenition]** incompetent.
9   *Yao xue dei shihou* **[T4]** *jiu de xue.*
           When it's time [T4] to learn [you] really have to learn.

92 Cosmopolitan Mandarin in the Making of Beijing Yuppies

In the above excerpt, Rebecca—the youngest chief representative and the cream of the crop of local Chinese banking professionals—stresses having a realistic view about oneself and a sense of modesty, citing a colloquial Beijing saying, "one has to admit incompetence" (line 6). She reiterates the importance of learning. This realistic and modest persona is again accompanied by the use of CM features in words that are usually pronounced with local features, that is, *yidian* 'a bit' without rhotacization (line 2), *qishi* 'in fact' without lenition (line 4), and *juede* 'feel' with a full tone (T2) in the second syllable (line 4), and *shihou* 'when' with a full tone (T4) in the second syllable (line 9). Only when she starts citing the Beijing saying does she use the local feature, lenition, in three occurrences of *jiushi* as *jiuri* 'that is' (lines 5 and 7) and 'really are' (line 8). Rebecca's styling of herself as an accomplished investment banker with a realistic and modest view of herself is achieved through heavy use of CM. Absence of rhotacization, minimal lenition, and frequent use of full tone in neutral tone environments make her speech sound hyper-enunciated, careful, and effortful. As I discuss next, her linguistic style is in stark contrast with that of her subordinate David, the deputy representative who is 12 years her senior and has 14 years of experience in *waiqi*.

David started his *waiqi* career in 1983 when foreign banks had just started opening representative offices in China. With a bachelor's degree in English, he was hired as an assistant to the chief representative of a European bank, one of the ten foreign banks permitted to establish their representative office in China in the early 1980s. He had worked for the same bank for 10 years before joining the current company about 3 years before the interview. In his words, "unlike other *waiqi* comrades who jump [jobs] more often, my [job] history is very simple." His use of the word *tongzhimen* 'comrades', an (address) term widely used in pre-reform China, to refer to the *waiqi* cohort, is intended to be witty, as *waiqi* is the so-called capitalist operations in China in opposition to socialism and communism, symbolized by the term *tongzihimen* 'comrade'. Referring to the others as "comrades" also reflects his view of *waiqi* professionals as a community where he sees himself as a veteran among his comrades. In the summary of his work history at the beginning of the interview, David used more BM features than Rebecca. He also used many English expressions, for instance, <u>salary package</u>, <u>rep office</u>, <u>investment banking</u>, <u>project financing</u>, and <u>capital market financing</u>. Unlike Rebecca, who had a degree in international business, David joined *waiqi* in the early 1980s primarily because of his English language skills. Hence, one would expect that (like Rebecca) learning would have been crucial in his career development from an assistant to the chief representative to a deputy representative. However, as we see from the excerpts below, learning is not mentioned.

The following extracts are drawn from David's description of three levels of *waiqi* employees: The lower level (e.g., service people, secretaries), the middle level (to which he belongs), and the top level (e.g., chief representatives, managers). In his view, "the <u>local basis</u>, their <u>salary package</u> is not as high as that of those <u>expatriates</u>, but **[+lenition]** the work **[-interdental]** they do is that of

Cosmopolitan Mandarin in the Making of Beijing Yuppies **93**

the <u>cornerstone</u>." He further elaborates on the "cornerstone" work of the local, middle level professionals:

Excerpt 3.7 David: "You shoulder the function of educating them"

1   *ZHONG ceng ne,*
    MIDDLE level,
2   *jiuri* **[+lention]** *shuo women* **[T0]** *zheixie ren ne,*
    that's **[+lention]** to say people like us **[T0]**,
3   *zaiyewu* **[T0]** *shang ne,*
    in terms of professional work **[T0]**,
4   *shi CHENG-SHANG* **[-lenition]** *-QI-XIA*
    [we] are the connecting link between the upper [-lenition] and lower levels.
5   *Gen shangbiar* **[+R, T0]** *baochi lianluo.*
    Keep in contact with the upper level **[+R, T0]**.
6   *Shangbiar* **[+R, T0]** *baokuo,*
    The upper level **[+R, T0]** includes,
7   *nide* <u>expatriates</u> *de ZHONGGUO ji de daibiao.*
    your representatives who are CHINESE <u>expatriates</u>.
8   *Shi yi zhong biejiao hao goutong de.*
    [They] are the kind who are easier to communicate with.
9   *Yinwei dui shichang bijao liaojie.*
    Because [they are] familiar with the market.
10 *WAIguo ren ne,*
    FOREIGNers,
11 *ni jiu jianfu zhe ne,*
    you shoulder,
12 *dui ta jinxing* <u>education</u> *de zheige yige gongneng.*
    the function of <u>educating</u> them.

In this excerpt, David fashions himself as the mediator between his upper-level management and lower-level local employees. Earlier in the interview, he described himself as the local intermediary between his foreign employer and the Chinese customer and bureaucracy. Learning on his part is not mentioned; instead, he emphasized his role as an educator for his foreign superior (lines 10–12). He told me that in the 13 years working under a foreign representative, he had worked with about six different representatives. According to him, such a turnover rate was too high, because "for every foreign representative, it takes at least a 2- to 3-year process from unfamiliarity to being knowledgeable about the China market." It is frustrating for him that his representatives left right at the time when they were becoming familiar with the China market:

*Ni **HAO:3bu0 rong2yi0** jiao chulai* **[T0]** *yige* **[T0]***, ta zou* **[-interdental]** *le.*
*You **took so much pain** to complete teaching one, s/he left **[-interdental]**.*

94 Cosmopolitan Mandarin in the Making of Beijing Yuppies

The image of the local intermediary-educator, knowledgeable of the workings of the Chinese market, is styled with the use of Beijing local features in all potential environments with only three exceptions in the above extracts. First, in the quote about the cornerstone work that the local professionals do, the second syllable onset of the word *gongzuo* 'work' is pronounced as [ts] rather than the interdental "alley saunterer" variant. The same nonlocal variant is used in the word *zou* 'left' in the quote above about his frustration over the turnover rate. Third, when describing his role as an intermediary in Excerpt 3.7, in line 4, he uses the Chinese idiom *cheng-shang-qi-xia* 'connecting link', within which the second syllable initial in *-shang* can be potentially lenited but is not. This is because each syllable of this idiom was pronounced with emphasis.

His otherwise frequent use of rhotacization, lenition, and neutral tone contribute to a casual, relaxed, and legato style in sharp contrast to the enunciated, controlled, and staccato style of Rebecca. Note that the expression *hao3bu0 rong2yi0* 'very difficult', which typically has a full tone in each syllable *hao3bu4 rong2yi4*, is pronounced with a neutral tone in every other syllable. The neutral tone syllable—unstressed and shorter—alternating between a stressed and longer full-tone syllable—creates a poetic effect, making his speech sound rhythmic but also conveying vividly his frustration.[13] Such a double-trochee effect is in sharp contrast to that of a double spondee if the expression were pronounced with a full tone in all four syllables, *hao3bu4 rong2yi4*. The poetic effect of neutral tone shows up again in the next part of his interview when he highlights his distinction from some other *waiqi* professionals.

In addition to presenting himself as a mediator and educator, David distinguishes himself from some middle- and high-ranking *waiqi* professionals who he thinks "have a feeling of superiority" and act like "superior Chinese." He declares himself to be the "*ta1-ta0-shi2-shi0*" 'steady and reliable' kind who "do not have inordinate desires" (e.g., asking for ever-higher salaries) but who "take the initiative to accomplish their work" and "position themselves as an upright person in society." Finally, he summarizes his view of *waiqi* employees:

Excerpt 3.8 David: "I for sure am the feet-on-the-ground type"

1 *ZO::NGjie* **[-interdental]** *lai kan,*
   To SUMMARIZE **[-interdental]**,
2 *wo geren juede* **[T0]**,
   I personally feel **[T0]**,
3 *buguan zhei san* **[-interdental]** *deng shi na yige*
   no matter which of the three **[-interdental]** ranks
4 *WO kending shi nei bijiao jiao3-ta0*[T0]*-shi2-di4 neizhong* **[-lenition]**.
   I for sure is the feet-on[T0]-the-ground type [-lenition].

David's self-characterization as a reliable employee who takes initiative at work and keeps his feet on the ground reminds us of Rebecca's principle of diligence

Cosmopolitan Mandarin in the Making of Beijing Yuppies **95**

and having a realistic view of herself. However, unlike Rebecca, who presents her professional persona with features of CM, David's realistic, down-to-earth persona is instantiated through the use of neutral tone in the two focal expressions, both four-character idioms, *ta1-ta0-shi2-shi0* 'steady and reliable' and *jiao3-ta0-shi2-di4* 'feet on the ground'.[14] The first consists of two monosyllabic reduplications in which the use of neutral tone in the reduplicated syllable is expected in both BM and Standard PTH (C. Li and Thompson 1981, 28–29; Lu 1995, 27). In the second expression, *jao3-ta4-shi2-di4*, the second syllable of this expression has a falling tone (T4) in Standard PTH. David's use of a neutral tone (the tone with the shortest duration) instead after the falling-rising (T3) (the tone with the longest duration), *jiao3-ta0-shi2-di4*, exaggerates the contrast in the duration and stress between the first and second syllable. In contrast to the measured regularity produced by the use of all full-tone syllables, such uses of a neutral tone alternating with a full tone add variation to stress and tempo, again making his speech rhythmic. Note also that the neutral tone is the only local feature used in the above extract. He used the nonlocal variants of the other variables in all the potential environments in lines 1, 3, and 4. Considering that in this part of the interview, he distinguishes himself from some other *waiqi* professional of similar and higher rank, the poetic effect produced by the neutral tone vivifies his self-claimed reliable and down-to-earth persona, but the use of other nonlocal features keeps this persona not too closely aligned with the image of a local Beijinger.

3.7 Local Excess vs. Cosmopolitan Restraint

As shown in the previous excerpts, in addition to features of CM, both Rebecca and David used local features to signal contrast. In Rebecca's quotation and explanation of the local Beijing saying, "one really has to admit incompetence," she used lenition to distinguish a modest, humble attitude in contrast to one that is unrealistically self-conceited (Excerpt 3.6 lines 5–8). Similarly, David used the neutral tone when describing himself as the "down-to-earth" kind of guy to set himself apart from those "superior Chinese." Both speakers used local features and expressions to index a realistic attitude and persona with which the speakers aligned themselves with, but each speaker accomplished this by drawing on different features. In the examples below, local features are used to create an image of excess from which the yuppies disaligned themselves.

Recall in Chapter 2, Sarah described the ostentatiously adorned parvenus. Part of Excerpt 2.1 is repeated below where the use of variants are marked:

Excerpt 3.9 Sarah: "Famous brands from head to toe"

1 *Zou* [**-interdental**] *zai* [**-interdental**] *dajie shang,*
   Walking [**-interdental**] in [**-interdental**] the street,

2 *ni kanjian* [**T0**] *chuande te piaoliang* [**T0**], ((*te* for *tebie* 'very' is a local expression))

96 Cosmopolitan Mandarin in the Making of Beijing Yuppies

you see **[T0]** (one) wearying **very** pretty **[T0]**,
3   *yisher* **[+R]** *mingpair* **[+R]**.
     famous brands **[+R]** from head to toe **[+R]**.
4   *Dai* **yi** *DA jin biao.* ((**yi** for *yi-zhi* 'one' without the classifier *–zhi is a local*
     expression))
     Wearing **a** BIG gold watch.
...
8   *Ye shi baofa hur* **[+R]**.
     (They) are also (known as) upstarts **[+R]**.

Preceding this excerpt, Sarah was discussing the importance of a professional image for *waiqi* professionals. There was a noticeable change in style
when she began to describe the excessive use of famous brands by the new
rich. In addition to a neutral tone, the "Beijing flavor" of her speech is intensified with the repeated use of rhotacization in *yisher mingpair* 'famous
brands from head to toe' (line 3), the local intensifier *te* for 'very' (line 2),
and the absence of the classifier *zhi* or *kuai* in 'a big gold watch' (line 4).
Together, with the use of rhotacization in the term *baofahur* 'upstart' in line
8, the intensified use of local features propels the image of material and
stylistic excess away from the cultured cosmopolitan with which she herself
is associated.

Beijing features were also used in Terry's description of (a) wealthy young
men who engage in conspicuous consumption to show off their wealth (Excerpt
3.10) and later (b) *baofahu*s, who are members of his club but whom he deemed
as lacking in taste and morality (Excerpt 3.11):

Excerpt 3.10 Terry: "<u>Dunhill</u> from head to toe"

1   *You shi***hou** **[T0]** *ni kanjian* **[T0]** *HENduo youqian de nan hai zi* **[T0]**,
     Sometimes **[T0]** you see **[T0]** many rich young kids **[T0]**,
2   *yishuir* **[+R]** *de <u>Dunhill</u>.* ((*yishuir* is a local expression))
     (wearing) Dunhill from head to toe **[+R]**.
3   *Cong shang dao xia QUAN douri* **[+lenition]** *mingpair* **[+R]**.
     From top to bottom all are **[+lenition]** designer brands **[+R]**.

Excerpt 3.11 (from Excerpt 2.2) Terry: "Not all members are like us"

1   *Tamen* [*baofahur*] *ye shi bujiang gongde de.*
     They [upstarts] don't care about public morality.
2   *Biru shuo,*
     For example,
3   *yantour* **[+R]** *a mandir* **[+R]** *reng a,*
     littering the floor **[+R]** with cigarette butts **[+R]**,
4   *sui dir* **[+R]** *tu tan a*
     spit freely on the floor **[+R]**.

Recall that in Chapter 2, Terry presented himself as disdaining the ostentatious behavior and style of other wealthy people. In both excerpts above, local features mark his description of the examples of ostentatiousness. In Excerpt 3.10, the excess adornment with designer brands is accompanied by the use of rhotacization and lenition in the key descriptors: 'from head to toe' (line 2), 'all are' (line 3), and 'designer brands' (line 3). Similarly, in his description of the *baofahur*'s behavior of lacking "public morality" in Excerpt 3.11, rhotacization was used three times in all the potential environments: 'cigarette butts' in line 3 and 'floor' in lines 3 and 4.

As pointed out earlier, in Chapter 2, the content of the talk describes the ostentatious and sumptuous Other with inferior taste and morality. The use of the local variants in such descriptions shown above adds another layer of meaning to that conveyed through the content of the talk. This indirect indexical meaning is localness, the kind of localness that invokes *tu* and *su* (or *tuqi* and *suqi*), being 'rustic', 'uncouth', and 'unrefined', in opposition to *yang* 'Western, modern, stylish' and *ya* 'elegant, refined'. In this way, the content and the style of the talk work together to link material and stylistic excess to localness and its associated negative qualities. Disassociating from such local images of excess, the yuppies present themselves as cosmopolitan urbanites with restraint, or in Sarah's words *you neihan* (see Excerpt 2.1), the ability to exercise self-control.

It should be pointed out that the yuppies' appeal to restraint is on the basis of superior economic status, not the pre-reform principle of restraining from materialism in the well-known expression *jian-ku-pu-su* 'hardworking-plain-living'. Self-control exercised under economic freedom distinguished the yuppies as cosmopolitans with taste and *dangci* 'class' from those other nouveaux riches. This is also reflected in Catherine's juxtaposition between the lifestyles of the affluent yuppies and the "uncouth private proprietors who can't afford to be rich": a cultivated lifestyle that refrains from the trappings of extravagant materialism versus one of 'eating-drinking-whoring-gambling' (see Excerpt 2.3). As she further explains in the excerpt below, a lifestyle with "taste" is what she aspired to. The linguistic style of her explanation is overwhelmingly cosmopolitan, combining full tone (lines 1, 12, 13), non-rhotacization (line 4), minimal lenition (one occurrence in line 5), and English expressions (lines 6, 7, 13).

Excerpt 3.12 Catherine: "I like very much people with taste"

1   *Wo juede* **[T2]** *shenghuo fangshi shi*
     I feel **[T2]** lifestyle is,

2   *yige qujue yu nide geren xingge*[15] *he nide aihao.*
     one depends on your disposition/personality and your likings.

3   *Lingyige jiushi* **[-lenition]** *jingji jichu.*
     Another is **[-lenition]** economic foundation.

4   **Zong [-interdental]** *tan qian keneng you yidian* **[-R]** *su,*
     Talking about money all the time [-interdental] may be a bit [-R] of poor taste,

98 Cosmopolitan Mandarin in the Making of Beijing Yuppies

5 *danri* [+lention] *queshi* [-lenition] *ta shi hen zhongyao de jichu.*
   but [+lention] it is actually [-lenition] a very important foundation.
6 *Wo ziji* [-interdental] *jiao ta shi mission* [E] *ye hao*
   I myself [-interdental] call it mission [E]
7 *huozhe* [-lenition] *motto* [E] *ye hao,*
   or [-lenition] motto,
8 *jiushi* [-lenition] *ni bu neng wei qian er huo zhe.*
   that is [-lenition] you can't live for money.
9 *danshi* [-lenition] *mei qian ni ye huo bu liao.*
   but [-lenition] you also can't live without money.
10 *Huozhe* [-lenition] *shuo,*
   Or [-lenition] in other words,
11 *mei qian ni jiu bu neng gaishan shenghuo.*
   without money you can't improve life.
12 *Suoyi wo juede* [T2] *wo shi,*
   So I feel [T2] I am,
13 *wo feichang xihuan you taste* [E] *de ren.*
   I like very much people with taste [E].

3.8 Conclusion

As newly emergent social groups in China are seeking semiotic means to create distinctions, language inevitably becomes a key resource in the styling of new social distinctions. As pointed out in the Introduction, the de-elitized Standard PTH, or "common speech," symbolizing pre-reform socialist egalitarianism becomes inadequate when faced with demands for signaling differentiation from "commonness." Particularly for the upwardly mobile and outwardly looking cosmopolitan Chinese like the Beijing yuppies, the national standard language, which is also their native dialect, falls with the trappings of being regional (Beijing, Northern China, mainland China) in the context of the emergence of a transnational Chinese linguistic market. The discussion presented in this chapter demonstrates that the yuppies are creating a cosmopolitan style of Mandarin by drawing on linguistic features from Standard PTH, non-mainland Mandarin varieties, and English. Cosmopolitan Mandarin is markedly different from Beijing-Mandarin-based PTH exemplified in the speech of the China Central Television (CCTV) broadcasters. What makes it distinctive is the limited use of the linguistic features that are the hallmarks of the official Standard PTH—rhotacization and neutral tone.[16] Thus, although the yuppies use significantly less local Beijing features than the state professionals, their linguistic style is not "superstandard" in the sense of the superstandard English used by, for example, White American teenage nerds in Bucholtz's study (2001). Rather, their linguistic style is a bricolage of elements of Mainland Standard Mandarin, the innovative use of the full tone, and English. CM thus defies the norms of

Cosmopolitan Mandarin in the Making of Beijing Yuppies **99**

standardness and extends the indexical potential of supralocalness beyond the regional-political confines of mainland China. Such a supraregional linguistic style gives meaning to the distinctiveness of a Beijing yuppie. Differentiating themselves from the state professionals and the local nouveau riche, the yuppies draw on CM to present themselves as cosmopolitan professionals.

Furthermore, borrowing Ulrich Beck's metaphor, their cosmopolitanism has "'roots' and 'wings' at the same time" (2002, 19). If CM is understood as the wings of their cosmopolitanism, it is rooted and meaningful **in the local context of Beijing and mainland China.** Localness is shown to be crucial in the yuppies' distinction-making project: (1) in providing the foil for the yuppies to differentiate themselves from relevant local types; and (2) locally salient linguistic resources are used to index contrast between themselves and others. In this way, their cosmopolitan identity becomes not only meaningful to themselves but also interpretable and meaningful to others.

My analysis of the bricolage of salient linguistic resources to create a new Mandarin style highlights, on the one hand, the *agency* of the yuppies actively constructing their styles, and on the other hand, that their agency is *mediated* (Ahearn 2001). That is, it is conditioned by a multitude of factors, particularly: (1) the imbued cultural values of the linguistic variables; (2) the reconfiguration of the standard language market as part of the economic transformation; and (3) the historical emergence of this professional group as the first generation of *waiqi* professionals, which contributed to the gendered career trajectories and the aesthetic labor constituting the company's symbolic capital.

The next chapter explores the use of CM in another prime locale of rising social distinctions: television programs promoting a new middle-class cosmopolitan lifestyle. It further examines the ways in which the emergence of CM and new social distinctions is a mediated process. Examining the use of CM in mass media offers a lens into the mediatization of both the new linguistic style and a new middle-class distinction: I show that features of CM are deployed by the program's hosts to create a cosmopolitan, trendy persona and consumption-based lifestyle. CM is simultaneously both part of the metasemiotic discourse that organizes, interprets, and evaluates a diverse range of signs (including consumer products and behaviors) and the means through which those signs are linked to a cosmopolitan urbanite and the lifestyle represented in the TV program.

Notes

1 Rhotacization causes phonemic changes in finals that do not end with central and back vowels. Norman (1988, 144) summarizes the changes as the following: "(1) the syllabic endings *i* and *n* are dropped [as in Examples 2, 3, 4, and 5], (2) front vowels become centralized, and (3) final *ng* fuses with *r* to form a nasalized retroflexed vowel."

2 As described in note 1, rhotacization of the final causes the loss of the syllabic ending *n* in *wan2* 'play', *ben3* 'classifier for books, albums', *jin* 'today', and locative suffixes *-bian* and *-mian*.
3 [tʂ] is syllabified.
4 [ɻ] is syllabified.
5 Although no formal study has been done on this feature, a footnote in the *Hanyu Fangyan Cihui 'Chinese Dialect Vocabulary'* describes the interdental variant as an accent feature of some speakers in the southern part of the city (Linguistics Group 1995, 8n12). In my data, the use of the interdental variant does not correlate with the participants' geographic origin in Beijing. However, as this result is based on a small number of speakers, a larger sample is needed to investigate the geographic distribution of this variant.
6 If the speaker's native dialect is a Southern variety.
7 A VARBRUL weighting value above 0.5 indicates that a factor favors the occurrence of the variant in question; a value below 0.5 indicates a disfavoring effect.
8 Treating the full-tone variant as a marker of "yuppieness" would be an analysis that takes correlation itself as the social meaning of the linguistic feature. Treating it as indexing an aspiration to being a Hong Konger or a Taiwanese would assume that the indexicality of the full-tone variant is fixed, that is, it indexes an association with Hong Kong and Taiwan.
9 I do not assume a discrete linguistic division between the two markets. Neither do I assume that the yuppies participate only in the transnational Chinese linguistic market and the state professionals only in the MSP linguistic market. Rather, as language users in general, both groups are engaged in multiple linguistic markets. Working for international companies engages the yuppies primarily in a transnational Chinese linguistic market, and working for state-owned enterprises engages the state professionals primarily in the MSP linguistic market.
10 For example, *wuguan duanzheng* 'having regular features', is a euphemistic way to describe people who are physically attractive in a particular way. Hence, a requirement that job seekers should have "regular features" is another way of saying "ugly people and those with physically visible abnormalities or deformities should not apply."
11 Original quote in Chinese: "*Xiang Zhongguo duiwai guangbo yuan shuo hua. Guoji-hua Putonghua, you yang weir, yong de cir bu xiang yiban laobaixing de richang yong ci, bijiao wen.*"
12 The different career trajectories leading to differential significance of linguistic skills for the careers of *waiqi* women and men is also noted in Ong's (2008) discussion of Chinese yuppies in Shanghai.
13 Various authors have written on the duration of Mandarin tones. T3 is longer than T2, which in turn tends to be longer than T1 and T4 (e.g., Nordenhake and Svantesson 1983; Yu 2010).
14 Other researchers also find the use of local and colloquial linguistic features in the performance of down-to-earth and practical masculine personae (e.g., Kiesling 1998; Pujolar 1997).
15 The Chinese word *xingge* can be translated as 'personality', 'character', or 'disposition'.
16 These two features are specifically taught and drilled in Chinese language classes that use Beijing Mandarin as the standard. They are also included in the *Putonghua* Proficiency Test.

References

Agha, Asif. 2003. "The Social Life of Cultural Value." *Language & Communication* 23 (3–4):231–273.

Agha, Asif. 2007. "Recombinant Selves in Mass Mediated Spacetime." *Language & Communication* 27 (3):320–335.

Ahearn, Laura M. 2001. "Language and Agency." *Annual Review of Anthropology* 30 (1):109–137.

Bakhtin, Mikhail M. 1981. *The Dialogic Imagination: Four Essays.* Translated by Caryl Emerson, and Michael Holquist. Edited by Michael Holquist. Austin, TX: University of Texas Press.

Baranovitch, Nimrod. 2003. *China's New Voices: Popular Music, Ethnicity, Gender, and Politics, 1978–1997.* Berkeley, CA: University of California Press.

Barmé, Geremie R. 1992. "The Greying of Chinese Culture." *China Review* 13:13.11–13.52.

Beck, Ulrich. 2002. "The Cosmopolitan Society and Its Enemies." *Theory, Culture and Society* 19 (1–2):17–44.

Benor, Sarah B. 2001. "Sounding Learned: The Gendered Use of /t/ in Orthodox Jewish English." In *Penn Working Papers in Linguistics: Selected Papers from NWAV 2000,* edited by Tara Sanchez, and Daniel E. Johnson, 1–16. Philadelphia, PA: University of Pennsylvania Department of Linguistics.

Blum, Susan D. 2004. "Good to Hear: Using the Trope of Standard to Find One's Way in a Sea of Linguistic Diversity." In *Language Policy in the People's Republic of China: Theory and Practice since 1949,* edited by Minglang Zhou, and Hongkai Sun, 123–141. Boston: Kluwer.

Blum, Susan D. 2005. "Nationalism without Linguism." In *The Contest of Language: Before and Beyond Nationalism,* edited by Martin W. Bloomer, 134–164. Notre Dame, IN: University of Notre Dame Press.

Bourdieu, Pierre. 1977. "The Economics of Linguistic Exchanges." *Social Science Information* 16 (6):645–668.

Bourdieu, Pierre. 1984. *Distinction: A Social Critique of the Judgment of Taste.* Translated by Richard Nice. Cambridge, MA: Harvard University Press.

Bourdieu, Pierre. 1991. *Language and Symbolic Power.* Translated by Gino Raymond, and Matthew Adamson. Cambridge, MA: Harvard University Press.

Bucholtz, Mary. 2001. "The Whiteness of Nerds: Superstandard English and Racial Markedness." *Journal of Linguistic Anthropology* 11:84–100.

Butler, Judith. 1999. *Gender Trouble: Feminism and the Subversion of Identity.* 10th Anniversary ed. New York: Routledge.

Chao, Yuen Ren. 1968. *A Grammar of Spoken Chinese.* Berkeley, CA: University of California Press.

Chao, Yuen Ren. 1976 [1961]. "What Is Correct Chinese?" In *Aspects of Chinese Sociolinguistics: Essays by Yuen Ren Chao,* selected and introduced by Anwar S. Dil, 72–83. Stanford, CA: Stanford University Press.

Chen, Shuixian. 2006. *"Gang-Tai Diqu Cihui dui Putonghua de Yingxiang"* ("Influence of Vocabulary from the Region of Hong Kong-Taiwan on *Putonghua*"). *Sino-US English Teaching* 3 (8):59–64.

Chen, Songlin. 1991. *"Shehui Yinsu dui Yuyan Shiyong de Yingxiang: Jiu Dangqian Min Yue Yu Re de Taolun"* ("Effects of Social Factors on Language Use: A Discussion on the Current Fever of Min and Cantonese"). *Yuwen Jianshe (Philology Construction)* 1:32–33.

Chen, Xian. 1997. *"Zajiao Zhongwen"* ("Hybrid Chinese"). *Xiaofei Zhinan (Consumption Guide),* September 17, 9.

Cheshire, Jenny, Paul Kerswill, Sue Fox, and Eivind Torgersen. 2011. "Contact, the Feature Pool and the Speech Community: The Emergence of Multicultural London English." *Journal of Sociolinguistics* 15 (2):151–196.

102 Cosmopolitan Mandarin in the Making of Beijing Yuppies

Duanmu, San. 2000. *The Phonology of Standard Chinese*. Oxford: Oxford University Press.

Erbaugh, Mary S. 1995. "Southern Chinese Dialects as a Medium for Reconciliation within Greater China." *Language in Society* 24 (1):79–94.

Gal, Susan. 2016. "Sociolinguistic Differentiation." In *Sociolinguistics: Theoretical Debates*, edited by Nikolas Coupland, 113–136. Cambridge: Cambridge University Press.

Gold, Thomas B. 1993. "Go with Your Feelings: Hong Kong and Taiwan Popular Culture in Greater China." *The China Quarterly* 136:907–925.

Guo, Youpeng. 1990. "The Use of *Putonghua* and Dialects in the City of Shiyan, Hubei Province." *Chinese Philology* 219:427–432.

Harrell, Stevan. 1993. "Linguistics and Hegemony in China." *International Journal of the Sociology of Language* 103:97–114.

Hoffman, Lisa M. 2010. *Patriotic Professionalism in Urban China: Fostering Talent*. Philadelphia, PA: Temple University Press.

Irvine, Judith, and Susan Gal. 2000. "Language Ideology and Linguistic Differentiation." In *Regimes of Language*, edited by Paul V. Kroskrity, 35–84. Santa Fe, NM: School of American Research Press.

Jin, Can, and Gong Bai. 1993. *Jing Weir: Toushi Beijing Ren de Yuyan (Beijing Flavor: Examining the Language of Beijingers)*. Beijing: Zhongguo Funü Chuban She (China Women's Publishing House).

Kiesling, Scott Fabius. 1998. "Men's Identities and Sociolinguistic Variation: The Case of Fraternity Men." *Journal of Sociolinguistics* 2 (1):69–99.

Kubler, Cornelius C. 1985. "The Influence of Southern Min on the Mandarin of Taiwan." *Anthropological Linguistics* 27 (2):156–176.

Lao, She. 1984 [1979]. *Zheng Hong Qi Xia (Under the Red Banner)*. In *Lao She Wen Ji (Anthology of Lao She)*, Vol. 7, 179–306. Beijing: Renmin Wenxue Chubanshe (People's Literature Publishing House).

Li, Charles N., and Sandra A. Thompson. 1981. *Mandarin Chinese: A Functional Reference Grammar*. Berkeley, CA: University of California Press.

Linguistics Group. 1995. *Zhongguo Fangyan Cihui (Chinese Dialect Vocabulary)*. Beijing: Character Reform Publishing House.

Liu, Xinwu. 1985. *Zhong Gu Lou (Bell Drum Tower)*. Beijing: Remin Wenxue Chuban She (People's Literature Publishing House).

Liu, Xinwu. 1997. *Hongtong Chuanzi (Alley Saunterers)*. Beijing: Beijing Yanshan Chuban She (Beijing Yanshan Publishing House).

Lou, Chen. 2003. *"Bailing Liren: Dianya zhong de Shishang"* ("White-Collar Beauty: Fashion in Elegance"). *Yiyao yu Baojian (Medicine and Healthcare)* 11:5.

Lu, Yunzhong. 1995. *Putonghua de Qing She yu Erhua (Neutral Tone and Rhotacization in Putonghua)*. Beijing: Shangwu Chuban She (Commercial Press).

Lü, Zhimin. 1994. *Hua Su Wei Ya de Yishu: Jing Wei Xiaoshuo Tezheng Lun (The Art of Transforming the Popular to the Literary: Characteristics of Beijing Flavor Novels)*. Beijing: Zhongguo Heping Chuban She (China Peace Publishing House).

Nordenhake, Magnus, and Jan-Olof Svantesson. 1983. "Duration of Standard Chinese Word Tones in Different Sentence Environments." *Lund University Working Papers in Linguistics* 25:105–111.

Norman, Jerry. 1988. *Chinese*. Cambridge: Cambridge University Press.

Ong, Aihwa. 1997. "Chinese Modernities: Narratives of Nation and of Capitalism." In *Ungrounded Empires: The Cultural Politics of Modern Chinese Transnationalism*, edited by Aihwa Ong, and Donald M. Nonini, 171–202. New York, NY and London: Routledge.

Ong, Aihwa. 2008. "Self-Fashioning Shanghainese: Dancing Across Spheres of Value." In *Privatizing China: Socialism From Afar*, edited by Li Zhang, and Aihwa Ong, 182–196. Ithaca, NY: Cornell University Press.

Podesva, Robert J., Roberts, Sarah J., and Campbell-Kibler, Kathryn. 2002. "Sharing Resources and Indexing Meanings in the Production of Gay Styles." In *Language and Sexuality: Contesting Meaning in Theory and Practice*, edited by Kathryn Campbell-Kibler, Robert J. Podesva, Sarah J. Roberts, and Andrew Wong, 175–189. Stanford, CA: CSLI Press.

PSCSG. 2004. *Putonghua Shuiping Ceshi Shishi Gangyao (The Implementation Guidelines for the Putonghua Proficiency Test)*. Beijing: Commercial Press.

Pujolar, Joan. 1997. "Masculinities in a Multilingual Setting." In *Language and Masculinity*, edited by Sally Johnson, and Ulrike H. Meinhof, 86–106. Oxford: Blackwell.

Qian, Nairong. 1995. *Modern Chinese Linguistics*. Beijing: Beijing Language Institute Press.

Ramsey, S. Robert. 1987. *The Languages of China*. Princeton, NJ: Princeton University Press.

Rand, David, and Sankoff, David. 1990. "GoldVarb Version 2.0: A Variable Rule Application for the Macintosh." Montreal: Centre de Recherches Mathématiques, Université de Montréal.

Sankoff, David, and Suzanne Laberge. 1978. "The Linguistic Market and the Statistical Explanation of Variability." In *Linguistic Variation: Models and Methods*, edited by David Sankoff, 239–250. New York, NY: Academic Press.

Shen, Susan Xiaonan. 1990. *The Prosody of Mandarin Chinese*. Berkeley, CA: University of California Press.

Silverstein, Michael. 2003. "Indexical Order and the Dialectics of Sociolinguistic Life." *Language & Communication* 23 (3–4):193–229.

Tang, Zhixiang. 2001. *Dangdai Hanyu Ciyu de Gongshi Zhuangkuang jiqi Chanbian: Jiushi Niandai Zhongguo Dalu, Xianggang, Taiwan Hanyu Ciyu Xianzhuang Yanjiu (Synchronic Status and Evolution in Contemporary Chinese Vocabulary: Research in the Chinese Vocabulary of Mainland China, Hong Kong, and Taiwan in the 1990s)*. Shanghai: Fudan Daxue Chuban She (Fudan University Press).

Wang, Li. 1958. *Hanyu Shi Gao (History of Chinese)*. Beijing: Kexue Chuban She (Science Publishing House).

Xi, Boxian. 1995. *"Zui li Na Lai 'Re Doufu'?: Shitan Beijing Tuyin"* ("Where Does the 'Hot Tofu' in the Mouth Come from?: Discussion of Beijing Vernacular Sounds"). *Yuwen Jianshe (Philology Construction)* 12:5–8.

Xiandai Hanyu Cidian (Modern Chinese Dictionary). 1998. Beijing: Shangwu Yinshuguan (Commercial Press).

Yang, Dongping. 1994. *City Wind of Season: The Cultural Spirit of Beijing and Shanghai*. Beijing: Oriental Press.

Yang, Mayfair Mei-hui. 1997. "Mass Media and Transnational Subjectivity in Shanghai: Notes on (Re)Cosmopolitanism in a Chinese Metropolis." In *Ungrounded Empires: The Cultural Politics of Modern Chinese Transnationalism*, edited by Aihwa Ong, and Donald M. Nonini, 287–319. New York, NY and London: Routledge.

Yu, Alan C. L. 2010. "Tonal Effects on Perceived Vowel Duration." *Laboratory Phonology* 10:151–168.

Zhang, Lihang. 1994. *Beijing Wenxue de Diyu Wenhua Meili (The Beauty of the Regional Culture of Beijing Literature)*. Beijing: ZhongguoHeping Chuban She (China Peace Publishing House).

Zhang, Qing. 2001. *Changing Economy, Changing Markets: A Sociolinguistic Study of Chinese Yuppies*. Ph.D. Dissertation. Stanford, CA: Stanford University.

Zhang, Qing. 2007. "Cosmopolitanism and Linguistic Capital in China: Language, Gender and the Transition to a Globalized Market Economy in Beijing." In *Words, Worlds, and Material Girls: Language, Gender, Globalization*, edited by Bonnie S. McElhinny, 403–422. Berlin: de Gruyter.

Zhang, Qing 2008. "Rhotacization and the 'Beijing Smooth Operator': The Social Meaning of a Linguistic Variable." *Journal of Sociolinguistics* 12 (2):201–222.

Zhao, Danian. 1996. "*Jingwei Xiaoshuo. Beijing Ren. Beijing Hua*" ("Beijing Flavor Novels. Beijing People. Beijing Speech"). *Qianxian (Frontline)* 5: 50–52.

Zhao, Yuan. 1991. *Beijing: Cheng yu Ren (Beijing: The City and Its People)*. Shanghai: Shanghai Renmin Chubanshe (Shanghai People's Publishing House).

Zhu, Wanjin, and Jianmin Chen. 1991. "Some Economic Aspects of the Language Situation in China." *Journal of Asian Pacific Communication* 2 (1): 91–101.

4

COSMOPOLITAN MANDARIN IN THE MAKING OF A NEW CHINESE MIDDLE-CLASS CONSUMER

4.1 Metasemiotic Discourse and the Mediation of New Social Distinction

When I was conducting my research with the yuppies in Beijing, *Trends Gentleman*, "the first-of-its-kind glossy magazine" (Lakshmanan 1997, D1), was inaugurated and later became the Chinese edition of *Esquire*. It was considered the "bible" for affluent Chinese men who had plenty of money but needed guidance on "proper" ways to consume and enjoy a new lifestyle with taste (ibid.). The Chinese translation of Paul Fussell's (1983) *Class: A Guide through the American Status System*[1] was one of the best sellers in 1998 (Lin 2009). It has in effect become a popular "lifestyle guidebook" for many Chinese white-collar professionals and petit bourgeoisie urbanites (Lin 2009, 2). In a similar fashion, the 2002 Chinese translation of David Brook's (2000) *Bobos in Paradise* became an instant bestseller and generated "bobo fever" in urban China (Wang 2005a, 534). These have joined numerous other commercial magazines and mass media products to offer "proper" guidance for the growing fledgling Chinese consumers (e.g., Song and Lee 2012; Sun 2015; Xu 2009). Mass media play a crucial role in the re-emergence of social distinctions and the rise of consumerism, without which the "valorization of difference" (Dirlik 2001, 16) in the reform era would not have been possible. They constitute a major force in creating and orientating people to distinctions and styles on multiple scales of differentiation, including age, gender, and class (Donald and Zheng 2009; Hooper 1998; Song and Lee 2012; Wang 2005b; Xu 2009).

Building on recent developments in anthropological and media studies (Ginsburg, Abu-Lughod, and Larkin 2002; Livingstone 2009; Mazzarella 2004, 2012; Peters 1997), my analysis in this chapter illustrates how media is a reflexive and constitutive process of mediation. The lifestyle television program examined in this chapter thus does not represent what is happening in the off-screen

106 Cosmopolitan Mandarin

world, nor does it try to identify what cultural values are important to its audience and adjust its message accordingly (Mazzarella 2012, 220). Rather, it interprets, categorizes, and constructs social realities, relations, and particular types of audiences in ideology-laden ways (Couldry 2003; Hjarvard 2008; Mazzarella 2012; McQuail 2002). The mass-mediated constitution of emerging consumer cultures and new middle-class identities, including the important role of television in the process, have been documented widely in Asia, including Nepal (Liechty 2003), India (Mankekar 1999; Nakassis 2016), Singapore, Taiwan, and China (Lewis, Martin, and Sun 2012; Sun 2015; Xu 2007, 2009). But the question remains: How do the media mediate the construction of distinction? In other words, how is the semiotic process of mediation carried out?

This chapter addresses the above question by examining the use of Cosmopolitan Mandarin (CM) in a television program on consumption and lifestyle. Such programs have become immensely popular in China (Sun 2015). In this chapter, I take my analysis further and investigate three specific ways that CM is integral to emerging new social distinctions. First, by examining the speech of the program's hosts, the analysis reveals an expanded range of linguistic elements that constitute CM and provides evidence for an expanded social domain of people who use CM (Agha 2007, 169). I discuss how the television hosts are cultural intermediaries (Bourdieu 1984) or metacultural experts (Urban 2001) who, as explained in detail later, are pivotal generators of meanings and values in the semiotic process of mediation (Wright 2005, 110). Second, the analysis reveals an expanded range of the social meanings of CM (Agha 2007, 169). Third, the chapter illuminates that the making of new social distinction is a process of mediation relying on language functioning as a meta-sign; specifically, through metasemiotic discourse, mass media, in this case, the television program, mediate the construction of distinction.

Through examining CM in metasemiotic discourse, I show that the television program mediates the construction of distinction by grouping a diverse range of signs—including consumer products and behaviors—and linking them to urban middle-class consumer personae and a cosmopolitan lifestyle. Crucially, my analysis illustrates the ways in which mediation takes place through metasemiotic discourse, or discourse about signs, which creates meanings and values for the signs involved (Agha 2011a; Inoue 2007). Although such semiotic mediation[2] of social distinction always takes place in everyday off-screen and offline lives, the mediatization of new social distinctions emphasizes that social change and more generally "everyday practices and relations are increasingly shaped by mediating technologies and media organizations" (Agha 2011b; Hepp 2014, 50–52; Livingstone 2009, 4).[3] Thus, my work here highlights that the importance of examining mediatized metasemiotic discourse lies in the fact that television programming, such as the one in this study, and mass media in general, are sites of mediation where the connection among signs, their meanings, and messages about meanings and values are produced and made known to a large number of people (Agha 2007, 2011b; see also Coupland 2014). Although messages about signs, including linguistic signs, generated through such mass mediation do not guarantee (uniform forms of) uptake and recontextualization (Agha 2011a, 2011b), mediatization leads to "a greater cultural reflexivity" (Hjarvard 2008, 130)—including "sociolinguistic reflexivity" (Coupland 2014, 78)—and a heightened awareness of alternative choices (Hjarvard 2008, 130), including socially meaningful, alternative ways of speaking (e.g., Walters 2003, 88). Thus, as shown in this chapter, the use of CM in television juxtaposes this innovative Mandarin style against the conventional Beijing-Mandarin-based PTH and contributes to increased awareness of their difference. Such reflexivity is particularly important in sociolinguistic change as social actors come to be aware of and recognize different and new ways of doing things—including using language—and their social significance (Coupland 2014, 76).

One type of social actor who plays a pivotal role in the semiotic process of mass mediation and mediatization of new social distinction is what Bourdieu refers to as "cultural intermediaries (the most typical of whom are the producers of cultural programmes on TV and radio...)" (1984, 325). As indicated in the opening discussion, the demand for cultural intermediaries continues to grow in China with the rise of consumerism and new lifestyle choices (see also Featherstone 2007, 19). These intermediaries are a type of social actors of particular importance in this study on mediation of new social distinction—and in any study on cultural change—because of the pedagogical work they do in helping (Chinese) consumers know how to engage with and orient to consumer products and how to use and organize them appropriately (Cronin 2004; Maguire and Smith 2010, 2012). They interpret and evaluate the meaning and value of products and behaviors, thus shaping consumer tastes and dispositions (Bourdieu 1984, 230; Macquire and Matthews 2010; Nixon and Du Guy 2002, 497; Wright 2005, 110). In this sense, cultural intermediaries are similar to what Urban refers to as "metacultural experts," people who provide expert judgments about "similarities and differences—continuity with the past and change [or newness]" (2001, 3). Their opinions play a vital role in making cultural change recognizable to the public as their judgments "get encoded in mass-disseminated forms such as magazine or journal articles, or television or radio commentary" (ibid., 235). The hosts of the television program discussed in this chapter are just such cultural intermediaries and metacultural experts; their talk thus deserves special attention to reveal the meaning-making process in the making of a new middle-class cosmopolitan consumer, another crucial discursive domain where new social distinction is constructed.

I provide a description of the television program in Section 4.2 and analyze the linguistic characteristics of the hosts' talk in Section 4.3. Section 4.4 focuses on an analysis of the metasemiotic discourse through which the hosts construct a new middle-class consumer. The conclusion summarizes the findings and the indexical values of CM revealed through the analyses.

108 Cosmopolitan Mandarin

4.2 *S Information Station*: "Leader in Distinctive Individualistic Consumption"

The television program analyzed in this chapter is *S Qiangbao Zhan* 'S *Information Station*', with the letter 'S' as the initial of the English word 'shopping'. It is a shopping-lifestyle program broadcast on the 'Metropolis Channel' (*Dushi Pindao*) of Tianjin Television Station in the city of Tianjin, 120 kilometers southeast of Beijing.[4] A half-hour weekly program, it is aired at 7:30 p.m. on Friday and rerun at 10:30 a.m. on Saturday and 3:30 p.m. the following Tuesday. The 16 episodes of the program used for the analysis in this chapter were recorded from May to October 2005 and March 2006. Self-styled as "the leader in distinctive and individualistic consumption," the program seeks to "provide information about trendy and cutting-edge consumption and detailed practical guidance on shopping," in the hope of bringing to the audience "enjoyment through information and happiness in consumption" (TJTV 2005). The slogan of the program is "*jiang* shopping *jinxing daodi!*" 'carry shopping through to the end', a play on a well-known communist revolutionary slogan "*jiang geming jinxing daodi*" 'carry the revolution through to the end'. It was originally the title of an article written by Mao Zedong for the Xinhua News Agency on the New Year's Eve of 1948, one year before the Chinese Communist Party and the People's Liberation Army defeated the Nationalists in 1949. Since then, it has become one of the most widely quoted slogans in political movements and campaigns. Replacing "revolution," that is, the communist revolution for political power, with the English word "shopping," the keyword of the program, the show reappropriates the slogan to turn the revolution into one in the realm of consumption. Indeed, what the show intends to do is to take on the role of leader and trendsetter in the current consumer revolution.

The program consists of four major segments. *Liuxing Dianji* 'Trends Spotting' is about what is stylish and fashionable in the season. It "disseminates the latest information on consumption," including "the latest style trends, new and unique commodities, cultural activities, and good books and music" (ibid.). *Jietou Sou Ku* 'Street Cool Hunting' "finds trendy, cutting-edge and new individualistic shops, recommends individualistic single items" (ibid.). *Chengshi Quan Gonglüe* 'Complete Metropolitan Strategies' is about how to live a city life. It deals with "eating, drinking, playing, entertaining, clothing, food, residence, transportation and travel," and "provides knowledge on consumer products and shopping techniques" (ibid.). *Jietou Duidui Peng* 'Shopping Partner' is a segment in which one of the hosts goes to a shopping mall as the "shopping partner" to accompany a guest shopper, offering her expert advice for the consumer's shopping mission.

Based on the consumer products and their prices, the shopping venues, and the guest consumers featured in the program, it is clear that *S Information Station* is intended for an audience of young, urban, white-collar professionals with high purchasing power. In the 16 episodes analyzed in this chapter, the consumer products, many of which are of international brands, range from clothing and fashion accessories, beauty products, and sports gear to home products (e.g., furniture, fine bone china, home accessories), electronics (e.g., digital cameras, cell phones), and wedding event services. It also introduces new ways of urban living, such as home aromatherapy treatment, gift-giving on special occasions (e.g., anniversaries, housewarming), making cocktails, brewing and drinking coffee, and going to parties after work. Such practices are often presented as shared globally. Hence, as illustrated later, the audience of the television show is not addressed as Tianjin-based locals but as sophisticated consumers living a cosmopolitan lifestyle (see also Wang 2005a, 540).

The program's two female hosts are Liu Ling and Yu Yuan, both Tianjin natives. Young, good-looking, and ebullient, they enact the program's theme and mission through their on-screen performance. They draw on linguistic and other semiotic resources to create a stylish cosmopolitan persona, an authority in trends and a new consumption-based urban lifestyle. As metacultural experts or cultural intermediaries, they provide expert opinions on urban living; fashion trends; what, where, how to buy; and how to mix and match to create tasteful styles. In other words, they prescribe particular "consumer regimens" (Liechty 2003, 34) for trendy middle-class consumer-urbanites. Furthermore, and similar to presenters in other consumption and lifestyle programs, they serve as role-models—including ways of speaking—for the particular types of audience constructed through the programs (e.g., Davies 2003; Jaworski et al. 2003). In *S Information Station*, the hosts literally serve as consumer models by trying on clothing and accessories and performing the role of customers consuming (new) services (e.g., image design and wedding event service). In what follows, I first examine the major linguistic features of the hosts' speech style and how they are used to create their persona as experts on style and taste. Then, I analyze their metasemiotic discourse that creates meaning and value for a diverse range of consumer goods and behaviors, linking them to an urban middle-class consumer persona and a cosmopolitan consumption-based lifestyle.

4.3 Linguistic Features of the Hosts' Speech Style

Before presenting the data, I provide a brief explanation of the official regulations concerning language use in the Chinese broadcasting media. In October 2000, the "Common Language Law" was passed, stipulating that PTH should be used as the language of radio and television broadcasting. In the following year, the city of Tianjin's Committee on Language and Character and the Committee on Education issued a circular on the examination and evaluation of the status of PTH in the city, in an effort to prepare for the pending evaluation by the state Ministry of Education and the Working Committee on Language and Character in 2003 (Nankai Daxue 2002). As required by the circular, radio

110 Cosmopolitan Mandarin

and television broadcasters and professional program hosts were to use Standard PTH in their programming. Moreover, they were required to take the *Putonghua Shuiping Ceshi* 'Putonghua Proficiency Test' (hereinafter, PSC) and obtain the certificate of the highest proficiency level of Grade 1-A. According to the information published on the Tianjin Television website, by the end of 2004, "all broadcasters and hosts have obtained Grade 1-A Certificate of the PSC" (TJTV 2004). This means that the two hosts had taken the PSC and that their PTH proficiency level had been certified to be Grade 1-A. The data collection period for the study presented in this chapter coincided with a time when a series of government regulations were issued to even more strictly reinforce the use of PTH in the broadcasting media. First, in April 2004, the State Administration of Radio, Film, and Television (SARFT), the top government broadcasting authority, initiated the "Purification Project," aiming to purge from television programs, radio, and films, "harmful" elements that may affect the well-being of young people in China (SARFT 2004). To this end, radio and television broadcasting personnel were required to adhere to Standard PTH. They were prohibited to mix PTH with foreign languages and imitate Hong-Kong and Taiwan accents (ibid.). Then in September 2005, SARFT rolled out "The Self-Disciplining Conventions of Radio and Television Broadcasters and Hosts in China," showing more determination to "protect the purity and standard of the national language" (SARFT 2005).[5] These regulations are intended for broadcasting personnel to serve as norm keepers and exemplary speakers of Beijing-Mandarin-based Standard PTH. However, as the following analysis shows, despite the tightened government control on language use in the broadcasting media, the two hosts of *S Information Station* are norm breakers whose linguistic style is not in conformity with the official regulations.

In contrast to the conservative Standard PTH of their newscaster colleagues, the stereotypic exemplary speaker of the standard language, the hosts' speech style is innovative with respect to the use of new lexical items, (English–Mandarin) code-mixing, and innovative sound features. Each aspect of their speech is described below to show that the hosts' speech style is similar to that of the Beijing yuppies examined earlier, in the sense that they use a cosmopolitan style of Mandarin.

4.3.1 Innovative Lexical Items

One type of innovative lexical items used by the hosts consists of expressions that have recently found their way into PTH to fill lexical gaps, as shown in Table 4.1. Although some of them are included in the 2003 edition of *Xinhua Xin Ciyu Cidian* (hereinafter, XXCC), 'Xinhua Dictionary of New Expressions', none is found in the 2005 edition of *Xiandai Hanyu Cidian* (hereinafter, XHC), *Modern Chinese Dictionary*, the most authoritative dictionary published in China. From 'aromatherapy' to 'bubble bath', from 'table runner' to 'vacuum

Cosmopolitan Mandarin **111**

TABLE 4.1 Vocabulary of New Urban Lifestyle[7]

New consumer products	New ways of urban living and practices	New concepts and urban characteristics
hongxi hu 'vacuum pot' (vacuum coffee brewer), unaware of its use in Taiwan and Hong Kong (Survey)	**huoshui yangsheng guan** 'spa', referring to the commercial establishment offering health and beauty treatment, also used in Taiwan and Hong Kong (Survey)	**an jie** 'mortgage' (XXCC 2003, 3), also used in Hong Kong but not Taiwan (Survey)
huaban 'skateboard', also used in Taiwan and Hong Kong (Survey)	**hunda** calque of English 'mix and match', also used in Taiwan but not Hong Kong (Survey)	**jianyue** 'minimalist', 'less-is-more', used to describe styles of fashion and décor that are minimalist and refined, also used in Taiwan and Hong Kong (Survey)
jingyou 'essential oil', also used in Taiwan and Hong Kong (Survey)	**paopao yu** 'bubble bath', also used in Taiwan and Hong Kong (Survey)	**ku** 'cool, fashionably attractive', a loanword from English (XXCC 2003, 187), also used in Taiwan and Hong Kong (Survey)
moka hu 'moka pot', also used in Taiwan and Hong Kong (Survey)	**shoushen** 'slim, make oneself thinner by such means as exercising and dieting', loanword from Japanese, spread to Taiwan and then to Hong Kong and mainland China (XXCC 2003, 295), also used in Taiwan and Hong Kong (Survey)	**linglei** 'nonconformist', 'unconventional', 'original', 'unique' (XXCC 2003, 203), also used in Taiwan and Hong Kong (Survey)
zhuoqi 'table runner', unaware of its use in Taiwan and Hong Kong (Survey)	**xiangxun liaofa** 'aromatherapy', also used in Taiwan and Hong Kong (Survey)	**zhuang shan** 'clothing clash', resemblance in clothing, considered a fashion faux pas (XXCC 2003, 428), also used in Taiwan and Hong Kong (Survey)

coffee brewer', from 'slimming' to avoiding 'clothing clash' at a party, from being 'cool' to being 'nonconformist', these expressions are about new consumer products, new concepts and practices of urban living, and new urban characteristics. They constitute the vocabulary of an urban lifestyle that is distinctively

112 Cosmopolitan Mandarin

new (nontraditional) and cosmopolitan (nonlocal). New expressions such as these directly index newness and cosmopolitan urbanism in that denotationally they refer to new consumer products, practices, concepts, and desirable urban characteristics that are different from what is considered the "traditional" and the "local." Although this study does not intend to investigate the source(s) of the innovative lexical items found in the data, a small, written questionnaire survey was conducted to find out whether they were also used at all in Taiwan and Hong Kong. Six respondents from Hong Kong and five from Taiwan participated in the survey.[6] The judgments of the respondents were quite consistent. The summary of the responses for each expression is presented following the English translation of the term in Table 4.1.

In addition to the above type of innovative lexical items, the hosts use many new expressions that do not necessarily denote newness or cosmopolitanism but that carry an indexical value of being "trendy" (unconventional, nontraditional) and "cosmopolitan" (nonlocal). These include Mandarin expressions such as those listed in Table 4.2 and the English words in Table 4.3. The difference between the set of Mandarin expressions in Table 4.1 and those in Table 4.2 is that members of the latter group do not fill lexical gaps, as all have equivalents in the existing PTH lexicon. The main "communication sources" (Spitulnik 1998, 47) of these expressions are popular culture and computer-mediated communication, e.g., the two English based loan-words *xiu* 'show' and *kiu* 'cute', and *meimei* 'pretty girl'. The adverb *man* 'quite' or 'very' and exclamation particle *wa* 'wow' have long been in use in some Southern varieties, for instance, Shanghai *hua* and Cantonese. Similar to neutral tone, they have come to take on special social significance in PTH since the influx of Hong Kong and Taiwan popular culture products in the mainland market. It is the contrast between these new forms and their conservative PTH counterparts that gives indexical value to the innovative expressions. Furthermore, the indexical meaning of "trendiness" and "cosmopolitanism" is brought out through the hosts' motivated act of employing an innovative form instead of its conventional counterpart.

The indexical meaning as conveyed by the above items is especially highlighted in conversations between a host and a guest participant in which the former employs an innovative expression whereas the latter uses the conventional term, as shown in (4) in Table 4.2. In this example, from the segment "Shopping Partner," the guest shopper Yang is looking for a birthday gift for her mother. Commenting on a potential candidate, a silk scarf, she uses the conventional PTH adverb *ting* 'quite' or 'very' to modify *piaoliang* 'pretty'. In the next turn, the host Liu expresses her agreement with Yang but describes the scarf as *man piaoliang*, using the trendier, new form *man*. Another interesting aspect of this example is the co-occurrence of features in the speech of Yang and Liu. In Yang's speech, *ting* co-occurs with another conventional PTH feature, that is, the neutral tone of the second syllable in *piao4liang0*. In contrast, in

TABLE 4.2 "Trendy" Expressions

"Trendy" expressions	Conservative Putonghua
xiu 'show' (verb or noun) a loanword from English, used in Taiwan Mandarin and spreading to mainland China (Huang 2003, 43; XXCC 2003, 372), also used in Taiwan and Hong Kong (Survey)	*zhanshi* (verb) 'show, display' *biaoyan* (noun) 'show, performance'
(1) <showing a hair accessory, "Trend Spotting", 10/8/05> Liu: *women rang ta zhuan guoqu, gei dajia* **xiu** **[L]** *yi xia.* 'let's ask him to turn around, show **[L]** it to us.'	
kiu 'cute' a loanword from English, also used in Taiwan and Hong Kong (Survey)	*ke'ai* 'adorable', 'cute'
(2) <discussing clothing accessories, "Shopping Partner", 8/19/05> Liu: *Ruguo chuanshang zheyang yi jian yifu, daishang yi ge zheyang xiao lianzi, yiding hui rang ren ganjue feichang* **kiu** [L] *de* 'If (you) wear a piece of clothing like this (a pair of grey pants), matching it with a small chain like this (a thin metallic silver belt), (you) will for sure look very **cute [L]**'.	
meimei 'pretty girl' a popular term referring to a pretty girl, used most often in online communication (XXCC 2003, 454), also used in Taiwan and Hong Kong (Survey)	*meili de nü hai* 'pretty girl'
(3) <introducing the owner of a coffee shop, "Street Cool Hunting", 9/24/05> Liu: *Na women xianzai jieshao de zhejia dian de dianzhu, yi wei piaoliang* **[T4]** *de* **meimei [L]**. 'The owner of the [coffee] shop we're introducing now is a **pretty [T4]** girl **[L]**.'	
man (adverb) + adjective 'quite', 'very' In XHC (2005, 914) *man* is marked as "dialectal." This adverb is used in certain Southern varieties such as the Shanghai dialect and also used in Hong Kong Cantonese and Taiwan Mandarin (Survey).	*ting* 'quite', 'very'
(4) <shopping for a birthday gift for Yang's mother, Yang asking for Liu's opinion on a silk scarf, "Shopping Partner," Yang = guest shopping partner, 9/17/05> Yang: *Liu Ling, wo juede zhetiao si jin* **ting** *piaoliang* **[T0]** *de. Ni juede zenmoyang.* 'Liu Ling, I think this silk scarf is **quite** pretty **[T0]**. What do you think.' Liu: *Shi* **man [L]** *pianliang* **[T4]** *de. Ni mama yingding hui xihuan de.* 'It is **quite [L] pretty [T4]**. Your mom will definitely like it.'	
hao (adverb) + adjective 'very, so' As an intensifier, this adverb is used more often in Southern varieties whereas Beijing and Tianjin Mandarin speakers tend to use *zhen*. See example in (5).	zhen 'very, so'
wa (exclamation) 'wow' expressing surprise and/or admiration In conventional Standard PTH *wa* is an onomatopoeia describing the sound of vomiting or crying (XHC 2005, 1395). It is used in Taiwan Mandarin and Hong Kong Cantonese (Survey)	*aya, oyo*
(5) <commenting on the achievement of a competitor in "Super Shopping Show," 10/22/05> Liu: **Wa [L]**, **hao [L]** *LIHAI* **[T4]** *a.* 'Wow **[L]**, so **[L]** AMAZING **[T4]** ah.'	

114 Cosmopolitan Mandarin

addition to using the innovative adverb *man*, Liu pronounces the second syllable of *piao4liang4* with a full tone, another innovative feature discussed in Section 4.3.3. I take up the issue of co-occurring innovative features in Section 4.4.

4.3.2 Code-Mixing

In addition to lexical innovations in Mandarin, the hosts' speech is interspersed with English expressions. Almost all the code-mixing cases found in the data are single word insertions, as shown in Table 4.3. Items marked with an asterisk in the top of the list are English expressions associated with elements of new urban lifestyles and popular culture, for instance, "townhouse," a new type of private residence, "download," and "e-mail," new telecommunication technology and practice, "hip hop," a new popular music genre, "spa," new health and beauty service and venue, a new trend of "DIY" practice, "Carrie," Carrie Bradshaw, a popular culture character from the American hit series *Sex and the City*, and the Japanese "Hello Kitty." These English expressions index newness and cosmopolitanism. Such indexical meaning is derived from their referents—which refer to something new—as well as English, a new code in Chinese interaction and one associated with global trends. However, these expressions all have PTH equivalents that are themselves lexical innovations, and their use is gaining currency in the contemporary culture of consumption. The use of English here adds authenticity and helps the hosts assert their authority as experts in a new cosmopolitan lifestyle.

Another set of English words, shown in Table 4.3, without the asterisk mark, do not refer to elements of newness, trendiness, or cosmopolitanism, and again, most of them have PTH equivalents. In contrast to the English words discussed above, the indexical value of this set derives from the contrast between the two codes. These words include the program's keyword "shopping"; the routine expressions in the segment "Shopping Partner," such as "partner," referring to the participant who will share the shopping experience with the host, and "let's go," used to signal the beginning of a shopping mission; "hi," used to greet the audience at the beginning of each episode and the participants during the show; and "bye-bye," used at the end of each episode. "Hi," "bye-bye," and "okay" are also often used by young show business celebrities as well as hosts in programs about show business. They are also very popular among young Chinese urbanites. "Office" and "OL" (office lady) are words associated with the white-collar professionals, particularly those working in the local branches of international corporations, who are part of the show's prominent target audience. Such English words create the sense of trendiness and cosmopolitanism, which would be lost if they were replaced by their PTH equivalents. The analysis of the two sets of English expressions shows that the use of English creates slightly different indexical meanings: In expressions that refer to newness, English conveys an additional layer of indexical meaning

Cosmopolitan Mandarin 115

TABLE 4.3 English Expressions

English	Putonghua
*Carrie (Carrie Bradshaw)	*Kaili*
*download	*xiazai*
*e-mail	*dianzi youjian*
*DIY	*ziji dongshou*
*hip hop	*xi ha*
*Hello Kitty	*Kaidi Mao*
*spa	*huo shui yangsheng guan*
*townhouse	*lianti bieshu*
bye-bye	*zaijian*
Hawai'i	*Xiaweiyi*
high (in a cheerful spirit, see also Huang (2004, 45))	*jingshen zhenfen, qingxu gao'ang*
Hi	*ni hao*
let's go!	*zanmen zou ba!*
logo	*tuxing biaozhi, hui biao*
office	*bangong shi*
okay	*hao ba*
OL (office lady)	
model	*mote*
partner	*huoban, dadang*
party	*juhui, paidui*
pose	*zishi (noun), bai zishi (verb)*
shopping	*gouwu*
VIP	*guibin*

of authenticity and authority in fashion and a new urban lifestyle; in expressions that do not refer to newness, the code itself indexes trendiness and cosmopolitanism.

4.3.3 Innovative Sound Features

The most innovative aspect of the hosts' speech style is their limited use of rhotacization and frequent realization of a neutral tone as a full tone. Although rhotacization is a salient feature of Beijing Mandarin (BM) (see Section 3.2.1) and optional in most cases, it is considered a norm in Standard PTH. Such a norm is reflected in the fact that words with syllable rhymes that "*must be rhotacized* in colloquial speech are treated as independent lexical entries" in *The Modern Chinese Dictionary* (XHC 2005, 3; emphasis added). Rhotacization is also one of the tested items in the PSC. A list of 189 words with syllable rhymes that can be rhotacized is given in the *Putonghua Shuiping Ceshi Shishi Gangyao* (hereinafter, PSCSG), '*The Implementation Guidelines for the Putonghua Proficiency*

116 Cosmopolitan Mandarin

Test' (PSCSG 2004, 247–251). From this list a minimum of four such words are to be included in the PSC.

Like rhotacization, neutral tone, one of the local BM features described in Chapter 3 (Section 3.2.3), is also considered a norm in Standard PTH. In *The Modern Chinese Dictionary*, words with a neutral tone are explicitly marked in their pinyin transcriptions. A list of 545 words with syllables that must be pronounced with a neutral tone is provided in the PSCSG (2004, 238–246). In the PSC, a minimum of three such words must be included to test the speaker's ability to identify and pronounce them correctly.[8] Considering that the two hosts had obtained the highest level of proficiency in the PSC and that their native Tianjin dialect shares the two features with BM, their limited use of rhotacization and frequent use of full tone in place of a neural tone are shown to be part of their strategic deployment of language to produce a distinctive style.

4.3.3.1 De-rhotacization

Rhotacization is rarely used in formal speech, such as newscasting, but often used in casual, colloquial speech. As introduced earlier, one of the program's objectives is to make shopping and consumption a joyful experience, in which case the use of rhotacization would be consistent with the overall casual and jovial style of the program. As shown in example (6), when addressing each other, the hosts sometimes rhotacize each other's given name, a familiar practice among Beijing and Tianjin Mandarin speakers to signal endearment. The rhotacized locative particle *zher* 'here', which is conventionalized in the *Modern Chinese Dictionary* (XHC 2005, 1727), is also used.

(6) <in a hair accessory store, "Trends Spotting," 10/8/2005>

Yu: *Liu Lingr* **[R+]** *a, ni bushi yao gei wo bianhuan zaoxing ma? zenmo dai wo dao zher* **[R+]** *lai le?*
Liu Ling**r** **[R+]**, aren't you going to have my style changed? Why are you taking me here **[R+]**?

However, in view of the casual and jovial style of the program, it is quite unexpected that the hosts had such a low rate of rhotacization at 13.7% (see Table 4.4) across the recorded episodes. It can be argued that the interactions in the program, although casual in style, were somewhat scripted and rehearsed, like those in entertainment programs in general (Coupland 2001). Thus, the

TABLE 4.4 Limited Use of Rhotacization

Potential environment	% of rhotacization
526	13.7% (n = 72)

Cosmopolitan Mandarin **117**

percentage of usage alone cannot tell us much about the social significance of the hosts' limited use of rhotacization.

The following examples illustrate that the low frequency of rhotacization is not predicated on the scriptedness of the program. Like their use of lexical innovations, non-rhotacization, or rather **de-rhotacization**, is a motivated act of the hosts: They do not use rhotacization in the same environment as the participants' speech, as shown in excerpt (7), nor in the linguistic environment that favors it, as illustrated in example (8).

(7) <discussing skateboards in a trendy sports gear store, "Street Cool Hunting," 9/10/05, S = store owner>

S: *Na women xianzai kan yixia tade banmianr* [**R+**].
      Let's now take a look at the deck [**R+**] of the skateboard.
Yu: *Banmian* [**R-**].
      The deck [**R-**].
S: *Dui, tade huaban mianr* [**R+**], *yiban tade banmianr* [**R+**] *you san zhong.*
      Right, the deck [**R+**] *of the skateboard, usually there're three types of decks* [**R+**].
Yu: *Na san zhong banmian* [**R-**] *ne?*
      Which three types of decks [**R-**]?

In the above example, the store owner uses rhotacization in all three occurrences of *(ban)mian* 'deck' as *(ban)mianr*, but Yu repeats *banmian* twice without rhotacization. Such contrast between the hosts and participants becomes even more striking in a pragmatically salient environment favoring rhotacization, as illustrated in (8). The frequently used minimal response *meicuo* 'right'— signaling interactional alignment—is expected to be rhotacized as *meicuor* in casual speech of Tianjin and Beijing Mandarin speakers of PTH. This is how it is produced by Zhang, manager of a wedding planning company. In contrast, Yu does not rhotacize in either occurrence. In fact, the hosts used *meicuo* 52 times in the 16 episodes and none was rhotacized. De-rhotacization in this environment is stylistically salient especially considering the friendly, casual style of the program.

(8) <discussing wedding planning companies and their services, 8/26/05, Zhang = manager of a wedding planning company>

Yu: *Gangcai zai wuli women shuodao hunqing de xianchang buzhi shi hen zhongyaode.*
       Just now when inside we mentioned that the decoration of the site of the wedding ceremony was very important.
       Dangran wo juede chedui dui xinren laishuo yeshi feichang zhongyaode.
       Of course I think the motorcade is also very important for the bride and groom.
Zhang: *Meicuor* [**+R**]. *Xianzai xinrenmen yuelaiyue zhuzhong hunli de meige xijie.*

118 Cosmopolitan Mandarin

	Right **[+R]**. Nowadays brides and grooms are paying more and more attention to every detail of the wedding ceremony.
Yu:	*Meicuo* **[-R]**. Right **[-R]**.
Zhang:	*Qishi yingxin de chedui zai zhengge hunli de guochengzhong ye zhanyou yege feichang zhongyao de weizhi.* In fact the motorcade for the couple is also very important in the whole wedding process.
Yu:	*Meicuo* **[-R]**. Right **[-R]**.

Example (9) represents another linguistic environment that favors rhotacization as well as neutral tone: with locative participles. In Mandarin, locative particles, such as *zhe* 'here', *wai* 'outside', *li* 'inside', often occur with one of the suffixes *–bian* 'side', *-mian* 'surface', and these suffixes are often rhotacized (Lu 1995, 27; Shi 2004) and take a neutral tone (Li and Thompson 1981, 391; Lu 1995, 27). As shown in (9), Liu breaks both conventions by using de-rhotacization and a full tone.

(9) <describing a jacket, "Shopping Partner," 8/19/05>
Liu: *Ranhou ye you yige hudiejie, ji zai zhe-**bian*** **[R-; T1]**.
Then there is also a bow, tied on this side **[R-; T1]**.

As summarized in Table 4.5, the hosts' use of other locative particles of the same type, namely *na-bian* 'there', *li-bian* 'inside', *li-mian* 'inside', and *wai-mian* 'outside', consistently shows the same tendency of not rhotacizing the suffixes. In this way, de-rhotacization brings the hosts' speech style into sharp contrast with the local colloquial style of the show's participants on the one hand and the conventional style of PTH on the other.

TABLE 4.5 Locative Particles with Non-rhotacized Suffixes

Number of locative particle with suffix	*Number of non-rhotacized suffix*
li-bian 'inside': 10	10
zhe-bian 'here': 36	36
nei/na-bian 'there': 16	15
li-mian 'inside': 59	57
wai-mian 'outside': 8	8

4.3.3.2 Full Tone in a Neutral Tone Environment

The use of a full tone in a neutral tone environment is another salient feature characteristic of the two hosts' speech. In example (10a), the second syllable of

Cosmopolitan Mandarin **119**

piao4liang0 'pretty' carries a neutral tone in Standard PTH, but Liu uses the full (high-falling) tone, *piao4liang4*, instead. In contrast, in the same segment a few minutes later, in (10b), the participant shopper uses the neutral tone in the second syllable of the same word.

(10a) <discussing fashion trends, "Shopping Partner," 8/19/05>

Liu: *V zi ling haoxiang jin nian bijiao liuxing, nazhong mingxing canjia aosika doushi xihuan luchu suogu, hen piao**liang** [T4]*
The V-neck seems in fashion this year. The celebrities attending the Oscars all like to expose their collarbones, very pretty **[T4]**.

…

(10b) <participant shopper trying on a jacket, "Shopping Partner," 8/19/05, Men = guest shopping partner>

Men: *Wo juede zhejian yifu ting piao**liang** [T0]*.
I think this piece is quite pretty **[T0]**.

The hosts are also found using a full tone in environments where a neutral tone is "obligatory" in Standard PTH, as in example (11),

(11) <discussing coffee culture at a coffee shop, "Street Cool Hunting," 9/24/05>

Yu: *Na xianzai women jiu lai kan-**kan** [T4] kafei dou [R-] ba.*
Then let's take a look **[T4]** at the coffee beans **[R-]**.

In the above excerpt, *kan-kan* 'look-look' ('take a look') is a case of reduplication in which the reduplicated morpheme is monosyllabic. In such a construction, the second syllable takes a neutral tone in Standard PTH (see Li and Thompson 1981, 28–29; Lu 1995, 27), but Yu uses a full tone instead. The hosts also use a full tone in the nouns with the second syllable *–zi*. For example, instead of *ku4zi0* 'pants' with a neutral tone in the second syllable, it was produced as *ku4zi3* with a falling-rising tone. However, according to the *Guidelines for the Implementation of Putonghua Proficiency Test*, for this type of nouns, the *–zi* syllable "must be pronounced with a neutral tone" (PSCSG 2004, 238). Among the 265 occurrences of such nouns used by the hosts, 32, or 12% of the *–zi* syllable, are pronounced with a full tone. Although the percentage is quite low, it is an especially salient stylistic move because it happens in an environment that requires a neutral tone in Northern Mandarin and Standard PTH. It is worth mentioning that this is the linguistic environment where the neutral tone is categorically realized among the Beijing yuppies.

The analysis in this section demonstrates that the two hosts do not follow closely the Standard PTH norms on rhotacization and neutral tone. The fact that they are native Northern Mandarin speakers and, as television professionals, have passed the PSC with a rate of over 97% correctness provides strong evidence that the hosts are engaged in a motivated act of styling. Their performance of styling becomes particularly salient when they de-rhotacize and use

120 Cosmopolitan Mandarin

a full tone in linguistic environments that particularly favor the conventional variants of rhotacization and neutral tone. Combined with the other types of innovative elements, their linguistic style is also cosmopolitan, that is, non-conventional and supraregional. This Cosmopolitan Mandarin style contrasts sharply with the conservative Standard PTH in news broadcasting, also known as *boyin qiang* 'broadcasting accent'. Their linguistic style, combined with their makeup, hairstyle, accessories, clothing, and smile, projects a youthful, trendy, and ebullient image that is antithetical to the conservative, serious, and solemn image of the CCTV newscasters.

In the next section, I analyze the talk of the hosts to show that CM is part of the metasemiotic discourse that groups and evaluates a diverse range of consumer products and behaviors and links them to a particular type of new social persona—a cosmopolitan urban consumer—and a new lifestyle. As discussed at the beginning of this chapter, such metasemiotic discourse generates meanings and values for the signs involved. It is through the discourse about signs that meanings of new social distinction are created. Furthermore, the following analysis emphasizes that the meaning of distinction is created not only denotationally and explicitly through the content of the talk, that is, what the hosts talk about, but more important, *how* they talk about the signs by employing linguistic resources and discourse strategies. CM is shown to be a crucial constitutive component of the metasemiotic discourse and meaning generating resource.

4.4 Constructing a New Middle-Class Consumer

Talk about consumption, fashion, and lifestyle practices constitutes the bulk of the program. However, such metasemiotic discourse about commodities and ways of doing things is ultimately about a particular kind of consumer that the show targets, as shown in excerpt (12), which is part of a segment on white-collar male fashion, including business attire, casual wear, and accessories. At the beginning of this segment, not shown in the excerpt below, Yu observes that the time-reporting function of watches is diminishing due to the popularity of mobile phones. She also notes, however, a new trend of one person owning multiple watches: "designer/famous brand watches with formal business attire from Monday to Thursday, and casual style watches with casual wear on Friday and the weekend." She points out that "**elegant** (*youya*) people will find that many new styles of watches are tailor-made for them. In addition to the **minimalism** (*jianyue*) that characterizes their exterior designs, their plates of different and pleasant colors can reveal the **unique taste** (*dute pinwei*) of the individual" (*S Information Station*, 9/17/2005). Immediately preceding the excerpt, she points out that "accessories are very important for a high-end business outfit" (ibid.).

In lines 1–9 of (12), the hosts make the generalizing observation that the wallet, leather belt, and watch are three important accessories for high-ranking white-collar professionals and that such items should be of high quality and intricate workmanship. In line 9, Liu emphasizes that "men **must** use these items made by famous brands." The word *mingpai* 'famous brand' is pronounced without rhotacization. Yu continues in line 10, linking commodities of famous brands to one's *shenfen* 'identity', which is pronounced with a falling tone instead of a neutral tone on the second syllable. Finally, in line 11, Liu drives home the message that you are what you wear. Her statement that "(you) yourself are also a famous brand" accomplishes "semiotic consubstantiality" (Silverstein 2006, 485), whereby the value and prestige associated with famous-brand commodities are transferred to the consumer of the commodities. Again in this statement, the key term *mingpai* 'famous brand' is produced without rhotacization. When this segment comes to an end, an image is conjured up of a high-ranking white-collar business professional dressed in, and accessorized with, high-end, famous, presumably international, brand names. What is significant in this excerpt is that words that express the key ideas of the segment, 'identity' and 'famous brands,' are produced using the innovative forms rather than their conventional PTH alternatives. In this example, de-rhotacization and full tone are merged with the content of the talk to bring about a stylish and cosmopolitan image of a high-ranking business professional.

(12) <discussing three fashion accessories for men: watch, wallet, leather belt, "Trends Spotting," 9/17/2005>

1 Yu: *Women kandao, yiban gaoji bailing,*
     We see that, in general high-ranking white-collar professionals,

2   *dui zhe sanyang wuping dou feichang zhongshi.*
     pay a lot of attention to these three items.

3 Liu: *Erqie, women lai kan yixia* **[R-]** *ta de xijie.*
     And, let's look at the details.

4   *Youqi shi yixie hao yidian* **[R-]** *de,*
     Especially some a bit **[R-]** nicer,

5   *zhiliang bijiao gao de yixie pidai a.*
     better quality leather belts.

6   *baokuo qianjia shoubiao.*
     including wallets and watches.

7   *tade zuogong doushi feichang jingxide.*
     the workmanship is very intricate.

8 Yu: *Meicuo* **[R-]**.
     Right **[R-]**.

9 Liu *Erqie wo juede nanren zhexie dongxi* **[T0] YIDING** *yao yong mingpai* **[R-]**.
     And I think for men, they **MUST** use these items **[T0]** made by famous brands **[R-]**.

10 Yu: *Dui, zheyang dehua, caineng tixian zijide shenfen* **[T4]**.

122 Cosmopolitan Mandarin

Right, only in this way can it reflect (one's) own identity **[T4]**.
11 Liu *Gaosu ni ziji ye shi mingpai* **[R-]**.
Telling you that (you) yourself are also a famous brand **[R-]**.
12 Yu: *Meicuo* **[R-]**.
Right **[R-]**.

The above talk valorizes the ideology that commodities and consumption symbolize the status of the self. Furthermore, the talk about the consumption of watches and other accessories not by virtue of their utilitarian value but their aesthetic value and the prestigious status of their brand positions the imagined consumer (i.e., the high-ranking white-collar professional) and by extension, the program's intended audience, as consumers with the "taste of luxury." According to Bourdieu (1984, 177), the taste of luxury (or freedom) is a lifestyle of the bourgeoisie whereas the "taste of necessity" is characteristic of the working class. In the context of contemporary China, such a new lifestyle is in stark contrast to the traditional way of life that emphasizes the virtue of *jiejian* 'frugality'. This contrast is realized not only through the content of the metasemiotic discourse, or talk about the social import of commodities, linking the consumer to their construed value, but also *how* the content is produced, that is, by combining linguistic elements of an innovative CM style.

As shown in excerpt (12) above and much of the program, the talk about fashion and consumption is not merely about possessing certain commodities. As Liechty explains in his study of the new middle class in Nepal, "middle-class consumption is less about *having* or *possessing* than it is about *being* and *belonging*" (2003, 35). The metasemiotic discourse about high-end commodities constructs the consumer as a person of privileged socioeconomic status belonging to a community of individuals who share the taste of luxury. Similarly, in excerpt (13), discussion about the elements of a fashionable outfit creates an image of an urban professional woman that transcends the specifics of place (Tianjin, China) and regional identity (mainland Chinese), positioning her as belonging to a world of urban women sharing a similar lifestyle.

(13) <discussing outfits, "Trends Spotting," 9/3/05>
1 Liu: *Ni kan wo zhe limian* **[T4; R-]** *shi mianhua* **[T1]** *laika de xiao beixin*
[R-].
Look, what I'm wearing inside **[T4; R-]** is a cotton **[T1]** Lycra
tank top **[R-]**.
2 *zai jiashang* **[T0]** *zhezhong bijiao liuxing de*
plus **[T0]** this kind of fashionable
3 *zhezhong liangshanshan de xiaoguo.*
this kind of sparkling effect.
4 *Dan yinwei shi laika,*
But because it's Lycra,

5		*ta keyi yi zhuai jiu keyi bian qunzhang* hhhhh
		when stretched, it can become a dress hhhhh
6	Yu:	*Danshi hh ta tanxing ye henhao,*
		But hh it has great elasticity,
7		*jiu hh shouhuiqu le.*
		it hh shrinks back [when let go].
8	Liu:	*Dui a dui a, yinwei shi qiutian,*
		Right right, because it's fall,
9		**yiding** *yao you yige zheyang de jiake,*
		you **must** have a jacket like this one,
10		*erqie shouyao feichang hao de.*
		and it's very nice that it has a narrow waistline.
11	Yu:	*En.*
		Yeah.
12	Liu:	*Zai* **dapei** *shang zheyang yige fang shepi,*
		And **match** it with a faux snakeskin [bag] like this one,
13		*ruguo shi* <u>**office**</u> **[E]** *de hua, wo juede ye* **man** **[L]** *hao.*
		if [you go to the] <u>**office**</u> **[E], I think it's also pretty [L] nice.**
14		*Suiran you yidian* **[R-]** *tiaoyue,*
		Although it's a little **[R-]** breezy,
15	Yu:	*keyi dang gongwenbao lai yong.*
		it can be used as a briefcase.
16	Liu:	*Ruguo ni wan***shang** **[T4]** *qu* **party** **[E]** *de hua,*
		If you go to a <u>**party**</u> **[E] in the evening [T4],**
17		*keyi chuan limian* **[T0; R-]** *nage xiao beixin* **[R-].**
		(you) can wear that little tank top **[R-]** inside **[T0; R-].**
18		*Yeshi wanquan meiyou wenti de.*
		It'd also be totally fine.

In lines 1–12, the hosts explain how individual items of clothing—a cotton-Lycra tank top with sparkles and a jacket—and accessory, a faux snakeskin bag, are configured into a stylish ensemble. Both Liu and Yu demonstrate their familiarity with and discernment of what is trendy and stylish in the fall season, a tank top with sparkles (lines 1–7), and a jacket with a narrow waistline (lines 8–10). Liu authoritatively instructs that this kind of jacket is a "must-have" for the fall season (line 9). In lines 13 through 18, Liu creates a hypothetical scenario for the audience-viewer in which she is a stylishly dressed and accessorized woman working in the office during the day and going to parties at night. Such a stylish and busy lifestyle is also shared by many urban professional women in other parts of the world. The hypothetical world of the trendy and cosmopolitan lifestyle is created through the content of the talk as well as through a clustering of innovative features that constitute the cosmopolitan linguistic style. In lines 13 through 18, all three types of innovative features are

124 Cosmopolitan Mandarin

used in all but one potential environment, i.e., lexical item *man* 'quite, pretty' (line 13), English words, "office" (line 13) and "party" (line 16), and the two sound features (lines 14, 16, 17).

In addition to projecting the intended audience as cosmopolitan middle-class consumers by locating them in hypothetical worlds, the hosts position them vis-à-vis familiar and salient social images and characters. The familiarity is often presented as shared knowledge between the hosts and their audience, the invocation of which can be used as a strategy to signal in-group membership (Bucholtz 1999; Talbot 1995). In *S Information Station*, the assumed shared familiarity is often about pop culture personalities, as shown in the following excerpt and later in example (15). In this part of the show, the hosts discuss the importance of using hair accessories as a way to avoid *zhuang shan* 'clothing clash' at parties (line 5). "Clothing clash," a neologism, refers to a new fashion faux pas of wearing the same or similar piece of clothing as someone else.

(14) <in a fashion accessory store, "Street Cool Hunting," 10/8/05>

1	Liu:	*Xianzai, women you haoduo jihui,*
		Now, we have lots of opportunities,
2		*jiu keyi wai**mian** [T4; R-] canjia yixie huodong.*
		can participate in activities outside **[T4; R-]** (of the home).
3	Yu:	*Mei**cuo** [R-].*
		Right **[R-]**.
4		**Party** **[E]** *a:, erqie zai toushi shang,*
		Like **parties** **[E]**, and regarding hair accessories,
5		*ruguo ni pa gen ren **zhuangshan** [L] de hua,*
		if you're afraid of **clothing clash [L]** (with someone),
6		*bufang zai toushi shang xia yixie gong**fu** [T0].*
		why not put some effort in hair accessories.
7		*Women lai kan yi kan canjia **party** [E] you shenme toushi.*
		Let's take a look at what hair accessories (we can wear) at **parties** **[E]**.
		((trying on accessories, 4 lines omitted))
12	Liu:	*Ei, liangge jiandan de toushi jiu you ganjue.*
		Eh, two simple hair accessories can produce a different effect.
13		*Erqie, zhengti ganjue shi bu shi tebie xiang dianshi ju li de,*
		And, the overall effect, doesn't it resemble very much in the TV drama,
14		CD *lide,* **Carrie** **[E]**.
		in the CD, **Carrie** **[E]**.
15		*Yinwei tamen dou xiguan yong yige sijin.*
		Because they all have the habit of using a silk scarf.

In their discussion about strategies to achieve uniqueness, the hosts recommend wearing hair accessories at parties to avoid "clothing clash" (lines 4–12). Liu then invokes the character of Carrie Bradshaw in the American television series *Sex and the City* as a role model of style and fashion sensibility (lines 13–14). Referring to her only by her English first name in line 14 instead of her name in Chinese transliteration (which is Kaili), the host projects the audience as being familiar with this pop culture icon of style, sophistication, and cosmopolitan femininity, as well as her stylish friends and their world (line 15). It is also noticeable that "clothing clash" co-occurs in this excerpt with the English word "party" (line 4 and 7) instead of the conventional PTH equivalent *juhui*.

The previous three examples and much of the metasemiotic discourse of the show highlight a familiar theme of consumer culture observed in Agha's (2011a) examination of lifestyle advertising. That is, consumption is a kind of labor that requires efforts from consumers to not only constantly consume but also to *select* individual tokens of commodities and *configure* them into a stylish and distinctive ensemble—a co-occurrence style (Agha 2007, 186). As shown in Table 4.6, the most frequently used words in the program reflect the emphasis on selection (*xuan, tiaoxuan*), configuration/coordination (*da, pei, dapei*), style (*fengge, feng*), and difference/differentiation/uniqueness (*butong, gexing, dute, yuzhongbutong*).

In the program, various co-occurrence styles are assembled by the hosts in the metasemiotic discourse, which imbues them with indexical meanings, such as privileged social status of the consumer (excerpt 12 and 14), uniqueness, stylishness, sophistication, and cosmopolitanism (excerpt 12, 13, and 14) (see also Agha 2011a, 42–43). Although explicit mentioning of linguistic signs is absent in the metasemiotic discourse, that is, how a stylish and cosmopolitan urbanite should talk and sound, CM is a part of the whole configuration and hence becomes "indexically congruent" (Agha 2007, 24; 2011a, 34) with the nonlinguistic elements of the co-occurrence style. An implicit metapragmatic message is thus created through the indexical congruency that binds a distinctive way of speaking—Cosmopolitan Mandarin—to a stylish, cosmopolitan consumer image and associated attributes discussed earlier. Furthermore, this indexical congruency is intentional: The elements of the co-occurrence styles—including speech—are presented in the metasemiotic discourse as fitting together, forming a configuration that is considered appropriate, e.g., for a high-ranking business

TABLE 4.6 Most Frequent Lexemes in *S Information Station*

Lexemes	Number of occurrence
xuan, xuanze, tiaoxuan 'choose'/'choice', 'select'	127
dapei, da, pei, hunda 'configure', 'match', 'coordinate', 'mix-and-match'	115
fengge, feng 'style'	96
butong 'different', 'difference'	75
gexing 'individuality'	19
dute, yuzhongbutong 'unique'	9

126 Cosmopolitan Mandarin

professional (excerpt 12) or a stylish and sophisticated professional woman (excerpt 13 and 14). The hosts' speech style is also designed to be congruent with their own youthful, trendy, and ebullient persona and the semiotic ensembles that they talk about in the show. In other words, the indexical congruency established in the metasemiotic discourse creates the impression of appropriateness for all the co-occurring signs, including the innovative speech style.

The indexical congruency and the consequential impression of appropriateness are the result of the evaluative and regimenting function of metasemiotic discourse. Indeed, the assemblage of style ensembles in the show is evaluated and regimented through explicit and implicit metadiscourse. Explicit evaluation include the hosts' overt judgment on the configurations, such as *ku* 'cool', *you gexing* 'having/showing individuality', *shishang* 'stylish', *you xiandai gan* 'modern', *youya de qizhi* 'elegant disposition', and so on. The hosts' evaluation in excerpt (12) is explicit, whereas excerpt (14) offers an example of implicit evaluation. Explicit regimentation is most often performed through the use of didactic expressions, including *yiding (yao)* 'must' (see excerpt (12) line 9 and excerpt (13) line 9; 57 occurrences), *tuijian* 'recommend' (32 occurrences), and *jianyi* 'suggest' (15 occurrences). Positive evaluation of the appropriate ensembles such as those in excerpts 12 through 14 positions the consumer in the company of other urbanites with comparable taste and style. Negative evaluation of the "wrong" or "inappropriate" assemblage locates the consumer on a par with characters of inferior taste and lower social status. As illustrated in the next example, the "wrong" color coordination is judged to be indexical of a rustic self.

(15) < Cuihua, "Shopping Partner," 8/19/05, Men = guest shopping partner>

1 Liu: *Zhe yifu chuan shang hui bu hui xiang **Cuihua** a.* (2)
          This outfit, wearing it would it (make the wearer) look like **Cuihua**.

2 Men: ((unintelligible))

3 Liu: *Wo juede **limian** [T4; –R] yinggai zai, bu yao zai, zai name nen ba.*
          I think inside **[T4; –R]** should, should not, should not have such a light color.

4   ***Hao* [L]** *Cui-* h h ***Cuihua*** ((exaggerated high pitch in Northeastern Mandarin accent))
          So [L] Cui- h h Cuihua.

In this episode of the "Shopping Partner," Men, the guest shopping partner, is planning to buy a jacket. Prior to the excerpt, Men goes to the fitting room to try on a third outfit, including a potential jacket to buy. In the excerpt, upon seeing Men coming back wearing a grass green jacket over a light pink shirt, Liu offers her evaluation. In line 1, she likens the wearer of such an outfit to a woman named Cuihua, with no additional information about who Cuihua is. After negatively evaluating Men's color coordination of the shirt and the jacket in line 3, Liu again evokes the character of Cuihua in line 4. Interrupting herself after the first syllable of the name, "Cui," and laughing, Liu repeats

"Cuihua," but shifts into a different voice, signaled by an exaggerated high pitch and the use of a stylized Northeastern Mandarin accent. The invocation of Cuihua is similar to the mentioning of Carrie (Bradshaw) in excerpt 14, assuming the shopper's and the audience's shared familiarity with the character. However, in this example the host invites Men and the audience to take an oppositional stance against the character.

Many mainland Chinese would associate the name Cuihua with a rural woman, but who is Cuihua in this example? She is a character in the song *"Dongbei ren dou shi huo Lei Feng"* 'Northeasterners are all living Lei Feng.' It was originally created in 1995 by Xue Cun, a singer-songwriter well known for his urban folk songs. The song has become immensely popular nationwide since 2001 because of its reproductions in Flash animated GIFs widely spread through the Internet (Liu 2013). Lei Feng was the model communist soldier and the icon of altruism introduced at the beginning of the book (see Introduction). The term *huo Lei Feng*, 'living Lei Feng', is a label for anyone who is selfless and going out of his or her way to help others. The song tells the story of a working-class or peasant Northeastern man helping a driver injured in a hit-and-run accident. After the driver's recovery, he invites the Northeasterner for a meal to thank him. The song ends with the Northeastern man calling Cuihua, presumably the waitress, in Northeastern Mandarin, *"Cuihua, shang suancai"* 'Cuihua, bring out the sauerkraut'. *Suancai* 'sauerkraut' is a simple, cheap local dish. The song reproduces the positive stereotype of a (male) Northeasterner as being kind-hearted, simple, and forthright. With the popularity of the song, *"Cuihua, shang suancai"* 'Cuihua, bring out the sauerkraut' spoken in the Northeastern accent has become a wide spread catchphrase, and Cuihua has also become a well-known figure of an unsophisticated rural woman.[9]

In this excerpt, the evaluation of the guest shopper's taste in color coordination in the metasemiotic discourse is both explicit and implicit. Explicitly, it links the outfit to the rural character of Cuihua in line 1. However, the punch of Liu's negative evaluation of Men's taste is linguistically performed—implicitly but in a palpable way—through the stylized realization of "Cuihua" in the Northeastern accent in line 4. The strategic stylization, signaled by Liu's self-interruption, laughter, exaggerated high pitch, and the shift to the Northeastern accent, involves vari-directional double-voicing (Bakhtin 1984, 193), which positions the speaker in opposition to the character Cuihua indexed through the voice in the local accent. In contrast to the previous examples of indexical congruency, the color combination of the outfit is judged to be indexically incongruent, resulting in an "inappropriate" ensemble linking the consumer to the "wrong" image of a rustic woman. The strategic stylization, itself an instance of intentional indexical incongruency, accentuates the inappropriateness of the whole configuration. By assuming shared familiarity with the character Cuihua, the host invites the shopper and the audience to take the same stance with her, disaligning themselves from what Cuihua represents, that is, *tu*, which encompasses rusticity and lack of sophistication.

128 Cosmopolitan Mandarin

4.5 Conclusion

The above analysis shows that metasemiotic discourse is a primary domain to examine how semiotic mediation is carried out in the making of new social distinction. Much of the hosts' talk is about creating ensembles or co-occurrence styles that are construed and evaluated to be stylish, tasteful, and cosmopolitan. As mentioned earlier, the components of such co-occurrence styles—including CM—are presented as indexically congruent such that they take on the above indexical values of the whole assemblage. Hence, although the hosts never explicitly talk about how such a stylish consumer-urbanite sounds, a message about the indexical value of CM is created through its prominent use in their metasemiotic discourse linking linguistic and nonlinguistic signs to characteristics of trendiness, taste, and cosmopolitan sophistication. Based on an ideology of appropriateness, these signs are taken to be fitting together, achieving the effect of looking—as well as sounding—"appropriate" for the consumer images (and their attractive attributes) enacted in the TV show. Furthermore, CM takes on an expanded range of social meaning as it is used to perform the hosts' youthful, ebullient, and convivial persona. Despite the didactic nature of the show and their talk, their persona—including their linguistic style—is not the serious, solemn kind often associated with traditional types of experts and figures of authority, such as teachers, scholars, and cadres. As the general style of the program is entertaining and fun-oriented, their talk is accompanied with laughter, smiles, jokes, impromptu singing, and clowning.[10] They are also often seen walking in locked arms with women guest shopping partners as female friends often do when they *guang jie* 'promenade the streets', meaning go (window) shopping. Thus, in addition to the indexical value of stylishness, tastefulness, sophistication, and cosmopolitanism, CM contributes to the enactment of the affective attributes of youthful ebullience and conviviality. Such attributes can be expressed through a wide range of linguistic resources, including dialectal elements and colloquial forms of a standard language (see Besnier 1990). What is new as shown from the hosts' employment of CM is the enactment of a new type of persona: a Chinese urbanite who combines stylishness and cosmopolitanism with youthful ebullience and conviviality.

This new persona is not unique to *S Information Station*. It is now commonly seen in entertainment programs on fashion, lifestyle, and popular culture. Furthermore, the use of CM is not unique to the television program examined here. During the data collection period of *S Information Station*, I also observed six other so-called *shishang* 'trendy' programs.[11] Their hosts' linguistic style is similar to that of *S Information Station*. It is even more widely spread in entertainment programs on Chinese television now. Such programs do more than exposing the audience to a new style of Mandarin: They contextualize CM such that the audience experiences it through its co-occurrence in semiotic ensembles such as the ones described in *S Information Station* and through its use by the hosts

Cosmopolitan Mandarin **129**

embodying a youthful, stylish, and jovial persona. As "iconic speakers" (Eckert 2000, 217), they play an important role in making the new linguistic style identifiable and attractive for others to recognize and imitate (Mendoza-Denton 2008). Furthermore, such television programs heighten the audience's awareness of the contrast between CM with its stylish, ebullient speakers and the conventional Beijing-Mandarin-based Standard PTH with its exemplary speakers, the serious and solemn newscasters of CCTV. The trendy, stylish, and glamorous personae invite positive perception and alignment from the audience and consequently positive perception of their speech style as being trendy, cosmopolitan, youthful, and ebullient. Repeated positive perception of their personae and speech style will lead to "a gradual sedimentation of habits of speech perception," which according to Agha (2007, 228), contributes to the enregisterment of CM, whereby the new linguistic style is recognized as distinctive and linked to the above appealing social attributes and images. However, the question remains: How is this new linguistic style recognized and interpreted by a larger population? This question will be addressed in the next chapter.

Notes

1 The Chinese title for the book is *Gediao—Shehui Dengji yu Shenghuo Pinwei*, which if translated back to English would be, *Style: Social Class and Taste in Life*. The Chinese title creatively captures three popular keywords of the time, "style," "class," and "taste," which draw the attention of anyone aspiring to a new middle-class tasteful lifestyle.

2 Agha defines semiotic mediation as "the generic process whereby signs connect persons to each other through various forms of cognition, communication and interaction" (2011c, 174).

3 Agha treats mediatization as a special case of mediation, defining it as "institutional practices that reflexively link processes of communication to processes of commoditization" (2011b, 163).

4 Tianjin is the neighboring city of Beijing, with a population of approximately 15 million (Tianjin Bureau of Statistics 2015). It is one of the four municipalities under the direct jurisdiction of the central government (*zhixia shi*). The other three are Beijing, Shanghai, and Chongqing.

5 More detailed discussion about the "Purification Project" and "The Self-Disciplining Conventions of Radio and Television Broadcasters and Hosts in China" is presented in Section 5.2.3.

6 Among the six Hong Kong respondents, five were graduate students at the City University of Hong Kong, and one was a lecturer at the Hong Kong Chinese University. All five Taiwanese respondents were graduate students at National Taiwan Normal University and University of Texas at Austin. I am grateful to Hsi-Yao Su and Fanny Lau for helping me conduct the surveys.

7 None of the expressions is found in the 2005 edition of *Xiandai Hanyu Cidian* (*Modern Chinese Dictionary*), but four are included in the 2012 edition. These are *anjie* 'mortgage', *jianyue* 'minimalist', *jingyou* 'essential oil', and *linglei* 'nonconformist'.

8 In Part Two of the PSC, test takers are given a list of multisyllabic words. These are used to test the speaker's level of standardness in the production of the syllable onset, rhyme, tone sandhi, neutral tone, and rhotacization. Regarding the last two features,

130 Cosmopolitan Mandarin

the test takers must identify which items in the word list are to be pronounced with a neutral tone and which can be rhotacized, and produce them correctly (PSCSG 2004, 2). Treating rhotacization and neutral tone as norms of Standard PTH and including them in the PSC put speakers of non-Northern Mandarin varieties in a disadvantaged position in the test. Because both are Northern Mandarin features, non-Northern Mandarin speakers have to acquire their usage from learning Beijing-Mandarin-based PTH. To prepare for the PSC, they resort to memorizing the word lists for rhotacization and neutral tone provided in the PSCSG. However, this would not be a problem for the two hosts in *S Information Station*, because their native Tianjin dialect shares these two features with Beijing Mandarin.

9 According to a survey, *Cuihua shang suancai* 'Cuihua bring out the sauerkraut' was ranked one of the top three most popular catchphrases among Chinese youth in 2003 (Chen and Yang 2003 quoted in Liu 2013, 149). For a discussion on the cultural significance of the song, see Liu (2013, 148–150).

10 Wanning Sun also observes that the style of Chinese lifestyle programs of costal, metropolitan channels, such as Shanghai Television, is "light-hearted, joking, fun-oriented" (2015, 27), whereas the pedagogical style of the national CCTV is top-down and serious and that of low-budget, local, rural television follows a "boring, textbook format" (ibid., 26).

11 These programs were (as of 2005): *MTV Tianlai Cun* 'MTV Village of Sounds of Nature', a popular music program, produced by MTV China, host Li Xia; *Qi Jiu Ba* 'Seven Nine Bar', a fashion-lifestyle program on *Lüyou Weishi* 'Travel Satellite Television', host Xiao Xue; *Shishang Fengyun Bang* 'Trends Chart', a fashion and celebrities program, produced by *Guangxian Chuanmei* 'Guangxian Media', host Li Siyu; *Yule Ren Wo Xing* 'Entertainment My Way', show business and celebrities program on *Lüyou Weishi* 'Travel Satellite Television', host Shen Ling; *Tiantian Xin Yi* 'Daily New Entertainment', entertainment news program on Tianjin Television Station, hosts Ding Peng and Hou Li; and *Just Music*, popular music program on Tianjin Television Station, host Hong Hai. The hosts of the six programs are all native speakers of Northern Mandarin.

References

Agha, Asif. 2007. *Language and Social Relations*. Cambridge: Cambridge University Press.

Agha, Asif. 2011a. "Commodity Registers." *Journal of Linguistic Anthropology* 21 (1):22–53.

Agha, Asif. 2011b. "Meet Mediatization." *Language & Communication* 31 (3):163–170.

Agha, Asif. 2011c. "Large and Small Scale Forms of Personhood." *Language & Communication* 31 (3):171–180.

Bakhtin, Mikhail M. 1984. *Problems of Dostoevsky's Poetics*. Translated by Caryl Emerson. Minneapolis, MN: University of Minnesota Press.

Besnier, Niko. 1990. "Language and Affect." *Annual Review of Anthropology* 19 (1):419–451.

Bourdieu, Pierre. 1984. *Distinction: A Social Critique of the Judgment of Taste*. Translated by Richard Nice. Cambridge, MA: Harvard University Press.

Brooks, David. 2000. *Bobos in Paradise: The New Upper Class and How They Got There*. New York, NY and London: Simon & Schuster.

Bucholtz, Mary. 1999. "Purchasing Power: The Gender and Class Imaginary on the Shopping Channel." In *Reinventing Identities: The Gendered Self in Discourse*, edited by

Mary Bucholtz, A. C. Liang, and Laurel A. Sutton, 348–368. New York, NY and Oxford: Oxford University Press.

Chen, Si, and Changzheng Yang. 2003. *"Qingshaonian 'Liuxingyu' Xianxiang Diaocha Baogao"* ("Survey on Youth's 'Catchy Expressions'"). *Zhongguo Qingnian Yanjiu (China Youth Research)* 2:55–63.

Couldry, Nick. 2003. *Media Rituals: A Critical Approach.* London: Routledge.

Coupland, Nikolas. 2001. "Stylization, Authenticity and TV News Review." *Discourse Studies* 3 (4):413–442.

Coupland, Nikolas. 2014. "Sociolinguistic Change, Vernacularization and Broadcast British Media." In *Mediatization and Sociolinguistic Change,* edited by Jannis Androutsopoulos, 67–96. Berlin: De Gruyter.

Cronin, Anne M. 2004. "Regimes of Mediation: Advertising Practitioners as Cultural Intermediaries?" *Consumption Markets & Culture* 7 (4):349–369.

Davies, Catherine Evans. 2003. "Language and American 'Good Taste': Martha Stewart as Mass-Media Role Model." In *New Media Language,* edited by Jean Aitchison, and Diana M. Lewis, 146–155. London: Routledge.

Dirlik, Arif. 2001. "Markets, Culture, Power: The Making of a 'Second Cultural Revolution' in China." *Asian Studies Review* 25 (1):1–33.

Donald, Stephanie Hemelryk, and Yi Zheng. 2009. "A Taste of Class: Manuals for Becoming Woman." *Positions: East Asia Cultures Critique* 17 (3):489–521.

Eckert, Penelope. 2000. *Linguistic Variation as Social Practice: The Linguistic Construction of Identity in Belten High.* Oxford: Blackwell.

Featherstone, Mike. 2007. *Consumer Culture and Postmodernism.* 2nd ed. London: Sage.

Fussell, Paul. 1983. *Class: A Guide through the American Status System.* New York, NY: Summit Books.

Ginsburg, Faye D., Lila Abu-Lughod, and Brian Larkin. 2002. "Introduction." In *Media Worlds: Anthropology on New Terrain,* edited by Faye D. Ginsburg, Lila Abu-Lughod, and Brian Larkin, 1–36. Berkeley, CA: University of California Press.

Hepp, Andreas. 2014. "Mediatization. A Panorama of Media and Communication Research." In *Mediatization and Sociolinguistic Change,* edited by Jannis Androutsopoulos, 49–66. Berlin: De Gruyter.

Hjarvard, Stig. 2008. "The Mediatization of Society: A Theory of the Media as Agents of Social and Cultural Change." *Nordicom Review* 29 (2):105–134.

Hooper, Beverley. 1998. "'Flower Vase and Housewife': Women and Consumerism in Post-Mao China." In *Gender and Power in Affluent Asia,* edited by Krishna Sen, and Maila Stivens, 169–192. London and New York, NY: Routledge.

Inoue, Miyako. 2007. "Things That Speak: Peirce, Benjamin, and the Kinesthestics of Commodity Advertisement in Japanese Women's Magazines, 1900 to the 1930s." *Public Culture* 15 (3):511–552.

Jaworski, Adam, Crispin Thurlow, Sarah Lawson, and Virpi Ylänne-McEwen. 2003. "The Uses and Representations of Local Languages in Tourist Destinations: A View from British TV Holiday Programmes." *Language Awareness* 12 (1):5–29.

Lakshmanan, Indira A.R. 1997. "China's Chuppie Revolution: The Name of the Game Is to Woo the Upwardly Mobile Consumer—and the State Condones It." *The Boston Globe,* April 29, D1.

Lewis, Tania, Fran Martin, and Wanning Sun. 2012. "Lifestyling Asia? Shaping Modernity and Selfhood on Life-Advice Programming." *International Journal of Cultural Studies* 15 (6):537–566.

132 Cosmopolitan Mandarin

Li, Charles N., and Sandra A. Thompson. 1981. *Mandarin Chinese: A Functional Reference Grammar*. Berkeley, CA: University of Berkeley Press.

Liechty, Mark 2003. *Suitably Modern: Making Middle-Class Culture in a New Consumer Society*. Princeton, NJ: Princeton University Press.

Lin, Songyu. 2009. "Mix and Match or Confusion?—Middleclass Taste in Contemporary China." *PORTAL: Journal of Multidisciplinary International Studies* 16 (2):1–9.

Liu, Jin. 2013. *Signifying the Local: Media Productions Rendered in Local Languages in Mainland China in the New Millennium*. Leiden: Brill.

Livingstone, Sonia. 2009. "On the Mediation of Everything: ICA Presidential Address 2008." *Journal of Communication* 59:1–18.

Lu, Yunzhong. 1995. *Putonghua de Qing Sheng yu Erhua (Neutral Tone and Rhotacization in Putonghua)*. Beijing: Shangwu Yinshuguan (Commercial Press).

Maguire, Jennifer Smith, and Julian Matthews. 2010. "Cultural Intermediaries and the Media." *Sociology Compass* 4 (7):405–416.

Maguire, Jennifer Smith, and Julian Matthews. 2012. "Are We All Cultural Intermediaries Now? An Introduction to Cultural Intermediaries in Context." *European Journal of Cultural Studies* 15 (5):551–562.

Mankekar, Purnima. 1999. *Screening Culture, Viewing Politics: An Ethnography of Television, Womanhood, and Nation in Postcolonial India*. Durham, NC: Duke University Press.

Mazzarella, William. 2004. "Culture, Globalization, Mediation." *Annual Review of Anthropology* 33 (1):345–367.

Mazzarella, William. 2012. "'Reality Must Improve': The Perversity of Expertise and the Belatedness of Indian Development Television." *Global Media and Communication* 8 (3):215–241.

McQuail, Denis. 2002. "The Media and Lifestyle: Editor's Introduction." *European Journal of Communication* 17 (4):427–428.

Mendoza-Denton, Norma. 2008. *Homegirls: Language and Cultural Practice Among Latina Youth Gangs*. Malden, MA: Blackwell.

Nakassis, Constantine V. 2016. *Doing Style: Youth and Mass Mediation in South India*. Chicago, IL: University of Chicago Press.

Nankai Daxue (Nankai University). 2002. *Tongyong Yuyan Wenzi Xuanchuan Shouce (Common Language Publicity Manual)*. Tianjin, China: Nankai Daxue Yuyan Wenzi Gongzuo Weiyuanhui (Nankai University Committee on Language and Script).

Nixon, Sean, and Paul Du Gay. 2002. "Who Needs Cultural Intermediaries?" *Cultural Studies* 16 (4):495–500.

Peters, John D. 1997. "Seeing Bifocally: Media, Place, Culture." In *Culture, Power, Place: Explorations in Critical Anthropology*, edited by Akhil Gupta, and James Ferguson, 75–92. Durham, NC: Duke University Press.

PSCSG. 2004. *Putonghua Shuiping Ceshi Shishi Gangyao (Implementation Guidelines for the Putonghua Proficiency Test)*. Beijing: Shangwu Yinshuguan (Commercial Press).

SARFT. 2004. "*Guangbo Yingshi Jiaqiang he Gaijin Weichengnian Ren Sixiang Daode Jianshe de ShiShi Fangan*" ("Implementation Plan for Strengthening and Improving the Spiritual and Moral Construction of [Chinese] Minors"). www.sarft.gov.cn/manage/publishfile/35/1716.html. Accessed May 20, 2005.

SARFT. 2005. "*Zhongguo Guangbo Dianshi Boyinyuan Zhuchiren Zilü Gongyue*" ("The Self-Disciplining Conventions of Chinese Radio and Television Broadcasters and Hosts"). www.sarft.gov.cn/manage/publishfile/35/3282.html. Accessed April 5, 2006.

Shi, Dingxu. 2004. *Peking Mandarin*. München: Lincom Europa.

Silverstein, Michael. 2006. "Old Wine, New Ethnographic Lexicography." *Annual Review of Anthropology* 35:481–496.

Song, Geng, and Tracy K. Lee. 2012. "'New Man' And 'New Lad' with Chinese Characteristics? Cosmopolitanism, Cultural Hybridity and Men's Lifestyle Magazines in China." *Asian Studies Review* 36 (3):345–367.

Spitulnik, Debra A. 1998. "The Language of the City: Town Bemba as Urban Hybridity." *Journal of Linguistic Anthropology* 8 (1):30–59.

Sun, Wanning. 2015. "Teaching People How to Live: *Shenghuo* Programs on Chinese Television." In *Chinese Television in the Twenty-First Century: Entertaining the Nation*, edited by Ruoyun Bai, and Geng Song, 17–32. Abingdon, Oxon; New York, NY: Routledge.

Talbot, Mary. 1995. "A Synthetic Sisterhood: False Friends in a Teenage Magazine." In *Gender Articulated: Language and the Socially Constructed Self*, edited by Kira Hall, and Mary Bucholtz, 169–182. New York, NY: Routledge.

Tianjin Bureau of Statistics. 2015. *2015 Tianjin Tongji Nianjian (2015 Statistical Yearbook of Tianjin)*. Tianjin: National Bureau of Statics Publishing House.

TJTV. 2004. *"Henzhua Yuyan Wanzi Gongzuo"* ("Conscientiously Working on Language and Script"). http://tjtv.enorth.com.cn/system/2004/12/13/000923026.shtml. Accessed July 25, 2005.

TJTV. 2005. "*S Qingbao Zhan*" ("S Information Station"). http://tjtv.enorth.com.cn/system/2004/12/13/000923026.shtml. Accessed July 26, 2005.

Urban, Greg. 2001. *Metaculture: How Culture Moves through the World*. Minneapolis, MN: University of Minnesota Press.

Walters, Keith. 2003. "Fergie's Prescience: The Changing Nature of Diglossia in Tunisia." *International Journal of the Sociology of Language* 163 (1):77–109.

Wang, Jing. 2005a. "Bourgeois Bohemians in China? Neo-Tribes and the Urban Imaginary." *The China Quarterly* 183:532–548.

Wang, Jing. 2005b. "Youth Culture, Music, and Cell Phone Branding in China." *Global Media and Communication* 1 (2):185–201.

Wright, David. 2005. "Mediating Production and Consumption: Cultural Capital and 'Cultural Workers'." *The British Journal of Sociology* 56 (1):105–121.

XHC. 2005. *Xiandai Hanyu Cidian (Modern Chinese Dictionary)*. 5th ed. Beijing: Shangwu Yinshuguan (Commercial Press).

Xu, Janice Hua. 2007. "Brand-New Lifestyle: Consumer-Oriented Programmes on Chinese Television." *Media, Culture & Society* 29 (3):363–376.

Xu, Janice Hua. 2009. "Building a Chinese 'Middle Class': Consumer Education and Identity Construction in Television Land." In *TV China*, edited by Ying Zhu, and Chris Berry, 150–167. Bloomington, IN: Indiana University Press.

Yang, Mayfair Mei-hui. 1997. "Mass Media and Transnational Subjectivity in Shanghai: Notes on (Re)Cosmopolitanism in a Chinese Metropolis." In *Ungrounded Empires: The Cultural Politics of Modern Chinese Transnationalism*, edited by Aihwa Ong, and Donald M. Nonini, 287–319. New York, NY and London: Routledge.

5

WARRING STANDARDS

Contesting the Enregisterment of Cosmopolitan Mandarin

> After a dozen or so years, when members of the neo-neo tribe who have grown up in *Gang-Tai qiang* become the mainspring of the mainland culture, the Chinese model for expressing sentiments will come to be unified, that is, to be unified to "*Gang-Tai Putonghua.*"
>
> *(Liu Xiaobo (1955–2017), 2010 Nobel Peace Prize Laureate, 2000)*

5.1 Introduction

In the previous chapters, I explore style from the production perspective in analyzing the linguistic composition of Cosmopolitan Mandarin (CM) and its use in the construction of new social distinctions by Beijing yuppies and hosts of trendy television programs. The analysis demonstrates that rather than merely reflecting social change, linguistic variation and innovation effect social change. Moving away from a traditional variationist approach to style that focuses on co-occurrence patterns, the analysis sheds light on style or styling as an emergent process. Elements associated with the style are variably employed in different contexts; the social meaning of the style emerges through (strategic) bundling of linguistic forms to create interstyle contrasts and through the deployment of stylistic forms in situated discourse.

In Chapters 3 and 4, I focus on the first two aspects of treating style as a sociohistorical process by exploring the "dialogic overtones" or the imbued cultural significance of the linguistic features and their bricolage by the Beijing yuppies and TV hosts to create social distinction. This chapter takes up another crucial aspect of style as a sociohistorical process: *enregisterment* (Agha 2007). Specifically, I examine the emergence of CM as *linguistic enregisterment,* the sociohistorical process "through which a linguistic repertoire becomes differentiable within a language as a socially recognized register of forms" (Agha 2007,

190) and is "linked to typifiable social personae or practices for a given population of speakers" (Agha 2007, 168). The concept of enregisterment offers a dynamic, reflexive approach to style beyond a focus on co-occurrence patterns and the construction of social meanings in the immediate discursive context or the here-and-now moments of interaction (e.g., Coupland 2010; Roth-Gordon and Woronov 2009). Such an approach foregrounds reflexivity and draws attention to the recognition, intelligibility, and interpretation of stylistic variation and its semiotic saliency among groups of language users in addition to the immediate users/interactants and the analyst (Agha 2007; Johnstone 2011). As reflexivity inevitably involves ideology, this approach necessarily treats ideology as integral to the production, interpretation, and analysis of styles. As Eckert argues, "ideology is at the center of stylistic practices" that involve "both the interpretation and production of styles" (2008, 456). Treating style as a sociohistorical process of enregisterment prompts us to ask questions that are crucial but have not been adequately addressed in the sociolinguistic study of styles: Specifically, how is the emergence of style fundamentally mediated by (changing) ideology, and how is it linked to broader sociopolitical issues? As CM is undergoing an early phase of enregisterment, investigating and demonstrating the process sheds light on its highly contested nature. This aspect of enregisterment has not been sufficiently explored in studies that focus on the expansion phase of the process, such as Agha's (2003) study on Received Pronunciation (RP) in Britain, and on styles and registers that have become relatively stable, such as the four perduring semiotic registers in Indonesia described in Goebel (2010) and Pittsburghese (Johnstone, Andrus, and Danielson 2006; Johnstone 2013). The two major questions I address in the analysis of CM in this chapter are below (see also Section 1.2.3.3).

1. How does a new style, including its salient components, come to be recognized (or made known)? Addressing this question requires examining a range of reflexive/metapragmatic activities and discourses from various social agents, individuals as well as institutions.
2. What are the metapragmatic messages that link (features of) a style to what stereotypic personae and social attributes? This question has to do with how the values of the style come to be established, maintained, negotiated, and contested. Addressing this question requires not only documenting metapragmatic typifications, but more important, showing regularities—recurring patterns—of typifications among a range of speakers. Such messages mediate the diffusion of a style or register and stabilize the cultural values and characterological figures linked to speech, as demonstrated in the case of RP and Pittsburghese. Although inconsistency is expected in register values (Agha 2007), competing valorizations expressed in metapragmatic messages are expected to be more prominent in styles and registers undergoing an early phase of enregisterment such as

136 Warring Standards

CM. Thus, an in-depth analysis of such competition and inconsistency in the cultural values associated with the style offers a good opportunity to reveal the different stakes and interests held by various social agents in the process of enregisterment. Metapragmatic messages thus constitute a site of ideological contestation where speech typifying messages are produced and manipulated by social agents—individuals and institutions—as tools for producing, regimenting, policing, and (de-)legitimizing social categories and boundaries, social positionings, ways of being, and so on (Moore 2011; Newell 2009; Roth-Gordon 2009; Silverstein 1993; Stroud 2004). As I show in this chapter, it is through such an analysis of the "micro" discursive level (e.g., commentaries on individual linguistic features from individuals in an interview, on a particular online discussion forum) that debates on CM's cultural values and its normativity vis-à-vis other relevant varieties are linked to "macro" level sociocultural models and (geo) political issues and projects.

To provide a comprehensive account of the emergence of CM, I also draw on Silverstein's (2003) concept of indexical order to analyze its enregisterment. The idea of the indexical order captures the contingent and fluid nature of indexicality and (re)construals of indexical values motivated by ideological engagement. For an indexical form of any indexical value, that is, an n-th order indexical form, an n+1st order indexicality is always immanent, motivated by a cultural-internal ideologically informed construal of the n-th order usage and its indexical meaningfulness (Silverstein 2003, 194, 212). The concept provides a framework to examine social meaning/indexicality as a reflexive and dialectic process, paying attention to both the presupposing and creative effects of language use as well as the metapragmatic function that mediates the pragmatics of language. Thus, indexical order links "the micro-social to the macro-social frames of analysis of any sociolinguistic phenomenon" (Silverstein 2003, 193). In the following analysis, I show how this framework can be used to embed linguistic innovation and change within broader processes of sociopolitical change.

My analysis shows that enregisterment and indexical order are inextricably linked (see also Silverstein 2003, 212–213). The latter is implicated in Agha's conceptions of enregisterment as well, for example, "processes whereby diverse behavioral signs (whether linguistic, non-linguistic, or both) are *functionally reanalyzed as cultural models of action*" (Agha 2007, 55; emphasis added). Such functional reanalysis must be achieved through a reflexive metapragmatic process, a cultural construal of some sort. This is more or less a semiotic movement across indexical orders, or a movement from n-th order to n+1st order indexicality. Indeed, a shift in indexical order is attested in the enregisterment of RP whereby a prestigious southeastern regional variety (n-th order index of localness and local prestige) has become a supraregional status emblem linked to a distinct scheme of cultural values (n+1st order indexicality; Agha 2003). A shift in indexical order is also shown to be the "defining dynamic" (Urciuoli 2010, 52) of the enregisterment of Pittsburghese (Johnstone 2013) and Copper Country English in Michigan's Keweenaw Peninsula (Remlinger 2009; Remlinger, Salmons, and Von Schneidemesser 2009). Such shifts in indexical orders are also indicated in other studies on enregisterment that do not explicitly engage the concept (e.g., Newell 2009; Smith-Hefner 2007). The endless or limitless cycle of tropic manipulation of cultural models or register norms discussed in Agha (2007) would be impossible without ideologically informed movement across indexical orders, in other words, re-construals or reinterpretations of enregistered norms.

5.2 Enregisterment of Cosmopolitan Mandarin

To become enregistered as an alternative supraregional Mandarin style to Beijing-Mandarin-based PTH and to index the meanings such as those when used by the Beijing yuppies and TV hosts examined earlier, CM and its constitutive features have to undergo a shift from an n-th order indexicality of geographical association, be it southern (China), Hong Kong, or Taiwan (see discussion in Chapters 3 and 4 on non-rhotacization, full tone, and lexical innovations from Southern varieties), to an n+1st order indexicality of social distinction. As shown in Table 5.1, the distinguishing features that constitute CM do not pose a threat to the national standard language at the n-th order indexicality, which focuses on geographical association. It is when these features are combined to form CM and take on an n+1st order indexicality of supraregional social distinction that CM comes to compete with Standard PTH and threatens to change the indexical field (Eckert 2008) of the national standard language.

TABLE 5.1 Contrasting Indexical Values of Standard *Putonghua* and Cosmopolitan Mandarin

Order of Indexicality	Standard Putonghua (rhotacization, neutral tone)	Cosmopolitan Mandarin (de-rhotacization, full tone)
n-th order indexicality: geographical association	Beijing, the North	The South, including Hong Kong and Taiwan
n+1st order indexicality: social distinction	Supraregional Chinese identity, modernity, national unity, social equality, and egalitarianism (based on discussion in Sections 0.5.1–0.5.4)	Cosmopolitan Chinese, being cultured and tasteful, stylishness, trendiness, sophistication, youthful ebullience and conviviality (based on analysis in Chapters 3 and 4)

138 Warring Standards

In the rest of the chapter, I demonstrate that contesting the enregisterment of CM is fundamentally an ideologically motivated battle over the n+1st order indexical values of CM and its constitutive features.

The following analysis of the enregisterment of CM is based on a diverse range of metapragmatic discourses covering a time span from 1994 to 2012. I use multiple forms of metapragmatic data to provide a better understanding of the schemes of cultural values associated with the new style than an analysis relying on a narrow range of data. Furthermore, a diverse range of data facilitates the discovery of regularities as well as offers a better chance of discovering fractionation in patterns of valorization, which sheds light on the social organization of reflexive practices and ideologies (e.g., Hill 1998; Rickford 1986; Schieffelin and Doucet 1998). I categorize the metadiscursive data following the scheme in Agha (2007, 151, Table 3.1): popular media and literary representations of the use and users of CM and its constitutive elements (Section 5.2.1), a metapragmatic label for CM (Section 5.2.2), government regulations on language use in the media (Section 5.2.3), other public sphere metadiscourses from online sources (including personal blogs, Internet forums, online commentaries from websites of newspapers and magazines) and print media, and commentaries elicited in interviews from my fieldwork (Section 5.2.4).

The data show, on the one hand, that certain patterns of evaluation recur and, on the other hand, varied and often competing cultural values co-exist, revealing a messy, contested indexical field. Thus, unlike an enregistered style that is linked to a set of relatively stable[1] and conventionalized cultural values and characterological figures, for example, RP recognized as an emblem of privileged social status (Agha 2003) and Pittsburghese linked to "the authentic Pittsburgher" (Johnstone 2009, 160), the cultural values of CM and its features are highly unstable. The unstableness, or more precisely, the unstableness of the n+1st order indexical value, is expected of a linguistic style in an early phase of enregisterment. The shift from an n-th order indexicality to an n+1st order valorization is fraught with contradiction and contestation, involving speakers/agents (both individuals and institutions) assigning certain interpretations/cultural values while excluding or rejecting others. This aspect of the enregisterment process has not been the focus of earlier studies on enregisterment. It is when a form or repertoire is enregistered, when its cultural values become stabilized and conventionalized in a community, that the social history of the contestation over indexical order (the process of selection and rejection) is forgotten or erased from the cultural awareness of contemporary users (Inoue 2004; Woolard 2004). The case of CM at the early stage of enregisterment thus offers a valuable opportunity to explore the complexities in the shift of indexical order. The analysis of the inconsistency and contestation over indexical order connects microlevel (meta)discursive practice to macrolevel sociopolitical issues and projects that are involved in the emergence of CM.

5.2.1 Popular Media and Literary Representations

An early example of metapragmatic typifications of the new linguistic style was found in a theatrical skit, or *xiaopin*,[2] broadcast nationwide during the 1995 annual CCTV Spring Festival Gala on the eve of the Chinese New Year, or *chun wan* as it is commonly called. A national event that draws hundreds of millions of viewers, it is the most popular show in China. The gala is also supposedly the most censored program on Chinese television as acts must undergo several rounds of selection and approval before they can be included in the final program of the gala (B. Zhao 1998). Every gala has set categories of performances, and comic skits belong to the *yuyan lei jiemu* 'language category performances'. The skits are performed to create humorous effects typically through parody or satire and thus serve as a form of social commentary (Du 1998). Additionally, like other acts in the Gala, they are intended to convey a message relevant to the sociopolitical themes of that year. Research has shown that this popular genre of performance at nationally televised media events such as the CCTV Spring Festival Galas has been utilized by the Chinese state as a venue to propagate party ideologies and official views, a new form of political propaganda through popular entertainment in the reform era (Gao and Pugsley 2008; Wang 2010).

The 1995 skit, *"Ruci baozhuang"* ("Packaging in such a way"), is performed by two famous comedians, Gong Hanlin and Zhao Lirong, who is also a well-known Chinese folk opera performer. The title explicitly frames the performance as a metapragmatic, or more precisely, metasemiotic event in which rules to organize signs—"packaging"—from multiple modalities (including speech, dress, body movements) are explained and carried out to achieve desired pragmatic effects. As mentioned earlier, the genre of *xiaopin* typically keys the performance as a parody, and so is the case in this 1995 skit.[3] As described in the CCTV's synopsis of the 1995 Gala, the skit "satirizes the packaging fever in show business" (CCTV 1995). It is about a manager and executive art designer (played by Gong) of the "Star Production Company" trying to package, or do a makeover of, a famous senior performer of the traditional Chinese opera, *Ping Xi* 'Ping Opera'[4] (played by Zhao, who is herself a legendary *Ping Xi* performer) for the shooting of a Ping Opera MTV, "a modern television artistic creation," in the words of the manager. For readers who are not familiar with the Chinese genre of *xiaopin*, imagine this performance as a skit on Saturday Night Live about the makeover of a legendary female version of Willie Nelson to become the next world rap superstar. The manager intends to "modernize" the opera to generate more profit. Throughout the skit, Zhao speaks in her native Tangshan Mandarin, a Northern Mandarin dialect used in *Ping Xi*. It is mutually intelligible with Beijing Mandarin (BM) and shares the features of rhotacization and neutral tone.

From the very beginning of the skit, Zhao, entering the stage wearing a conspicuously dowdy outfit carrying a flowery fabric tote bag, is portrayed as an

140 Warring Standards

elderly woman who is ignorant of the "modern" show business semiotics. In other words, she is unable to comprehend the signs that are assumed to index "modern" show business. For instance, she mistakes Gong for a woman due to his *xiaobiar* **[+R]** 'ponytail'; has trouble remembering and producing Gong's professional title *yishu zongjian* 'executive art designer'; misinterprets a sleeveless dress as an unfinished dress missing its sleeves and a back-revealing dress as "back not being sewn closed"; misinterprets "packaging" as wrapping up or covering up rather than wearing more revealing clothing. The following excerpt, at about 2 minutes into the skit, is about the packaging of her voice. To prepare her for the shooting of the MTV, Gong tells her, "the voice of your talk needs to be packaged" (lines 8 and 9). The packaging of her voice is done by getting rid of her local accent (lines 11–14) and by adding "a few trendy sounds" to make her more appealing (line 25). The linguistic packaging is done through the use of stereotypic features of CM, including English words "Hi" and "un-hum" (lines 31–34). After Gong demonstrates the "trendy sounds" for Zhao, she acknowledges that she can do it, too (line 39), which indicates that she recognizes—enregisters—the speech style that utilizes these "trendy features."[5] She demonstrates her competence in the trendy style through the use of stylized CM, including three salient features of CM (a, b, c) and a stereotypical southern feature (d):

a using a full tone in place of the neutral tone in *xianseng* **[T1]** 'Mister' (line 46); *xiaobianzi* **[T3]** 'ponytail' (line 47), *and piaoliang* **[T4]** (line 47);

b de-rhotacization saying "*xiaobianzi*" 'ponytail' (line 47) instead of *xiaobianr* 'ponytail' as she did at the beginning of the skit;

c the use of innovative intensifier *hao* 'very' (line 47);

d replacing retroflex *sh* with dental sibilant *s* in *xianseng* 'Mister' (line 46).

However, her competence in production is limited as shown by the reduced tempo of her speech and a hypercorrection in the use of the innovative intensifier by saying "***hao hao** piaoliang*" (line 47). The intensifier *hao* 'very', should not be duplicated here. The reduplication indicates that she is aware of the innovative use of *hao* but models its usage after "*hao* [intensifier] *hao-kan*" 'very pretty' or "*hao* [intensifier] *hao-chi*" 'very delicious', in which the first *hao* is an intensifier and the second *hao* is part of the compound adjective *hao-kan* 'pretty' and *hao-chi* 'delicious'.

Additional packaging includes giving her a Western stage name *Ma-la-ji-si* inspired by the American actress *Bo-ji-xiao-si* 'Brooke Shields', but when produced by Zhao it sounds like 'numbing-spicy-julienned-chicken.' She is given a revealing Western-style dress and hip-hop style clothing and taught hip-hop style singing and dancing, all of which are to appeal to an imagined modern, international audience and to generate more profit. At the end of the skit, after being forced to perform a well-known *Ping Xi* piece in hip-hop style, she revolts and reproaches, "It is the type of people like you [the manager] who have mangled our good stuff!"

Warring Standards **141**

In contrast to Zhao's character's predominant use of Tangshan Mandarin, the manager's speech is Standard PTH, with occasional use of stereotypical features of CM, particularly de-rhotaciation (line 20), full tone (line 24), replacing retroflex initial with dental sibilant (line 49), and English words "hi" (line 31) and "un-hum" (line 33) when demonstrating a new repackaged style of speaking. Some signs stereotypically associated with being effeminate are also used in the performance of this character, including exaggerated pitch range, exaggerated gestures, and elements of stereotypical feminine comportment.[6]

Excerpt 5.1 "Packaging in Such a Way"

...

1	Gong:	*Zai PAIshe zhiqian*
		Before the SHOOTING (of the MTV)
2		*wo zhunbei*
		I'm going to
3		*dui nin jinxing yici qu::anxin de BAOZHUANG.*
		co::mpletely REPACKAGE you.
4	Zhao:	*Baozhuang?*
		Package?
5	Gong:	*Shi a.*
		Yes.
6		*Baozhuang shi yizhong CHAOLIU.*
		Packaging is a TREND.
7		*HEN fuza de.*
		VERY complicated.
8		**Bifangshuo, nin jianghua de SHENGYIN,**
		For example, the VOICE of your talk
9		**ZHE:, jiu xuyao baozhuang.**
		THI:S, needs to be packaged.
10	Zhao:	*Na:: zar* [+R] *bao ei.* ((*zar* is a Tangshan localism.))
		How [+R] to wrap THA::T eh.
11	Gong:	*Nin tingting nin tingting.*
		Listen to yourself listen to yourself.
12		*NA: zar* [+R] *bao ei.* ((raised pitch, imitating Zhao in Tangshan dialect))
		How [+R] to wrap THA:T eh.
13		*BU XI:NG.*
		NO WA:Y.
14		*Nin zheige qiangdiaor* [R+] *YI:ding yao GA:Iyigai.*
		Your accent [R+] MU:st be CHA:nged.
15	Zhao:	*Gai bu liao la.*
		It can't be changed.
16		*Dou liushi duo nian la.*
		It's been more than 60 years.

142 Warring Standards

17		*Jiulian shuo menghua yeshi zhe weir* **[R+]**. ((audience laughter))
		I talk in this accent even when I'm dreaming.
18	Gong:	*YI::ding yao GA::I.*
		MU::St be CHA::NGED.
19		*Ben gongsi shi yao ba nin tuixiang guoji.*
		Our company wants to promote you to the global (market).
20		*peiyang chengwei shijie-ji de da: **pai** **[-R]** mingxing.*
		cultivate you to become a world-level bi:g shot **[-R]**.
21		*Yinci NIN jiangchu hua lai*
		Therefore when YOU talk
22		*ke QIANwan bu neng lao shi*
		It can NEVER be like
23		*zar* **[R+]** *a zar* **[R+]** *a zar* **[R+]** *a zar* **[R+]** *de.* ((raised pitch, in Tangshang dialect)).
		how **[R+]** ah how **[R+]** ah how **[R+]** ah how **[R+]**.
24		*Zhei yang**zi** **[T3]**,*
		This way **[T3]**,
25		**wo tiao ji ge SHI:mao de yuyin**
		I'll select a few TRE:Ndy sounds
26		**gei nin DIANZHUI yi xia.**
		to DECORATE you a bit.
27	Zhao:	*Hum.*
		Hum.
28	Gong:	*Bifangshuo*
		For example
29		*nin jianle ren he ta dazhaohu.*
		you see somebody and greet him/her.
30		*Nin jiu keyi zheyang.*
		You can do it like this.
31		*Ha:i* **[E]** ((English "hi," raised pitch))
		Hi: **[E]**
32	Zhao:	*Ha:i* **[E]** ((imitating Gong, raised pitch))
		Hi: **[E]**
33	Gong:	**Un-hum [E]**? ((English minimal response))
34	Zhao:	**Un-hum [E]**?
35	Gong:	h h h h
36		*Nin xuede* h *hai zhen xiang* h h. ((audience applause))
		You imitated h really well h h.
37		*Hao* h *hao* h *hao* h.
		Good h good h good h.
38	Zhao:	*Jiu ZHEme shuohua ya?*
		It's talking like THIS?
39		*Na wo ye HUI ya.*
		Then I CAN do it too.

40	Gong:	*Ou, nin hui shuo?* ((looking surprised))
		Oh, you can talk (like this)?
41		*Shuo yige wo tingting?*
		Say something for me?
42	Zhao:	**Hi [E]** ((raised pitch, exaggerated gestures))
43	Gong:	**Hi [E]**
44	Zhao:	**Un-hum [E]**?
45	Gong:	**Un-hum [E]**?
46	Zhao:	*Xianseng* **[T1]**, ((Standard PTH: *xian1sheng0*))
		Mister **[T1]**,
47		*ni de xiaobian* **zi** *[T3]* **hao** *[L]* *hao piaoliang* **[T4]** *a.* ((reduced tempo, hypercorrect use of innovative intensifier *hao* 'very'))
		your ponytail **[T3]** is **very[L]** very pretty **[T4]**.
48	Gong:	*A* h *ya:* h *laorenjia* h. ((audience applause))
		A h ya: h ma'am h.
49		*Ni jiangde zheshi* **zende** *mo.* ((**zende** should be **zhende** in Standard PTH. Here the retroflex initial is replaced with a dental sibilant))
		Was what you said real.
50	Zhao:	**Un-hum [E]**? ((conceitedly))
51	Gong:	*Shuode HAO.*
		(You) talk really WELL.
52		***Zhe jiushi YUYAN BAOZHUANG.***
		This is exactly LINGUISTIC PACKAGING.
53	Zhao:	***Zhe zou:shi bu rang ren haorhaor* [+R] *shuohua.*** ((switching to Tanshang dialect; audience laughter and applause))
		This is exactly not letting one talk normally [+R].

In "Packaging in Such a Way," there does not seem to be a single explicit message about the cultural value of the stereotypic forms of CM. Rather, the linguistic signs are linked to several things, all of which are precipitates of the transition to a market economy: (a) new character types that emerged through market reform, in this case, cultural entrepreneurs and pop-culture performers, and (b) social attributes, including being trendy, modern, and cosmopolitan. At the same time, they are linked to the "dark side" of a market economy, specifically, the eager pursuit of quick monetary gains at the expense of traditional Chinese cultural forms, commodification of hyperfemininity, and last but not least, mindless pursuit of Westernization. The cultural value of CM as shown through much of this skit is thus *ambivalent*, not explicitly positive or negative, but one aspect is clear: It is linked to the sociocultural transformations brought about by the market economy and is positioned in contrast to signs that putatively index traditional Chinese culture, including *Ping Xi* and its aging performer.

In addition to highlighting this contrast, another overarching metapragmatic message accentuates the absurdity of the new linguistic style, in Zhao's words, it is not a normal way of speaking (line 53). As the whole set of packaging

144 Warring Standards

strategies is the target of a parody, the audience is invited to *disalign* with all of them, including the linguistic device, that is, the packaged voice in CM. This invitation to disalignment becomes more explicit at the end of the excerpt. Responding to the manager's self-conceited comment, "This is exactly linguistic packaging" (line 52), the infuriated Zhao counters: "This is exactly not letting one talk normally" (line 53). At this moment, the intended message is loud and clear: Such a way of speaking is *not normal*. The audible laughter and applause from the audience members physically present at the gala may be prompted by (a) the humorous effect produced by the contrast between Gong's Standard Mandarin and Zhao's broad Tangshan dialect, and/or (b) their agreement with Zhao and thus laughing at the absurdity of the linguistic packaging. The second interpretation would indicate that the audience shares the intended disalignment. Whether or not such a disalignment happens is out of the control of the author, nominally the skit's writers, and the principal, who is likely to be a government authority of some sort.[7]

The above analysis demonstrates that one semiotic event may create multiple messages. The metapragmatic messages from the skit have the potential to reach hundreds of millions of viewers watching the show on Chinese New Year's Eve, more viewers in subsequent reruns of the show in the Spring Festival season, and even more viewers from further reruns in other entertainment programs all over China. As described above, one such message intended through this skit links CM to being fake and "not normal" (line 53). Hence, mass-mediated (meta)semiotic events like the CCTV Spring Festival Gala play a crucial role in the enregisterment process of CM. By juxtaposing it against other salient styles of Mandarin, the Spring Festival Gala facilitates heightened awareness and recognition of its distinctiveness among potentially large populations of mainland Chinese across space and time. Evidence of this is indeed found in a metalinguistic commentary 10 years later presented in Excerpt 5.18 below.

As the evaluation on (linguistic) normativity is ideologically informed (Cameron 1995, 180), we see from this skit an early indication that competing ideologies of normativity are at work in the enregisterment of CM. In the skit, the counter-valorization of the new style is communicated implicitly through the voice of the animator (the character Zhao) while the principal and the author of such a message remain invisible. I return to a discussion about the normativity debate in later examples of metapragmatic discourses (see Section 5.2.4.2). Finally, despite the potentially wide reach of the metapragmatic messages about the new style facilitated through the nationwide broadcasting of the gala, it is unpredictable whether the receivers, namely the audience of the skit, will align themselves with the messages. However, by putting the new Mandarin style on display, juxtaposed with the official standard language and a northern dialect, the nationally broadcast gala does contribute to a widespread *recognition* of the distinctiveness of the new Mandarin style.

The innovative linguistic style also catches the attention of literary writers. An early literary metapragmatic message about the new style appeared in a

1996 essay by the renowned novelist and essayist, Wang Xiaobo (1952–1997), "*Jingpianzi yu minzu zixinxin*" 'Beijing vernacular and national self-respect' (2006 [1996]). The essay presents several themes shared in many later metadiscourses about the innovative Mandarin style, including its characterological figures and amorality of its users in contrast to speakers of the authentic Beijing vernacular. A Beijing native, Wang exalts the "sublimity" of BM as "the most superb in Chinese speech" (2006 [1996], 159). Then he laments that such superiority has become a thing of the past, being replaced by "*Gang-Tai qiangdiao*" '*Gang-Tai* accent', which nowadays inundates radio and television broadcasting. The Chinese compound term *Gang-Tai* refers to Hong Kong and Taiwan. The examples given are "*hao ke'ai hao gaoxing ou*" 'very [innovative intensifier *hao*] adorable very [innovative intensifier *hao*] happy **oh** [sentence-final particle]', and "*Gang-Tai* accented" pronunciation of "*xiansheng*" 'Mister', involving the same stereotypic features used in the comic skit above. Although the written Chinese characters cannot represent the "*Gang-Tai* accented" pronunciation of *xiansheng*, it is presumably pronounced as *xian1sheng1* [T1] with a full tone on the second syllable; contrastively, in Beijing vernacular the second syllable is produced with a neutral tone. Linking "*Gang-Tai* accent" to broadcasters and female pop stars "whose speech is the most Hong Kong-Taiwanized," Wang offers a scathing remark (2006 [1996], 159):

Excerpt 5.2
Some of our fashionable young women mutilate their own language. They must be mentally masturbating the Hong Kong Dollar and the New Taiwan Dollar, because other than money these two places have nothing else that is appealing.

He further explains that the real issue with which he is concerned is not pronunciation but "the encroachment of Hong Kong-Taiwan culture on the mainland" and the contamination of the Chinese language as a result of the dominance of Hong Kong-Taiwan television dramas (Xiaobo Wang 2006 [1996], 160):

Excerpt 5.3
Those Gang-Tai TV dramas that are worse than dog shit are now dominating mainland television such that Chinese people cannot speak Chinese language well. Although Hong Kong and Taiwan are indeed wealthy, they do not have culture. Although our place here does not look anything special [we don't look glamorous], others still admire us. The so-called culture is accumulated dynasties after dynasties.

He recalls that in the early 1980s, young Beijing women working in hotels were notorious for their rude service attitude. However, despite their rudeness (Xiaobo Wang 2006 [1996], 160–161):

146 Warring Standards

Excerpt 5.4

They had honesty and integrity, and would not kiss up to rich people. ... Although it is not good to be rude, it is good to have national self-respect [*minzu zizunxin*]. When confronted with someone who wants to get intimate [a womanizer], a young woman would smack him in the face, which is justifiable; that's better than clinging her face to his. ... Nowadays, there are a lot more joint-venture hotels in Beijing where young women working there never rebuke their guests, but the old Chinese American customers never return. I suspect that it is because bird language[8] is spoken everywhere now so that it is not interesting to come back anymore.

In Wang's 1996 essay, stereotypic features of the innovative linguistic style are labeled "*Gang-Tai qiangdiao*" 'Hong Kong-Taiwan accent', which anchors the social provenance of the accent to a compound place of "Hong Kong-Taiwan" and by extension the people of "Hong Kong and Taiwan." The use of the term "accent" here is clearly ideological, as "Hong Kong-Taiwan accent" is not defined in linguistic terms. As discussed in more detail in the next section, *Gang-Tai qiang* 'Hong Kong-Taiwan accent' turns out to be the most widely used label for the innovative Mandarin style. In Wang's essay, the style is linked to radio and television broadcasters and to young women, particularly characters that have emerged in the market economy, namely, pop stars and women employees of joint-venture hotels. "*Gang-Tai* accent" is also associated with corrupt moral standards, including the pursuit of money (Excerpt 5.2), loss of national self-respect (Excerpt 5.4) and implied sexual promiscuity (Excerpt 5.4). A term of ideological stance, "accent" in this essay is used as a differentiating tool at several levels. The contrast between the authentic Beijing vernacular and "*Gang-Tai* accent" is recursively projected (Irvine and Gal 2000) onto a contrast between an authentic Beijing/Chinese culture with historicity and a *Gang-Tai* culture without history (Excerpt 5.3), and a temporal contrast between (a) a morally upright past with national self-respect up to the 1980s and (b) a contemporary period of weakened morality and loss of national self-respect. This last contrast is similar to that described in Hill (1998): a discourse of nostalgia in which a "pure" form of Mexicano language serves as a vehicle for "respect." In the case described here, the loss of the "noble" Beijing vernacular pronunciation is believed to result in a loss of linguistic means to express Chinese national self-respect, and the so-called *Gang-Tai* accent—when used by mainland speakers—is unfit for that indexical function. The loss of Chinese national self-confidence/respect would thus lead to *chunyangmeiwei*, a derogatory expression meaning 'blindly admiring everything foreign', or xenophilia. According to this ideology, "the mental masturbation of Hong Kong Dollar and the New Taiwan Dollar" are manifestations of such xenophilia.

Characterological figures in other media and literary representations are various types of young people, including *zhui xing zu* 'star-chasing tribe', or pop music fans (e.g., CCTV skit "*Zhui xing zu*" 'Star-chasing tribe' 1993), pop singers (CCTV skit "*Fuqin*" 'Father' 1995), young modern women (e.g., Y. Wang 1998), *xiao zi* 'the petite bourgeoisie' (e.g., Phoenix Television 2004; "petite bourgeoise women" in A. Zhang 2002), and *xin xin renlei* 'neo-neo tribe'[9] (eladies.sina 2002; Liu 2000; Wang and Lao 2000). In the first three examples, the characters are all young northern women who cross (Rampton 1995) from Standard PTH (in 'Star-chasing tribe' 1993 and Y. Wang 1998) and/or a Northern Mandarin dialect (Henan dialect in "Father" 1995) to stylized CM. In Y. Wang's 1998 short story, "*Mei zhehuishi*" 'There is no such thing', the label "*Gang-Tai qiang*" is used again to describe a young Beijing woman's speech style (Y. Wang 1998, 348):

Excerpt 5.5

Ke-ke was talking [*shuohuar*] to her grandmother, pouting like a spoiled child. Suddenly she saw a very pretty [*hen piaoliang*] hair stick on her grandmother's chignon. Using the **modern girls' habitual *Gang-Tai* accent**, she cried exaggeratingly, "<u>**wa**</u> [exclamation], Grandma's hair stick is **very** pretty **very** pretty [<u>***hao***</u> *piaoliang* <u>***hao***</u> *piaoliang*] ***wo*** [exclamation]!"

In the above excerpt, the contrast between the narrator's quoting voice in conventional BM (bold italic) and the quoted voice of "the modern girls' habitual *Gang-Tai* accent" (bold italic underlined) is represented through the use of rhotacization and the conventional intensifier "*hen*" 'very' for the former and the use of exclamations (*wa*, *wo*), and the stereotypic intensifier "*hao*" 'very' for the latter. The character-based Chinese script is less versatile in representing pronunciation features than an alphabet-based script such as English. Written representations of speech in Chinese most often reflect non-phonological features, except for those that can be represented in written characters, such as rhotacization. In the above excerpt, the young woman's utterance of "***hao*** *piaoliang* ***hao*** *piaoliang*" in "*Gang-Tai* accent" is presumably pronounced in a way similar to Zhao's performance of "***hao*** *piangliang4* **[T4]**" in Excerpt 5.1, with a falling tone in the third syllable rather than a neutral tone. Note that both *hao* and *wa* were used by the TV hosts in Chapter 4 (see Table 4.2 [5]).

5.2.2 The Metapragmatic Label "Gang-Tai Qiang" 'Hong Kong-Taiwan Accent'

The term *Gang-Tai qiang* 'Hong Kong-Taiwan accent' is the most widely used label to refer to a new way of speaking Mandarin distinctive from Standard PTH as illustrated in the previous examples. The label anchors the origin of the "accent" to a compound place of *Gang-Tai*, that is, Hong Kong and Taiwan. When used to describe a mainlander's Mandarin speech, the term specifically refers to the incorporation of so-called "Hong Kong-Taiwan" speech features in Standard PTH. Most often, the user of the term does not offer a definition (i.e., assumes an understanding of what the term refers to), but some do. The following are some representative definitions.

148 Warring Standards

In an article "*Xin xin renlei bi xiu: 2001 nian de ku ci yi lan*"'Neo-neo tribe must learn: a survey of cool vocabulary in 2001', *Gang-Tai qiang* is the top item in a list of "cool" diction that characterizes members of the "neo-neo tribe" (eladies.sina 2002; emphasis added):

Excerpt 5.6

Gang-Tai accent is in fashion among people working in business buildings: Intentionally [*guyi*] lengthening the last sound of a word, **intentionally** releasing half of a sound, **intentionally** pronouncing the fourth tone as the third tone and the second tone as the first tone. **Even a gal growing up in Beijing alleys, not even a week after she enters the business building, will she be unable to curl her tongue,** taking up the **soft, affectedly sweet, s-s-s crooked accent**: "'*nah*', *renjia deng ni yijing* '*man*' *jiu-le, ni* '*wei4shen3mo1*' [*wei4shen2me0* in Standard PTH and BM] *cai guolai?* [Translation: "**then**', I've waited for you for '**quite**' a long time, '**why**' did you get here just now?']

In the above description, young white-collar workers are identified as stereotypic users of *Gang-Tai qiang*. "Intentionally" is used three times to emphasize that *Gang-Tai qiang* is a designed way of speaking, an "unnatural" style deliberately performed by mainland, particularly Northern, Mandarin speakers. The descriptions of the "intentional" acts are vague at best, if not random. Lengthening the last sound of a word seems to refer to the stereotypic feature of lengthening the final vowel in sentence-final particles and/or exclamations. The description of the use of tones, replacing the fourth tone with the third and the second with the first, is random and makes no sense linguistically. However, the illustration of the accent transformation of "a girl growing up in the Beijing alleys" after becoming an office worker does fit into stereotypes of *Gang-Tai qiang*. With the loss of her ability to curl her tongue, presumably resulting in the loss of rhotacization and producing the retroflex initials as sibilants, her Beijing accent is replaced by a "crooked accent" full of sibilant sounds, namely *Gang-Tai* accent and characterized as "soft and affectedly sweet." The southern Mandarin expression "*dia-dia de*" 'affectedly sweet' describes the *sajiao* style of an adorable but petulant and spoiled child and of a young woman who deliberately acts pettishly charming as "a kind of romantic play" (A. Zhang 1995 quoted in Chan 1998, 39) or to "seek material or immaterial benefit from an unwilling listener" (Farris 1994, 13). The characterization of being "*dia*" is also found in many other evaluations of *Gang-Tai qiang*.

When citing the constructed girl's speech, the author used single quotation marks to highlight distinctive elements of *Gang-Tai* accent that make the voice "soft and affectedly sweet": an interjection '*nah*' (presumably with lengthened vowel), a stereotypic adverb '*man*' (quite), and tonal manipulation in '*wei4shen2me0*' (why) as '*wei4shen3mo1*'. It is interesting to note that the last cited form contains not only a replacement of neutral tone with a full tone

Warring Standards **149**

(tone 1) but also a representation of the Standard PTH tone 2 in *"shen2"* as tone 3 or a dipping tone contour *"shen3."*[10] This phenomenon of prescriptive tone 2 being realized as tone 3 (dipping contour tone) is documented among Taiwan Mandarin speakers in Sanders (2008) and Li, Xiong, and Wang (2006). The use of *'renjia'* in the quoted speech also adds to the softness and sweetness of the quoted voice. Originally meaning "other," *renjia* is used here as a first person pronoun, "a modest metaphoric distancing device," which is stereotypically used by girls and young women (Farris 1988, 292).

In an online article, Zhang Miaoyang (2011), chief voice-over artist and the Mandarin identification voice for Phoenix Television (Hong Kong), describes *Gang-Tai qiang* as *"budai juanshe, meiyou qingsheng"* (**'without [sounds made by] curling the tongue, without neutral tone'**). The sounds made by "curling the tongue" include two phonological features that contribute to the impression of tongue-curling, namely rhotacization and the retroflex syllable initials (and lenition of these initials described in Chapter 3); "without neutral tone" refers to the use of a full tone in a prescriptive neutral tone environment. Such an accent is again characterized as "affectedly sweet" and "soft" (ibid.).

According to the above descriptions, the major features of CM examined in Chapters 3 and 4 overlap with the major stereotypic features of *Gang-Tai qiang*, particularly non-rhotacization, full tone, the adverbs *hao* and *man*, sentence-final particles, and mixing English words in PTH. Such evidence attest to *Gang-Tai qiang* as a metalinguistic label for CM. Television entertainment program hosts, pop stars, white-collar professionals, *xin xin renlei* 'neo-neo tribe', and *xiao zi* 'the petite bourgeoisie'(e.g., Phoenix Television 2004), especially petite bourgeoisie women (e.g., A. Zhang 2002), are the social types most frequently associated with *Gang-Tai qiang*. Again, all of them are social types that have come about in the transition to a market economy. In the last two cases (Phoenix Television 2004 and A. Zhang 2002), *Gang-Tai qiang* is taken to be part of the cosmopolitan lifestyle of the Chinese petite bourgeoisie, described as "seeking quality of life, emphasizing individual indulgence, and participating in cultural consumption with taste" (A. Zhang 2002).

My discussion so far has demonstrated that major features that constitute CM are recognized as a new style of Mandarin distinctive from the conventional Standard PTH and linked to specific types of characterological figures. This provides strong evidence for the enregisterment of CM, which is currently most often labeled *Gang-Tai qiang*. The term has been in wide circulation, attracting attention from the media, the government, and Internet discussion forums over the past decade. For example, an online discussion related to this label on Tianya.cn, one of the largest Internet discussion forums in China (Jiang 2010), attracted 1,808 responses and was viewed 151,331 times between March 22 and May 8, 2012.[11] The following sections focus on metalinguistic discourses on *Gang-Tai qiang* to reveal the complexities of the cultural values associated with the new style of Mandarin in its early stage of enregisterment.

150 Warring Standards

5.2.3 The State's Counter-Enregisterment Efforts

CM as an alternative supraregional Mandarin style has caught the attention of the state-controlled media since the mid-1990s, as demonstrated earlier in the CCTV comic skit "Packaging in Such a Way." In such skits, the state plays the role of the invisible principal behind metapragmatic messages about the new linguistic style. Since 2000, the state has been engaged in counter-enregisterment efforts by producing explicit metapragmatic discourses condemning the so-called *Gang-Tai qiang*. The venues for such discourses are major state-controlled news media, such as the Chinese Communist Party's flagship newspaper, *Renmin Ribao (People's Daily)*, Xinhua News Agency, and China News Service and regulations on language use issued by government organizations. The state is waging an ideological war to contain the dissemination of a potential challenger to Standard PTH. It does this by means of pejorizing the term *Gang-Tai qiang*, stigmatizing the new style of Mandarin and its speakers so as to valorize the Beijing-Mandarin-based PTH. The pejoration is intended to regiment the $n+1$st order indexicality of CM and to prevent the potential sedimentation of positive evaluation and perception of the new Mandarin style and its distinctive features. The state's attack focuses particularly on television and radio hosts and broadcasters. This tactic is unsurprising, as these people are supposed to be the exemplary speakers of Standard PTH who play a pivotal role in processes of enregisterment (Agha 2007).

In 2000, *Guojia Tongyong Yuyan Wenzi Fa*, the 'National Common Language Law', was passed, stipulating that Standard PTH is the only language to be used in television and radio broadcasting. As mentioned in Chapter 3 (Section 3.5.1), radio and television broadcasters and program hosts, in addition to teachers and civil servants, are required to take the *Putonghua* Proficiency Test. Upholding the norms of BM, the proficiency test specifically tests the correct usage of rhotacization and neutral tone, labeling failure to produce these two features as "*yuyin quexian*" 'pronunciation deficiency' (PSCSG 2004, 3). Furthermore, the guidelines for the test identify incorrect pronunciation of neutral-tone words as a major cause of "*Gang-Tai* accent" (PSCSG 2004, 41; see quotation in Section 3.2.3). In the same year, in anticipation of the annual Putonghua Promotion Week in September, *Gang-Tai qiang* was in the headline of an award winning news report from China News Service, titled "Mainland promotes Putonghua, opposes *Gang-Tai* accent" (Xiaohui Wang 2000).[12] The article reported a nationwide trend of using *Gang-Tai qiang* in mainland television variety entertainment programs. The head of the Ministry of Culture was reported as criticizing some broadcasters and hosts "blindly imitating *Gang-Tai qiang*," which reflected "their lack of self-confidence in their own fine style of broadcasting and hosting" (ibid.). The article also reported that two hosts of a provincial-level variety entertainment program were disqualified from entering a major TV host competition because of "blatant imitation of *Gang-Tai qiang*" (ibid.). The emphasis on mainland speakers aping *Gang-Tai qiang* indicates an insistence on keeping it at the *n*-th order of indexicality as a regional "accent," one presupposing the speaker's geographical origin as Hong Kong-Taiwan, outside of the mainland. Hence, any mainlander's appropriation of the style and its elements is interpreted as imitation of someone else's native accent and thus must be motivated by linguistic insecurity in one's native accent—and therefore is inauthentic. Such an interpretation inevitably denaturalizes and illegitimates (Bucholtz and Hall 2004) the act of emulation as well as the emulators and paves the way for further negative construals of the imitators' characters, such as "lack of self-confidence" and lack of sound judgment, as indicated in the description "*blindly* imitating *Gang-Tai qiang*."

The counterattack against *Gang-Tai qiang* targeting hosts of television entertainment programs became intensified at the beginning of 2002, and the term was increasingly linked to negative values and attributes, such as inferior style, vulgarity, and linguistic and moral contamination. In January of 2002, the State Administration of Radio, Film and Television (SARFT) issued a circular titled "The prevention of bad tendencies in entertainment variety programs" (SARFT 2002). It accuses some programs of having "inferior style, nonsense and random content, and vulgarity" (ibid.). Among the seven major problems of entertainment programs, some hosts of variety shows are accused of "learning to speak *bu-lun-bu-lei de 'Gang-Tai qiang'*" (ibid.). The Mandarin idiom *bu-lun-bu-lei* means, "not resembling or fitting into any established type or category, used to describe something or someone that is not appropriate or not conforming to standards and norms" (*Xiandai Hanyu Cidian* 1993, 92). It is usually translated into English as 'neither fish nor fowl'. This expression is often used to describe deviancy or bad, awkward imitation.

Gang-Tai qiang is explicitly characterized as moral and linguistic contamination and a threat to the purity of the national language in a *People's Daily* article with a pugnacious title "Safeguarding the purity of the language of the homeland" (Zhong 2002).[13] Following the official definition of PTH (which emphasizes BM phonology as its norm and Northern Mandarin as its base dialect), the writer observes that the use of vulgar language is rampant in many popular newspapers and magazines and that nonstandard vernaculars are used to portray characters in films and television. S/he notes further that (ibid. 2002, 12):

Excerpt 5.7

the speech of hosts of many entertainment programs is full of **Gang-Tai qiang**....
...**Deliberate imitation of trendy accent to blindly pursue trendiness can only reflect a lack of creativity and self-confidence**. ...

In this article, *Gang-Tai qiang*, in company with vulgar language and nonstandard vernaculars, is treated among a pack of culprits that pose a threat to the purity and authority of the national language. "Trendy accent" in Excerpt 5.7 obviously

152 Warring Standards

refers to *Gang-Tai qiang*, but it is again interpreted as "deliberate imitation" and "unhealthy linguistic garbage" (ibid.) and is assigned an exclusive—"can only reflect"—$n+1$st order indexical meaning of "lack of creativity and self-confidence," which also depicts negative attributes of its speakers.

Official measures to clean up the "unhealthy linguistic garbage" were initiated in 2004 as part of the SARFT's *"Jinghua Gongcheng"* (Purification Project) aiming to "purge from films, radio, and television programs the thoughts, behaviors, language, and images which are harmful to the healthy development of minors" (SARFT 2004).[14] *Gang-Tai qiang* is among the 10 problem categories targeted (also called the "ten bans" of SARFT); others include crime and violence, pornography, feudal superstition and pseudo-science, self-serving, and mammonism (SARFT 2004). Targeting radio and television program hosts, the Purification Project requires (ibid.):

Excerpt 5.8

Firmly correcting the phenomenon of vulgarity and pandering to vulgarity (*di-su mei-su xianxiang*) found in program hosts' clothing, hairstyles, language, and overall style. ... To purify the linguistic environment, **crude and foul language is forbidden**; except for special needs, program hosts must use PTH. They should not mix PTH with foreign languages under the pretext of pursuing trendy speech styles. **Nor should they imitate the style of expression and pronunciation of *Gang-Tai* speech.**

Following SARFT's call for purification, more measures to monitor the language of broadcasters and program hosts were carried out in 2005. To curb the tendency of vulgarity and pandering to vulgarity (to use the terms from the SARFT 2004 document) or to *"tuosu"* 'shed vulgarity' or 'de-vulgarize' (F. Li 2005; Xu 2005; H. Zhang 2005; X. Zhang 2005; N. Zhao 2005), the China Radio and Television Society published "The Self-Disciplining Conventions of Chinese Radio and Television Broadcasters and Hosts" in 2005 (SARFT 2005). Closely following the guidelines of the "Purification Project," the Conventions reiterate that "broadcasters and program hosts should refrain from unnecessary mixing of foreign languages in PTH and from imitating Hong Kong-Taiwan accent and its style of expression" (ibid.). While *Gang-Tai qiang* is among 20 or so items in the Self-Disciplining Conventions, it takes the headlines of news reports on the Conventions and is linked to vulgarity, such as the one from *People's Daily* "Broadcasters and hosts stipulate conventions, cannot intentionally imitate *Gang-Tai qiang*" (Xu 2005; see also Guo 2005). The *People's Daily* website promptly publicized a list of program hosts who use *"Gang-Tai qiang,"* which included Li Xiang (female), He Jiong (male), Xie Na (female), and Li Xia (female) among others (People.com.cn[15] 2005a). The first three were hosts of one of the most popular television game-variety shows *"Kuaile Dabenying"* 'Happy Headquarters' produced by Hunan Satellite Television. Li Xia was the former host and video jockey of MTV China and *"Yule Xianchang"* 'Entertainment Live', produced by

Enlight Media. Young, ebullient, and glamorous, they are loved by many as exemplary speakers of a new Mandarin style and at the same time abhorred by others as notorious imitators of *Gang-Tai qiang*. In accusations of the causes for vulgarization tendencies, marketization is the culprit; it has led to the opportunist pursuit of high ratings and revenues and lowered quality of program hosts due to an over-emphasis on looks (H. Zhang 2005; Qiang and Wang 2007). The deputy director of SARFT charges that, "many hosts have merely a pretty face and gift of gab, but their own quality is not high. The vulgarity of programs thus reflects the vulgarity of the hosts themselves" (H. Zhang 2005, 11).

The official stance on *Gang-Tai qiang* is best summarized in an article in the *People's Daily Overseas Edition*, "*Cuo bu zai 'Gang-Tai qiang'*" 'The fault is not with "Hong Kong-Taiwan accent"' (Chen 2010). The article starts with an observation that it is now a common phenomenon that entertainers and media professionals in mainland China speak with a strong "*Gang-Tai qiang.*" The author explains that there is nothing wrong with speaking PTH with a *Gang-Tai* accent if one is from Hong Kong or Taiwan. However, it is wrong for Chinese mainlanders to speak with such an accent (Chen 2010, 3):[16]

Excerpt 5.9

[Speaking with a *Gang-Tai* accent] **is to be deliberately unconventional to appear superior or different from others; ... intellectually immature and blindly following trends and imitating; a dishonest person; ...** it reflects **superficiality and affectation...**

The above metadiscourses produced by the state and government organizations demonstrate that the state attempts to control the $n+1$st order indexicality of the new Mandarin style. Labeling it as *Gang-Tai qiang* creates an n-th order indexicality that locates its geographical origin and its "native" speakers *outside* of mainland China. Such indexicality enables $n+1$st order interpretations of mainlanders as illegitimate users and their use of *Gang-Tai qiang* as imitation and thus unnatural, inauthentic, and deviant. The imitated fake accent is in turn construed as reflecting the speaker's defective, problematic character, including lack of self-confidence and creativity, lack of sound judgment, low quality, opportunism, inferior taste or vulgarity, dishonesty, intellectual immaturity, and superficiality. Despite acknowledging that *Gang-Tai qiang* is connected to trendiness (e.g., in Excerpts 5.7 and 5.8), the official metadiscourses explicitly exclude and reject any positive interpretation of "trendiness" as an $n+1$st order indexicality. Instead, the government attempts to link Standard PTH to *shishang* 'stylishness/trendiness', as shown in the following officially approved slogans for the 2005 Putonghua Promotion and Publicity Week (Ministry of Education 2005):

Excerpt 5.10

Putonghua—shidai de xuqiu, **shishang de zhuiqiu**
'*Putonghua*—demand of the times, **pursuit of stylishness/trendiness**'

Putonghua—tong qingchun xieshou, **wenming yu he shishang bingjian**
'*Putonghua* and youth hand in hand, **civilized language and stylishness shoulder to shoulder**'

All such efforts are aimed at maintaining the normative and legitimate status of Beijing-Mandarin-based PTH, preventing positive perceptions of the new Mandarin style, and further preventing role alignment from mainland speakers.

It is not surprising that the state's counter-enregisterment efforts target heavily television entertainment program hosts—not only their language but also their image—as they are the state-designated exemplary speakers of Standard PTH. Outnumbering news broadcasters (see H. Zhang 2005)—the most conservative exemplary speakers of Standard PTH—the entertainment program hosts reach a wider audience and play a crucial role in the enregisterment of CM.

Recent reforms in the CCTV news programs indicate that the state is making efforts to change the images of the exemplary speakers, to make them look more attractive and appealing to the audience, particularly young viewers. For example, in July 2009, CCTV revamped some of its news programs in an effort to introduce more new and young news anchors who are "required to present a relaxed and amiable style" (Xinhuanet 2009). Recall that this is the style performed by the TV hosts of *S Information Station* in Chapter 4. The reform included giving a "*bian lian*" 'face change' to the Morning News program of CCTV-News (ibid.). These new anchors, such as Hu Die (anchor of "Morning News") and Guo Qiming (anchor of CCTV-News "24 Hours"), have incited much media coverage and online chatters about their attractive and stylish looks (e.g., ibid.; M. Li 2009).[17] More new and younger faces appeared in the CCTV flagship program *Xinwen Lianbo* 'Network News Broadcast' in 2011. Referred to as the *xin guo lian* 'new face(s) of the nation', the new anchors Ouyang Xiadan and Lang Yongchun are young and trendy (Ning 2011). Compared with the "*zhuangzhong yansu*" 'solemn and serious' style of their predecessors, the new anchors were reported to be "amiable" and "a bit ebullient" (Yang 2011). Such attributes again remind us of the persona of the TV hosts in Chapter 4. Using younger and (more) attractive news anchors and encouraging them to display amiability clearly show the state's efforts to "reform the packaging" (Xinhuanet 2009) of the exemplary speakers of the national standard language. Table 5.2 summarizes the state's counter-enregisterment tactics in regimenting the *n*+1st order indexicality of CM in the name of "*Gang-Tai qiang.*"

5.2.4 Other Public Sphere Metadiscourses

The state's campaign against *Gang-Tai qiang* incited heated discussions in the media and online discussion forums, which I analyze here. As mentioned in 5.2.2, a discussion on this topic at Tianya.cn attracted nearly 2,000 responses and was viewed 151,331 times in a two-and-a-half month period in 2012. The

TABLE 5.2 State's Construals of "*Gang-Tai Qiang*" vis-à-vis Standard *Putonghua*

Order of Indexicality	Standard Putonghua (rhotacization, neutral tone)	"Gang-Tai Qiang" (de-rhotacization, full tone)
n-th order indexicality: geographical association	Beijing, the North	Hong Kong and Taiwan
n+1st order indexicality: social distinction	Supraregional Chinese identity, modernity, national unity, social equality and egalitarianism, authenticity, moral uprightness, stylishness and trendiness (based on discussion in Sections 0.5.1–0.5.4 and Section 5.2.3)	Inauthenticity, neither fish nor fowl, lack of self-confidence, lack of sound judgment, vulgarity, superficiality, affectation, mammonism (based on discussion in Section 5.2.3)

following titles of articles and online discussion threads illustrate the contested nature of the debate over the cultural values of "*Gang-Tai qiang*":

- Why does "*Gang-Tai qiang*" matter so much? (*Nanfang Dushi Bao* 2004)
- "*Gang-Tai qiang*" "*Taiwan qiang*"—attacking tool fabricated by tongue-curling people (Xing-xun-bi-gong 2005, at tianya.cn)
- Tens of thousands signing to protest SARFT "*Gang-Tai qiang*" incident! What crime does "*Gang-Tai qiang*" commit? (Kuaile-cuojue 2005, at tianya.cn)
- "*Putonghua*" and cultural chauvinism (Yi-shi-ma-li 2008, at blog.sina.com.cn)
- Why nobody blames TV dramas full of Beijing vernacular, but so called *Gang-Tai qiang* should be despised (fedent 2009, at zzetyy.com).
- Southern accent is called *Gang-Tai qiang*, then why shouldn't Beijing vernacular and Northeastern dialect be called Manchurian accent? (softree 2008, at tianya.cn)
- Northern accent is superior? Southern accent is called *Gang-Tai qiang*? (Hen-jia-hen-hexie 2010, at tianya.cn.)

Many commenters share negative interpretations of *Gang-Tai qiang* as mainlanders' affected imitation of the native accent of people from Hong Kong and Taiwan and reflecting negative attributes of the imitator, similar to those seen in earlier examples (e.g., Zao-chun qingchen 2010). The following is a representative example from an online response to the topic "Media critique: Should hosts' '*Gang-Tai qiang*' be struck or not?" initiated by/on People.com.cn (2005b) soon after the publication of the SARFT "Self-Disciplining Conventions." *Gang-Tai qiang* is linked to hosts with attractive looks but low quality, who resort to it as a sex-appeal strategy, 'being coquettish' or *mai-nong-feng-sao*, to

156 Warring Standards

promote the viewing rate. The imitation is described with the Chinese idiom *dong-shi-xiao-pin* 'crude imitation with ludicrous effects' and is berated as being ridiculous, lamentable, self-deprecating, and superficial (219.137.212. 2005).

Excerpt 5.11

These hosts are mostly handsome guys and pretty girls .... They don't have much quality, can't talk much in front of the screen. To compete for viewing rate, they can only rely on being **coquettish**. But can't imagine the CCTV's hosts who have high cultural quality would also do **crude imitation with ludicrous effects**!!! **Extremely ridiculous**. ... **Lamentable**!!! How can they be so **self-deprecating**??? **Superficial** ah....

The evaluations of *Gang-Tai qiang* are not all derogatory and disparaging. The debate over the cultural values of *Gang-Tai qiang* challenges the taken-for-granted normativity and superiority of Standard PTH, specifically, its Beijing and Northern Mandarin basis. In the data presented below, valorizations of *Gang-Tai qiang* focus on two issues. First, the evaluations of *Gang-Tai qiang* are always in relation to other *hua* 'speech/dialects' or *qiang* 'accents', particularly *nanfang hua* 'Southern speech/dialects', and *beifang hua* 'Northern Mandarin', including BM. Second, the construals often draw on established and familiar cultural models of contrast at other levels. In Section 5.2.4.1, the very label *"Gang-Tai qiang"* is being challenged. I then show how the northern/Beijing-biased normativity of Standard PTH is contested (Section 5.2.4.2), and in Section 5.2.4.3 I present arguments for *Gang-Tai qiang* as an alternative Mandarin style (not a *difang kouyin* 'regional accent') to Standard PTH. In Section 5.2.4.4, I present recursive projections of the contrast between *Gang-Tai qiang* and Standard PTH onto other spatial and temporal scales.

5.2.4.1 Challenging the Label "Gang-Tai Qiang"

Many commenters challenge the validity of the label *"Gang-Tai qiang,"* for example, calling it "the greatest invention of the Chinese lexicon of the 21st century" (Feng-xing-xia 2005; also Chang-ting-yuan-man1 2005). Some question the presupposed linguistic basis for the "accent," pointing out the linguistic differences between Hong Kong Cantonese and Taiwanese or Southern Min and hence the groundlessness of the compound accent (e.g., Bai-jia-zi-fengle 2005; Jun-fei-fan 2005; Xing-xun-bi-gong 2005a). Excerpt 5.12 is from a thread titled "'Gang-Tai qiang' 'Taiwan qiang' attacking tool fabricated by tongue-curling people" (Xing-xun-bi-gong 2005a):[18]

Excerpt 5.12

People from Taiwan and Hong Kong would never use the term *"Gang-Tai qiang."* If there really is a so-called *Gang-Tai* accented *Putonghua* in the world, it might be the *Putonghua* spoken by people from Chao Zhou and Shan Tou.[19] ... But people from Taiwan and Hong Kong speak Southern Min and Cantonese respectively, therefore if one must find the so-called "*Gang-Tai qiang*", it can only be "*Chao-Shan qiang*" [Teochew accent]. Recently I found a welcoming phenomenon in the forum. Many people have already known that *Gang-Tai qiang* is a fabricated thing, but then a new term has emerged—"*Taiwan qiang*". This is what is called if one wants to condemn somebody, it's easy to trump up charges. ... **The so called "*Gang-Tai qiang*" and "*Taiwan qiang*" are nothing but an attacking tool of the tongue-curling people.**

The author applies her/his linguistic knowledge to explain that *Gang-Tai qiang* does not exist in reality.[20] By calling *Gang-Tai qiang* "an attacking tool of the tongue-curling people," the commenter implicitly suggests that those with vested interest in the term are northern speakers and those who uphold Northern Mandarin as the norm of PTH, as "tongue-curling" is commonly known to be associated with Northern Mandarin. Hence the term "*Gang-Tai qiang*" and the government's efforts to purge it from Standard PTH is viewed as targeting and discriminating against southern PTH speakers and privileging Beijing and Northern Mandarin speakers. Such a view is shared among other commenters (e.g., Mei-suo-mi-ya 2005; Chang-ting-yuan-man1 2005; Jun-fei-fan 2005). Many further contest the normativity and superiority of Beijing and Northern Mandarin (e.g., the discussion threads initiated by fedent 2009, Hen-jia-hen-hexie 2010, and numerous responses to these threads). As shown in the next section, "tongue-curling" and "tongue-curling sounds" (including rhotacization and retroflex initials), which are emblematic of BM and Standard PTH, often become the focal point of contention.

5.2.4.2 Challenging the Normativity, Authenticity, and Superiority of Beijing-/Northern-Mandarin-Based Putonghua

The superiority of Beijing and Northern Mandarin as the phonological, lexical, and grammatical norms of Modern Standard Chinese (both spoken and written) has been established since the early 20th century. Regarding the spoken standard language, ever since the adoption of BM as the phonetic basis for the National Language Romanization in 1926 (De Francis 1950), no other spoken Chinese variety has been able to challenge BM as the base dialect of the spoken standard language. The geographical and dialectal specificities of the "common speech" seem to have been forgotten. However, the debate on *Gang-Tai qiang* has incited counter-valorization of Beijing and Northern Mandarin as the standard norm.

As I discuss, in the following examples, many commenters object both to (a) *Gang-Tai qiang* being singled out as the culprit of non-standard speech and (b) the impunity endowed upon Beijing and Northern Mandarin. Many question the taken-for-granted "standardness" of Northern Mandarin (e.g., Bai-dan-mei 2005; Jun-fei-fan 2005; Jue-zhan-dou-shi 2005) and call for

158 Warring Standards

banning Beijing and Northern Mandarin accents on TV and radio (e.g., Hu-li-shao-ye 2005; KTV-ah-KTV 2005; lakaya 2005):

Excerpt 5.13 (Yun-an 2005)
If one wants to criticize others imitating *Gang-Tai* accent, then they have to simultaneously criticize those who imitate Beijing accent! **I don't think the two are different in terms of superiority and inferiority.**

Excerpt 5.14 (Rong-yan-lao-si-ji 2007)
I've found in many [television and radio] stations that the hosts' Beijing vernacular is very strong. Why aren't they criticized! In the regulation of the Broadcasting Association, why does it specifically focus on prohibiting imitation of *Gang-Tai* accent? **Why doesn't it blame that now many hosts speak in Beijing dialect with a curled tongue?**

In a similar way to the state metadiscourse that deauthenticates *Gang-Tai qiang* as a faked imitation and lacking a long history in contrast to the national language, some commenters contest the authenticity of Beijing and Northern Mandarin. A shared strategy of valorization and authentication among several posts claims historical continuity (Coupland 2003) of Southern Chinese from ancient Chinese and identifies emblematic features of BM, particularly rhotacization and retroflex initials, as the result of Manchu[21] influence brought about by the Manchu conquest, which established the Qing Dynasty. In this way, the base dialect of Standard PTH is conceived as being historically contaminated by non-Han and non-Chinese influence (e.g., Fa-ke-you-tu 2005; Zhen-mo-ming-qi-miao 2008; softree 2008; Hen-jia-hen-hexie 2010; Pigu-juntuan 2010; He-xin 2011). For instance, in Excerpt 5.15 below, from the thread "Northern accent is superior? Southern accent is called *Gang-Tai* accent?," the commenter Hen-jia-hen-hexie opposes the superiority of BM represented by "tongue-curling sounds," rhotacization, and a few stereotypic local expressions. In her/his view, southern accents are mislabeled as *"Gang-Tai qiang"* mainly due to what s/he calls *"yuqi zhuci"* 'modal particles' or sentence-final particles. The author explains that these particles are descendants of ancient Chinese, thus tracing the origin of *Gang-Tai qiang* to classical Chinese. S/he further legitimates the authenticity of southern Chinese as having a long history and the South as the origin of the Han/Chinese language. Finally, to devalue and delegitimize BM even further, s/he describes Beijing accent as "PTH with Manchu-Qing [Dynasty] enslaved rhotacization" and expresses her/his scornful attitude toward it by asking *"suan shenme dongxi?"* 'What is [this kind of PTH] supposed to be?':[22]

Excerpt 5.15 (Hen-jia-hen-hexie 2010)
You [polite form, sarcastic] speak in broad Beijing vernacular, tongue-curling sounds and rhotacization, but don't allow southerners to use modal particles passed down from the ancient [Chinese] language?

Generation after generation we like to say *"lieh" "wah" "geh" "youh"* [sentence-final particles], but these are regarded as *Gang-Tai qiang*. **You [polite form, sarcastic] with a mouthful of tongue-curling sounds can ascend to the hall of elegance?** Calling our modal particles *Gang-Tai qiang*? **Then *"zhi hu zhe"* [classical literary Chinese particles] are also antecedents of *Gang-Tai qiang lieh*!**

You [polite form, sarcastic] can always say in a grand manner *"zhe gala"* [this corner] *"na jijiao"* [that corner] *"sha wanyir"* [what is it].[23] Is what shitted out of your mouth Standard PTH? If southerners say *"hao haochi youh"* [very delicious *youh*] *"you-mei-you zhe yangzi yah"* [Isn't it like this *yah*] *"you-mei-you gao cuo lah"* [what's wrong *lah*],[24] then it is called *Gang-Tai qiang*? ...

Southern ancient language has a long history. Moreover the South is the origin of the Han language. The Southern dialects are numerous and complex, but they all habitually use many modal particles. **Just like ancient people like to say *zhi hu zhe ye* [classical literary Chinese particles]. This is our habit.** It's not your turn to point the finger at us.

Our PTH with southern habits is deemed *Gang-Tai qiang*? **Then what is your PTH with Manchu-Qing [Dynasty] enslaved rhotacization supposed to be?**

In the above excerpt, the most emblematic feature of BM, rhotacization, is conceived as the shameful linguistic consequence of Manchu-Qing conquest and enslavement of the Han Chinese and Han language. Similar claims of Southern Chinese varieties retaining more linguistic features from ancient Chinese than Beijing and Northern Mandarin are also documented among Southern Min speakers in DeBernardi (1991) and Su (2008) as a counter-valorization strategy against the politically dominant Taiwan *Guoyu* (Standard Mandarin in Taiwan). Such claims are partially supported by linguistic evidence. Some linguists (Norman 1988; Ramsey 1987) observe that some of the Southern varieties, such as Wu, Cantonese, and Southern Min, preserve more of the linguistic features found in Middle Chinese than Northern varieties, particularly the preservation of the *ru sheng* 'entering tone' and (more) final consonants. However, Hen-jia-hen-hexie's (2010) assertion above that the South is the origin of the Chinese language and that the southern sentence-final particles are descendants of the classical Chinese particles *zhi, hu, zhe*, and *ye* are unfounded.

Rhotacization is similarly challenged as the norm of Standard PTH in the following post by Bai-dan-mei (2005). In addition to objecting to the non-rhotacized PTH of southern announcers as nonstandard and being labeled as *Gang-Tai qiang*, the commenter perceives the difference in terms of different linguistic styles appropriate for different programs.

Excerpt 5.16
What exactly is Standard PTH? Is it what is spoken by Beijingers?
I found that CCTV news broadcasters all use rhotacization with many words,

160 Warring Standards

for example it is obviously "*Gongzhu Fen*" [place name in Beijing], but broadcasters must pronounce it as "*Gongzhu Fer*." If it's pronounced by southern broadcasters, it would be "*Gongzhu Fen*". But it's considered nonstandard PTH if pronounced like this [without rhotacization] by southern announcers. It's called *Gang-Tai qiang*, but CCTV broadcasters' "*Gongzhu Fer*" is regarded as "Standard PTH". Is this fair? Such examples are too many.

...

I can't imagine that hosts of variety entertainment programs use the newscast style. That would be too strange. I think the host's style should be appropriate to the style of the program. They can't be all the same.

5.2.4.3 Gang-Tai Qiang as an Alternative Style to Standard PTH

Similar to the above comment in Excerpt 5.16, many also view the so-called *Gang-Tai qiang* as an alternative style to express other feelings and emotions for which Standard PTH is inappropriate or inadequate (e.g., Planelove 2005; 4rain 2005; genzxc 2005; Zhuang 2005). In the following excerpt from Zhuang Liwei's (2005) essay "*Gang-Tai* Speech Is Also Chinese," Standard PTH is described as "harsh," "didactic," and "officialese." Likened to "linguistic rocks" (*yuyan shitou*), it is deemed too heavily charged with political intentions to express happy emotions of ordinary folks.

Excerpt 5.17
It would be a horrifying situation if folks from all over the country have to use *Putonghua* or Beijing accented *Putonghua* to express their happy feelings. In fact, there are reasons for the "invasion" of *Gang-Tai qiang*. If we don't reflect on and discard the harsh tone, didactic tone, and officialese from the mainland broadcast media, then other popular and lively substitutes will naturally "invade." **The large amount of political vocabulary and political tone in *Putonghua* are like pieces of linguistic rocks.**

Similarly, commenter 4rain (2005) contends that "all hosts speak PTH, but they just emphasize differences [with different accents]. ... Some people feel that **such a style of speech [*Gang-Tai qiang*] is adorable, ... has stronger amiability and easy reception. ... It feels weird to talk about intimate topics using authentic PTH**." As s/he goes on to explain why *Gang-Tai qiang* is popular and widespread in the next excerpt, we begin to see why the enregisterment of CM is a high-stake battle for the state:

Excerpt 5.18
American culture is (more) powerful (*qiang shi*), so we learn "bye bye ... OK! Yes." ***Gang-Tai* culture is powerful, so we of course have to learn from *Gang-Tai*.** If Beijing doesn't concede, it can strengthen its culture and cultural influence so that we'll talk with a Beijing accent. ... Think about how our

Gang-Tai qiang is formed. When we were young watching the Spring Festival Gala, some actors deliberately faked a *Gang-Tai* accent, like "Mister, your ponytail is very very-pretty lah......" [see Excerpt 5.1 lines 46–47].

The government certainly does not want to see the *Gang-Tai qiang* being linked to a "more advanced" culture whose center is not Beijing. Interestingly, at the end of this excerpt the commenter attributes the spread and uptake of *Gang-Tai qiang* by mainlanders to its use in mass-mediated events such as the CCTV Spring Festival Gala. S/he even cites an example of its use from the 1995 comic skit "Packaging in Such a Way" analyzed in Excerpt 5.1. This attests to my earlier observation that despite the wide reach of the state media, the principal and the author cannot control the reception of the intended (negative) message created in the skit. However, the contrast between the so-called *Gang-Tai qiang* and Standard PTH performed on stage is so palpable and memorable—even being remembered nearly a decade later by 4rain (2005)—that the CCTV Spring Festival Galas may have helped the propagation of the new Mandarin style.

Many also deemed Beijing/Standard Mandarin *tu* 'bumpkinish' or 'rustic' compared with *Gang-Tai qiang* and hence an inappropriate linguistic style for young, trendy characters and related social attributes (fedent 2009; Ren-dan-di-shi-yi 2003; Yu-rong-qiu 2009). In Excerpt 5.19 from the thread "Why nobody comments on TV dramas full of Beijing vernacular, but so-called *Gang-Tai qiang* is despised?," fedent (2009) first objects to the double standard applied to *Gang-Tai qiang* and BM in television. S/he then links Beijing vernacular to qualities of being "rustic, oily, and vulgar," which make it incompatible with young and glamorous characters in what is called "*ouxiang ju*"(idol television dramas), which are very popular among young people in China (fedent 2009).

Excerpt 5.19

A nice TV drama, good cast, good plot, but one always hears Beijing vernacular. "*War*" [play], "*shir*"[matter], a normal sentence, **when added rhotacization or exaggerated posterior nasal sounds,**[25] **will immediately make one feel rustic, oily/smooth, vulgar.** ... If Beijing vernacular is allowed to be spoken, why isn't *Gang-Tai qiang*? ... **Is it a good thing that after 50 years, ... everybody in the country will speak Beijing vernacular? Then China will really become a country of bumpkins.** With the economic development of the mainland, glamorous idol television dramas will appear sooner or later. I don't want to hear handsome guys and pretty women in the dramas speaking Beijing vernacular. It seriously affects the enjoyability of the drama.

The preceding sections (5.2.4.1–5.2.4.3) present evaluations of the new Mandarin style in relation to Beijing/Northern Mandarin and Standard PTH that challenges particular cultural values associated with the national standard language, i.e., normativity, superiority, authenticity, and legitimacy. The last

162 Warring Standards

two examples perceived *"Gang-Tai qiang"* as an alternative style to Beijing-Mandarin-based PTH due to the latter's indexical inappropriateness and inadequacy to express non-politically related emotions and to enact trendy, youthful, and glamorous characters. The social evaluations focus on particular salient linguistic features that differentiate the styles of Mandarin. In the next section, I further explore the contrast between *Gang-Tai qiang* and conventional PTH construed at broader scales and how such construals come about.

5.2.4.4 Gang-Tai Qiang vs. Putonghua: Recursive Construals

The social evaluations of *Gang-Tai qiang* vis-à-vis Northern/Beijing-Mandarin-based PTH do not come from nowhere—although *Gang-Tai qiang* is a relatively new phenomenon, the first-order contrast based on the geographical associations of the North and the South is reinterpreted drawing on pre-existing cultural models of differentiation familiar to many Chinese speakers. Through fractal recursivity (Irvine and Gal 2000), the contrast at one level is projected onto other spatial and temporal scales, specifically, that between China (and the East) and the West (e.g., Cheng-lang-ke 2012; Zhu-yue-yue 2011), the old and the young (e.g., Jue-zhan-dou-shi 2005; Yi-ming 2005), and the past and the present (e.g., Wang and Lao 2000).

The following long excerpt from my interview with an editor at a local television station includes several of such recursive renderings. Her comment that hosts of entertainment programs have "traits of *Gang-Tai* but not the real *Gang-Tai* accent" (lines 12–13) indicates that she does not see the hosts' linguistic style as an imitation or reproduction of someone else's *Gang-Tai* accent but rather as drawing on elements from Hong Kong and Taiwan ways of speaking.

Excerpt 5.20 <Interview with Li, 28, 7-25-2009>

1	QZ:	What are the TV station's current requirements of hosts.
2	Li:	The State Administration of Radio Film and Television
3		requires [hosts] to speak Standard *Putonghua*.
4		There are regulations in the (official) document.
...		
11	Li:	A:::, sometimes,
12		[Hosts of entertainment programs] have traits of *Gang-Tai*.
13		but it's not the REAL *Gang-Tai* accent.
14	QZ:	What do you think they sound like?
15		If I ask you to do it?
16	Li:	((in a higher pitch)) A::, how do you all feel about this *ne:::*?
		((lengthened sentence-final particle))
17		Audience **friends**? ((*pengyou-men* [T2]))
18		Hello everybody.

19		**Thanks.** ((*xiexie* [T4]))
20		Thank ((*xiexie* [T4])) you ((*nimen* [T2])) *ou:::.* ((lengthened sentence-final particle))
21		It's just like this.
22		But one may also say that **it's affectedly sweet.**
...		
34	Li:	China's **traditional** *Putonghua* **or**
35		**broadcasting style is very orthodox.**
...		
40		*Gang-Tai* **accent sounds quite casual quite leisurely,** I feel.
41		Maybe **traditional broadcasting style**
42		**young people will feel a bit bumpkinish.**
43		Like the grand programs of CCTV.
44		even though they are entertainment programs
45		they are still orthodox.
...		
58	Li:	**People feel that** *Gang-Tai* **is more advanced than us.**
59		**and also trendy.**
60		**So some people use** *Gang-Tai* **accent.**
61		**They won't use country accent right?**
62		**Country accent is for humor.**
63		*Gang-Tai* **accent will feel like**
64		**this person is fashionable/Western.**
65		**It's to learn from more advanced places.**
66		**Because** *Gang-Tai* **is more advanced than us.**
...		
72	Li:	For example.
73		**people will use a little foreign language in their talk.**
74		**You'll feel that it's trendy.**
75		**You might use a couple of words from America,**
76		**because you feel it's a developed country.**
77		**But it's not possible**
78		**you'll say a sentence in Ethiopian right?**
79		**Nobody will.**
80		**So you speak** *Gang-Tai* **accent again because**
81		**they are more advanced and trendier than us.**

In the first half of the excerpt, we see the contrasting characteristics associated with *Gang-Tai* accent and traditional *Putonghua* similar to those in earlier examples (e.g., orthodox vs. casual [lines 34–35, 40, 43–45], *tu* 'bumpkinish' vs. *yang* 'fashionable/Western' [lines 41–42]). From line 58, she further projects the contrast between the two styles onto several spatial scales, *Gang-Tai* vs. mainland (lines 58–60), urban vs. the rural (lines 61–66), developed world (represented by the United States) vs. underdeveloped world (represented by Ethiopia) (lines 72–79). In each of the pairs, the former (and its

164 Warring Standards

accent/language) are viewed as being more advanced and trendier than the latter. Although such recursive construals from an editor at a local television station will certainly not create enough jitters to put the (language) authorities on edge, similar interpretations from the vast online discussions and, as I present next, from more prominent voices will.

The stake in the enregisterment battle becomes more explicit in the recursive interpretations illuminated in the writings of eminent Chinese writers, including the 2010 Nobel Peace Prize Laureate Liu Xiaobo (2000), Wang Shuo and Lao Xia (2000),[26] and Yu Jie (2010). Liu and Yu are also dissident intellectuals and democracy activists whose many works are banned in the mainland.[27] Wang Shuo is a writer and novelist who is well-known for his Beijing vernacular writing style.

In Excerpt 5.21, Liu Xiaobo (2000) observes that since the 1990s, *Gang-Tai qiang* has rapidly spread in mainland China and has become the trendy language of young people. This is explained as related to a shift in the types of emotions or sentiments that are valorized in the pre-reform Mao era and the contemporary 1990s:

Excerpt 5.21

Mao era's uplifting politicized expression of grand/lofty emotions [*fan zhengzhi hua da shu xing*]... has been dominated by the **Gang-Tai model of secular minor sentiments**[28] in the 1990s. ... Especially the spoiled people of the neo-neo tribe, whenever they need to express emotions, they will use *Gang-Tai qiang*.

He further predicts, as quoted at the beginning of this chapter, that "the Chinese model for expressing sentiments will come to be unified ... to '*Gang-Tai Putonghua*.'" Although Standard PTH is not explicitly mentioned, Liu's comment makes it obvious that it will be replaced by *Gang-Tai* PTH. This is an audacious remark, going head to head against the official discourse that Beijing-Mandarin-based Standard PTH represents the unified voice of the people of China. In this excerpt, we see a clear example of recursivity: The contrast between *Gang-Tai qiang* and Standard PTH is reinterpreted as a temporal schism between the contemporary and the Mao era; a contrast in emotions is also mapped onto the temporal dichotomy.

Closely related to the temporal and emotional dichotomy mentioned in Liu (2000), the contrast between Standard PTH and *Gang-Tai qiang* is interpreted as a quality difference between the hard/harsh and the soft in Wang and Lao (2000). The soft *Gang-Tai qiang* and the hard Standard PTH is again mapped onto the temporal contrast between the contemporary and the pre-reform revolutionary past (ibid.):

Excerpt 5.22

Gang-Tai style soft *Putonghua* is now directly threatening the *Putonghua* based on Northern Mandarin [ibid., 227]. ... So the language of our generation ... has been completely overwhelmed by *Gang-Tai* bird language[29] [ibid., 228]. ... **The young people nowadays are accustomed to accepting the kind of soft, tender-feeling accent, unlike the hard slogans we were used to hear when we were young**[30] [ibid., 229]. ... *Gang-Tai qiang*'s immense popularity really sweeps away everything in a **tender-and-soft-as-water** manner [ibid., 232]. ... Its [*Gang-Tai qiang*] soft accent disables the red language ["formed after 1949"] among young people, the so-called sugarcoated bullet, whoever eats it becomes soft [ibid., 233].

The mapping of contrast in language onto quality, temporal, and other schemes of differentiation is similar to Harkness's (2011) examination of the Korean fricative voiceless gestures (FVGs). Variants of the same voiceless fricative sound are perceived as "soft" and "harsh," and these qualities are reinterpreted and mapped onto differentiations along the paradigms of class, time, and gender. In the Korean case, it is also the quality of "softness" that gets linked to the young, the modern, and the contemporary. Similar to the ascendancy of softness in the South Korean society, the increasing popularity of the "soft" *Gang-Tai qiang* is emblematic of change in the larger value system of the Chinese society. That is, it mirrors the change from the "harshness" of the pre-reform emphasis on cultural-political conformity and the struggle between "us," the revolutionary proletariat and "them," the counter-revolutionary enemies, to the "softness" of the postsocialist valorization and tolerance of different ways of expressing differentiation.

5.3 Conclusion

The analysis of metalinguistic discourses in this chapter reveals that the process of enregisterment is fraught with contestation. The multiple *n*+1st order indexical values of the new Mandarin in relation to Standard PTH are summarized in Table 5.3. When compared with Table 5.1, we see that the picture of indexicality presented there highlights consistent, positive social meanings of both, and absence of conflict in their indexical values. In sharp contrast, Table 5.3 reveals indexical inconsistency and conflict. Only by examining a large range of metapragmatic discourses produced by different speakers, including individuals and institutions, can we reveal such multiple construals from different and conflicting perspectives.[31] Ironically, in its efforts to regiment the *n*+1st order indexicality of the new style by restricting it to a regional accent—"*Gang-Tai qiang*"—and placing it outside of the mainland, the state has reminded many of the Northern provenance of the "common speech." As shown in the comments presented earlier, by highlighting the Beijing/Northern origin of PTH and linking it to attributes such as *tu* 'rustic', the enregisterment battle undermines the normativity and symbolic dominance of the standard language.

The analysis also demonstrates that enregisterment is a relational and contrastive process whereby the emergent Mandarin style and its salient features

166 Warring Standards

TABLE 5.3 *N*-th and *n*+1st Order Indexicality of Standard *Putonghua* and Cosmopolitan Mandarin

Order of Indexicality	Standard Putonghua (rhotacization, neutral tone)	Cosmopolitan Mandarin (de-rhotacization, full tone)
n-th order indexicality: geographical association	Beijing, the North	The South, including Hong Kong and Taiwan
n+1st order indexicality: social distinction	State and some individuals: supraregional Chinese identity, modernity, national unity, social equality and egalitarianism, authenticity, moral uprightness (based on discussion in Sections 0.5.1–0.5.4 and Section 5.2.3) Individuals: rustic, vulgar, inauthentic, orthodox, didactic, old, underdeveloped, hard/harsh, the past/Mao era	State and some individuals: "*Gang-Tai qiang*" Inauthentic, neither fish nor fowl, lack of (national) self-respect and confidence, lack of sound judgment, vulgar, superficial, affected, mammonism Beijing yuppies and TV hosts: cosmopolitan Chinese, being cultured and tasteful, stylishness, trendiness, sophistication, youthful ebullience and conviviality (based on analysis in Chapters 3 and 4) Individuals, popular media: trendy, cosmopolitan, soft, advanced, amiable, ebullient, non-political, young, casual, contemporary and the future/post Mao era

are most often recognized, typified, and evaluated vis-à-vis its most relevant Other style, that is, the Beijing-/Northern-Mandarin-based Standard PTH and its stereotypic features. At the same time, the construal of and contestation over the meanings of the new style will impact and reshape the indexical field of its relevant Other. As we have seen in the present study and in Table 5.3, when CM is interpreted as a deviant, affected *Gang-Tai qiang*, its relevant Other, Standard PTH is explicitly and implicitly construed as normal and authentic. On the contrary, when *Gang-Tai qiang* is believed to be the voice of the cosmopolitan, the young and trendy, and the contemporary and future, its counterpart—explicitly and implicitly—is associated with the regional/local, the bumpkinish, the old, and the past. Hence, the relational and contrastive nature of enregisterment is what makes the process prone to contestation.

This is why the state is keenly engaged in the counter-enregisterment battle in its effort to control the development of the postsocialist stylistic regime (see Chapter 1), because, as I explain below, which stylistic resource gets to index a supraregional Chinese identity and a modern unified Chinese nation is at stake. By examining the conflict over meanings at various planes of differentiation—the spatial, the temporal, and the sensual qualitative—the high stakes involved in the enregisterment process are revealed. It is not simply a matter of some young people's enthusiasm about pursuing trends and taking up a "trendy" accent. If the indexical values in the bottom right cell of Table 5.3 become stabilized and shared among a wide range of language users, CM will come to be an alternative and even competing stylistic resource for indexing a supraregional Chinese identity and a modern unified Chinese nation. Furthermore, it will come to challenge the indexical field/potential of Beijing-Mandarin-based PTH, whose indexical values will be limited to those presented in the middle bottom cell of the table.

In the final chapter of the book, I summarize the major findings from the investigation of the emergence of CM and reflect on the study's contribution to a style-based approach to sociolinguistic change. Drawing on the results of this chapter, I also offer a discussion about the future of CM.

Notes

1 I emphasize that "stablization" does not mean that the social evaluations are fixed or consistent across community members. As Agha's (2007) and others' works (e.g., Campbell-Kibler 2008; Johnstone and Kiesling 2008) have demonstrated, the cultural values attached to enregistered forms are not necessarily consistent among speakers.

2 *Xiaopin*, as a form of contemporary Chinese performing arts, which has grown in popularity since the mid-1980s, is understood by most Chinese as "short and comical theatrical performances" (Du 1998, 384). I adopt its English translation, "theatrical or comic skits," from Du (ibid.).

3 Du's (1998) research on televised *xiaopin* performances between 1984 and 1997 finds that about 60% of such comic skits in the first 5 years of the 1990s share the theme of parodying negative consequences of commercialism on people's behaviors, attitudes, and social relations.

4 *Ping Xi* 'Ping Opera' is a traditional Chinese opera originated in Tangshan, Hebei Province. Like many other traditional Chinese performing art forms, it is losing out to other "modern" performances in the market economy.

5 This is in effect, evidence for the enregisterment of CM.

6 I have not done a study on the perception of the two characters' styles. Two Chinese friends of mine who watched the skit commented on the effeminate style of the manager. One of them used the term *nüli nüqi* 'effeminate' (Gu Xiaojuan, personal communication); the other used the term *niangniang qiang* 'effeminate tone' (Xu Tao, personal communication). A colleague from Taiwan also characterized his overall style as *niang*, meaning effeminate (E Chen-chun, personal communication).

7 The humor of the skit is largely created through the incongruity between the semiotic materials used for the packaging and the target of that packaging. The former consists of the new linguistic style, Western style clothing, and hip-hop dancing and singing style. The latter consists of the elderly traditional Ping Opera performer, her local dialect, and her Ping-Opera performance style. The effectiveness of the humor depends on the audience sharing the recognition and understanding of such incongruity.

168 Warring Standards

8　*Niao yu* 'bird language' refers to speech that is unfamiliar or foreign, and hard to understand. Here 'bird language' refers to "*Gang-Tai* accent."

9　*Xin xin renlei* 'neo-neo tribe', according to Jing Wang (2005), refers to "Asia's hottest market segment. Members of this emerging tribe are in their late teens and early 20s and cross gender divisions. They have a symbiotic existence with high-tech communication gadgets. Their threshold for irreverence is immeasurable... [T]he Chinese term *xin xin renlei* is a transliteration of the Japanese term *shin shin jinrei* introduced to the mainland via Hong Kong and Taiwan" (2005, 545). "This is a generation known to care about nothing but 'fashion,' 'hair styles,' 'computer gadgets' and 'relationships'" (2005, 546).

10　The tonal manipulation is represented in Chinese characters as 为沈摸　for *wei4shen3mo1* whereas the prescriptive PTH pronunciation in characters should be 为什么　*wei4shen2me0*.

11　The discussion thread is titled "*Beijing qiang, Dongbei qiang, Gang-Tai qiang*, 818 *naxie bu haohao shuohua de yirenmen*" 'Beijing accent, Northeastern accent, Hong Kong-Taiwan accent, gossip about those performers who don't talk normally', initiated by Marklesgaybi on March 22, 2012 at 10:23:00. www.tianya.cn/public-forum/content/funinfo/1/3194918.shtml

12　This article was a winner of the 1999–2000 Ministry of Education Award for Excellent News Reports and (Research) Articles. See awardees list at www.ruiwen.com/news/4112.htm

13　The author's name is Zhong4 Yan2, 仲言, homophonous with zhong4 yan2 众言 'words from the masses', and zhong1 yan2 忠言 'honest/loyal advice'. Informed mainland Chinese readers would quickly recognize that a *People's Daily* article with such a penname reflects the view of the party-state. The full article is accessible at www.people.com.cn/GB/news/8410/20020929/833951.html

14　The "Purification Project" is one of four projects in the SARFT's "Implementation plan for strengthening and improving the spiritual and moral construction of Chinese minors."

15　People.com.cn is People's Daily Online, the online platform of the CCP's flagship newspaper *Renmin Ribao, People's Daily.*

16　The full article is accessible at http://paper.people.com.cn/rmrbhwb/html/2010-08/10/content_591962.htm#

17　Hu Die was voted by online fans as "the most beautiful anchorwoman of CCTV" (Xinhuanet 2009).

18　This thread was viewed 1,263 times and generated 54 responses.

19　Chao Zhou and Shan Tou are in eastern Guangdong Province. The author explains that *Chao-Shan hua* or Teochew is a Southern Min dialect, but its pronunciation is influenced by Cantonese and Hakka.

20　In an earlier post by the same author (Xing-xun-bi-gong 2005b), s/he observes that there is no *Gang-Tai qiang* in reality just as there is no *Dongbei-Xibei qiang* 'Northeastern-Northwestern accent' or *Jing-Jin qiang* 'Beijing-Tianjin accent'.

21　Manchu is a Tungusic language of Altaic.

22　The rhetorical question "*suan shenme dongxi*," literally translated as 'supposed to be what thing/matter', is used to express a tone of hatred and contempt toward someone or something. It is similar to calling someone or something "what a piece of shit" in English.

23　The three phrases are local expressions in Beijing Mandarin.

24　All three phrases end with a final particle.

25　The "posterior nasal sounds" (*hou bi yin*) are likely to be the commenter's perception of nasalized finals when a final with a nasal coda is rhotacized, for example, *wan* [wan] 'play' when rhotacized is pronounced as *war* [wãɻ].

26　The book *Meiren Zeng Wo Menghan Yao 'A Beauty Presents Me with Knockout Drops'* (Wang and Lao 2000) is a collection of dialogues between Wang Shuo and Lao Xiao on contemporary Chinese culture and literature. Lao Xia is believed by some to be the penname of Liu Xiaobo, the 2010 Nobel Peace Prize winner (see e.g., https://zh.wikipedia.org/wiki/刘晓波). Similarities are indeed found when comparing Liu's comments on *Gang-Tai* culture and *Gang-Tai* accent in his 2000 article and the essay "*Gang-Tai 'Putonghua' da Fanlan*" '*Gang-Tai 'Putonghua'* Runs Wild') in Wang and Lao (2000).

27 Yu Jie, less well known than Liu Xiaobo outside of China, has come to the attention of Western media with his 2010 book, a critique of the then Premier Wen Jiabao, *Zhongguo Yingdi: Wen Jiaobao* (*China's Best Actor: Wen Jiabao*) and his 2012 book *Liu Xiaobo: A Biography*. Both books were published in Hong Kong and banned in mainland China. He is now in exile in the United States (see, for example, Johnson 2012; Wong 2012).

28 *Shisu xiao qingdiao*, 'secular minor sentiments', refer to non-political and private, individual sentiments, in contrast to the "uplifting politicized expression of grand/lofty emotions" in Mao's era.

29 'Bird language', or *niao yu*, see note 8.

30 Both Liu Xiaobo (born in 1955) and Wang Shuo (born in 1958) were teenagers during the Great Proletariat Cultural Revolution (1966–1976).

31 The analysis produces a drastically different view of the enregisterment of PTH from the one presented in Dong's (2010) study, in which PTH is enregistered as an accent-free supralocal linguistic standard whose symbolic dominance is accepted and taken for granted.

References

Agha, Asif. 2003. "The Social Life of Cultural Value." *Language & Communication* 23 (3–4):231–273.

Agha, Asif. 2007. *Language and Social Relations*. Cambridge: Cambridge University Press.

Bucholtz, Mary, and Kira Hall. 2004. "Theorizing Identity in Language and Sexuality Research." *Language in Society* 33 (4):469–515.

Cameron, Deborah. 1995. *Verbal Hygiene*. London: Routledge.

Campbell-Kibler, Kathryn. 2008. "I'll Be the Judge of That: Diversity in Social Perceptions of (Ing)." *Language in Society* 37 (5):637–659.

Chan, Marjorie K.M. 1998. "Gender Differences in the Chinese Language: A Preliminary Report." In *Proceedings of the Ninth North American Conference on Chinese Linguistics*, edited by Hua Lin, Vol. 2, 35–52. University of Southern California, LA: GSIL Publications.

Coupland, Nikolas. 2003. "Sociolinguistic Authenticities." *Journal of Sociolinguistics* 7 (3):417–431.

Coupland, Nikolas. 2010. "Language, Ideology, Media and Social Change." *SPELL: Swiss Papers in English Language and Literature* 24:55–79.

Coupland, Nikolas. 2014. "Sociolinguistic Change, Vernacularization and Broadcast British Media." In *Mediatization and Sociolinguistic Change*, edited by Jannis Androutsopoulos, 67–96. Berlin and Boston, MA: de Gruyter.

DeBernardi, Jean. 1991. "Linguistic Nationalism: The Case of Southern Min." *Sino-Platonic Papers* 25:1–22.

De Francis, John. 1950. *Nationalism and Language Reform in China*. Princeton, NJ: Princeton University Press.

Dong, Jie. 2010. "The Enregisterment of Putonghua in Practice." *Language & Communication* 30 (4):265–275.

170 Warring Standards

Du, Wenwei. 1998. "Xiaopin: Chinese Theatrical Skits as Both Creatures and Critics of Commercialism." *The China Quarterly* 154:382–399.

Eckert, Penelope. 2008. "Variation and the Indexical Field." *Journal of Sociolinguistics* 12 (4):453–476.

Farris, Catherine S. 1988. "Gender and Grammar in Chinese: With Implications for Language Universals." *Modern China* 14 (3):277–308.

Farris, Catherine S. 1994. "A Semiotic Analysis of *Sajiao* as a Gender Marked Communication Style in Chinese." In *Unbound Taiwan: Closeups from a Distance*, edited by Marshall Johnson, and Fred Y.L. Chiu, 1–29. Chicago, IL: Center for East Asian Studies.

Gao, Jia, and Peter C. Pugsley. 2008. "Utilizing Satire in Post-Deng Chinese Politics." *China Information* 22 (3):451–476.

Goebel, Zane. 2010. *Language, Migration, and Identity: Neighborhood Talk in Indonesia*. Cambridge: Cambridge University Press.

Goodwin, Marjorie Harness. 1990. *He-Said-She-Said: Talk as Social Organization among Black Children*. Bloomington, IN: Indiana University Press.

Harkness, Nicholas. 2011. "Culture and Interdiscursivity in Korean Fricative Voice Gestures." *Journal of Linguistic Anthropology* 21 (1):99–123.

Hill, Jane H. 1998. "'Today There Is No Respect': Nostalgia, 'Respect,' and Oppositional Discourse in Mexicano (Nahuatl) Language Ideology." In *Language Ideologies: Practice and Theory*, edited by Bambi B. Schieffelin, Kathryn A. Woolard and Paul V. Kroskrity, 51–67. New York, NY: Oxford University Press.

Inoue, Miyako. 2004. "What Does Language Remember? Indexical Inversion and the Naturalized History of Japanese Women." *Journal of Linguistic Anthropology* 14 (1):39–56.

Irvine, Judith, and Susan Gal. 2000. "Language Ideology and Linguistic Differentiation." In *Regimes of Language*, edited by Paul V. Kroskrity, 35–84. Santa Fe, NM: School of American Research Press.

Jiang, Min. 2010. Authoritarian Deliberation on Chinese Internet. *Electronic Journal of Communication* 20 (3&4). http://ssrn.com/abstract=1439354.

Johnson, Ian. 2012. "China's 'Fault Lines': Yu Jie on His New Biography of Liu Xiaobo." *The New York Review of Books,* July 14, 2012. www.nybooks.com/blogs/nyrblog/2012/jul/14/china-fault-lines-yu-jie-liu-xiaobo/. Accessed April 9, 2013.

Johnstone, Barbara. 2009. "Pittsburghese Shirts: Commodification and the Enregisterment of an Urban Dialect." *American Speech* 84 (2):157–175.

Johnstone, Barbara. 2011. "Dialect Enregisterment in Performance." *Journal of Sociolinguistics* 15 (5):657–679.

Johnstone, Barbara. 2013. *Speaking Pittsburghese: The Story of a Dialect*. New York, NY: Oxford University Press.

Johnstone, Barbara, Jennifer Andrus, and Andrew E. Danielson. 2006. "Mobility, Indexicality, and the Enregisterment of 'Pittsburghese'." *Journal of English Linguistics* 34 (2):77–104.

Johnstone, Barbara, and Scott F. Kiesling. 2008. "Indexicality and Experience: Exploring the Meanings of /Aw/-Monophthongization in Pittsburgh." *Journal of Sociolinguistics* 12 (1):5–33.

Li, Aijun, Ziyu Xiong, and Xia Wang. 2006. "Contrastive Study on Tonal Patterns between Accented and Standard Chinese." In *Proceedings of the 5th International Symposium on Chinese Spoken Language Processing (ISCSLP)*, edited by Qiang Huo, Bin Ma,

Eng-Siong Chng, and Haizhou Li, Vol. 2, 25–37. n.p.: COLIPS. www.isca-speech.org/archive_open/archive_papers/iscslp2006/B3.pdf.

Moore, Robert. 2011. "'If I Actually Talked Like That, I'd Pull a Gun on Myself': Accent, Avoidance, and Moral Panic in Irish English." *Anthropological Quarterly* 84 (1):41–64.

Newell, Sasha. 2009. "Enregistering Modernity, Bluffing Criminality: How Nouchi Speech Reinvented (and Fractured) the Nation." *Journal of Linguistic Anthropology* 19 (2):157–184.

Norman, Jerry. 1988. *Chinese.* Cambridge: Cambridge University Press.

Rampton, Ben. 1995. *Crossing: Language and Ethnicity among Adolescents.* London: Longman.

Ramsey, S. Robert. 1987. *The Languages of China.* Princeton, NJ: Princeton University Press.

Remlinger, Kathryn. 2009. "Everyone up Here: Enregisterment and Identity in Michigan's Keweenaw Peninsula." *American Speech* 84 (2):118–137.

Remlinger, Kathryn, Joseph Salmons, and Luanne Von Schneidemesser. 2009. "Revised Perceptions: Changing Dialect Perceptions in Wisconsin and Michigan's Upper Peninsula." *American Speech* 84 (2):176–191.

Rickford, R. John. 1986. "Concord and Contrast in the Characterization of the Speech Community." In *Proceedings of the Fourteenth Annual Conference on New Ways of Analyzing Variation (NWAV-14)*, edited by Ralph W. Fasold, 1–31. Washington, DC: Georgetown University.

Roth-Gordon, Jennifer. 2009. "The Language That Came Down the Hill: Slang, Crime, and Citizenship in Rio De Janeiro." *American Anthropologist* 111 (1):57–68.

Roth-Gordon, Jennifer, and Woronov, Terry E. 2009. "Youthful Concerns: Movement, Belonging, and Modernity." *Pragmatics.* 19 (1):137–151.

Sanders, Robert. 2008. "Tonetic Sound Change in Taiwan Mandarin: The Case of Tone 2 and Tone 3 Citation Contours." In *Proceedings of the 20th North American Conference on Chinese Linguistics (Naccl-20)*, edited by Marjorie K.M. Chan, and Hana Kang, 87–107. Columbus, OH: Ohio State University.

Schieffelin, Bambi B., and Rachelle Charlier Doucet. 1998. "The 'Real' Haitian Creole: Ideology, Metalinguistics, and Orthographic Choice." In *Language Ideologies: Practice and Theory*, edited by Bambi B. Schieffelin, Kathryn A. Woolard, and Paul V. Kroskrity, 285–316. New York, NY: Oxford University Press.

Silverstein, Michael. 1993. "Metapragmatic Discourse and Metapragmatic Function." In *Reflexive Language: Reported Speech and Metapragmatics*, edited by John Lucy, 33–58. New York, NY: Cambridge University Press.

Silverstein, Michael. 2003. "Indexical Order and the Dialectics of Sociolinguistic Life." *Language & Communication* 23 (3–4):193–229.

Smith-Hefner, Nancy J. 2007. "Youth Language, *Gaul* Sociability, and the New Indonesian Middle Class." *Journal of Linguistic Anthropology* 17 (2):184–203.

Stroud, Christopher. 2004. "Rinkeby Swedish and Semilingualism in Language Ideological Debates: A Bourdieuean Perspective." *Journal of Sociolinguistics* 8 (2):196–214.

Su, Hsi-Yao. 2008. "What Does It Mean to Be a Girl with *Qizhi*? Refinement, Gender and Language Ideologies in Contemporary Taiwan." *Journal of Sociolinguistics* 12 (3):334–358.

Urciuoli, Bonnie. 2010. "Entextualizing Diversity: Semiotic Incoherence in Institutional Discourse." *Language & Communication* 30 (1):48–57.

172 Warring Standards

Wang, Xiao. 2010. "Entertainment, Education, or Propaganda? A Longitudinal Analysis of China Central Television's Spring Festival Galas." *Journal of Broadcasting & Electronic Media* 54 (3):391–406.

Wong, Edward. 2012. "From Virginia Suburb, a Dissident Chinese Writer Continues His Mission." *The New York Times*. February 25, 2015. www.nytimes.com/2012/02/26/world/asia/yu-jie-dissident-chinese-writer-continues-his-work-in-us.html?pagewanted=all&_r=0. Accessed April 9, 2013.

Woolard, Kathryn A. 2004. "Is the Past a Foreign Country? Time, Language Origins, and the Nation in Early Modern Spain." *Journal of Linguistic Anthropology* 14 (1):57–80.

Zhang, Aiping. 1995. "Another Look at *the Sajiao* Phenomenon." ms, Ohio State University.

Zhao, Bin. 1998. "Popular Family Television and Party Ideology: The Spring Festival Eve Happy Gathering." *Media, Culture and Society* 20 (1):43–58.

Metadiscourse Database

"Fuqin" ("Father"). 1995. Skit performed in the 1995 CCTV Spring Festival Gala. http://ent.cntv.cn/special/C13396/classpage/video/20091209/101784.shtml. Accessed November 19, 2009.

"Ruci Baozhuang" ("Packaging in Such a Way"). 1995. Skit performed in the 1995 CCTV Spring Festival Gala. http://ent.cntv.cn/special/C13396/classpage/video/20091209/101797.shtml. Accessed November 19, 2009.

"Zhui Xing Zu" ("Star-Chasing Tribe"). 1993. Skit performed in CCTV's 35th Anniversary Celebration Gala "Tonight Belongs to You" (*Jinxiao shuyu ni*). http://space.tv.cctv.com/video/VIDE1242022020381151. Accessed May 10, 2009.

218.25.126. 2009. *"Nanfang Kouyin bei Chengwei Gang-Tai Qiang, Name Jing Pianzi he Dongbei Hua shi bu shi Yinggai Jiaozuo Manren Qiang ne?"* ("Southern Accent Is Called Hong Kong-Taiwan Accent, Then Shouldn't Beijing Vernacular and Northeastern Dialect be Called Manchurian Accent?"). Posted on March 14. http://ido.3mt.com.cn/Article/200903/show1337984c12p1.html

219.137.212.*. 2005. Response to People.cn.com 2005b. Posted on November 27 at 07:31:42. http://202.99.23.223:8080/bbs_new/filepool/htdoc/html/c272b24c06a4a059f672c73b41e42eb5872e3ed9/b2037230/1_2037230_1.html

4rain. 2005. Response to Kuaile-cuojue 2005. Posted on September 16 at 23:57:34. http://tianya.cn/bbs/post-funinfo-90652-1.shtml

Bai-dan-mei. 2005. Response to Kuaile-cuojue 2005. Posted on September 17 at 18:23:47. http://tianya.cn/bbs/post-funinfo-90652-1.shtml

Bai-jia-zi-fengle (Spendthrift-gone-crazy). 2005. Response to Kuaile-cuojue 2005. Posted on September 17 at 22:30:30. http://tianya.cn/bbs/post-funinfo-90652-1.shtml

CCTV. 1995. *"Ruci Baozhuang"* ("Packaging in Such a way"). http://ent.cntv.cn/special/C13396/classpage/video/20091209/101797.shtml. Accessed November 19, 2009.

Chang-ting-yuan-man1. 2005. Response to Kuaile-cuojue 2005. Posted on September 18 at 12:39:12. http://tianya.cn/bbs/post-funinfo-90652-1.shtml

Chen, Xiaoxing. 2010. *"Cuo Buzai 'Gang-Tai Qiang'"* ("The Fault Is Not With 'Hong Kong-Taiwan Accent'"). *Renmin Ribao Haiwai Ban (People's Daily Overseas Edition)*. August 10, 3.

Cheng-lang-ke. 2012. Response to Marklesgaybi 2012. Posted on March 25 at 02:11:17. www.tianya.cn/publicforum/content/funinfo/1/3201595.shtml

eladies.sina. 2002. *"Xin-Xin Renlei Bi Xiu: 2001 Nian de Ku Ci Yi Lan"*("Neo-Neo Tribe Must Learn: A Survey Of Cool Vocabulary in 2001"). http://eladies.sina.com. cn/2002-01-16/49069.html. Accessed August 25, 2003.

Fa-ke-you-tu. 2005. Response to Xing-xun-bi-gong 2005. Posted on August 23 at 10:11:50.

fedent. 2009. *"Weimao Dianshiju li Daochu Doushi Jing Pianzi Mei Ren Shuo, Suowei Gang-Tai Qiang jiuyao bei Ren bs Ah?"* ("Why Nobody Comments On TV Dramas Full of Beijing Vernacular, But So Called Hong Kong-Taiwan Accent Would Be Despised?"). Posted on November 14 at 21:32:00. www.zzetyy.com/plains. php?p_funinfo_1_1696362

Feng-xing-xia. 2005. Response to Xing-xun-bi-gong 2005. Posted on September 19 at 17:12:51.

genzxc. 2005. Response to Kuaile-cuo-jue 2005. Posted on September 16 at 20:27:27.

Guo, Muhua. 2005. *"Guang Dian Zong Ju Fa Zilü Gongyue Yanjin Zhuchiren Lan Yong Gang-Tai Qiang ji Fangyan"* ("SARFT Publishes Self-Disciplining Conventions to Prohibit Hosts Randomly Use Hong Kong-Taiwan Accent and Regional Dialects"). *Jin Bao*, September 14. http://politics.people.com.cn/GB/1027/3692832.html

He-xin. 2011. Response to *"Weishenme Da Duoshu Ren Ting Dongbei Weir Putonghua hui Juede Tu huozhe bu Shufu, Ting Xiang Gang Taiwan Qiang Putonghua jiu Juede Haihao?"* ("Why Most People Would Feel Rustic and Uncomfortable When Listening to Northeast-Accented, but Hong Kong-Taiwan Accented *Putonghua* Is Alright?"). Posted on November 13. www.butno.net/14686.

Hen-jia-hen-hexie (Very-fake-very-harmonious). 2010. *"Beifangren jiu Gaoren Yideng? Nanfang Kouyin jiu Jiao Gang-Tai Qiang?"*("Northerners are Superior? Southern Accent Is Called Hong Kong-Taiwan Accent?"). Posted on December 27 at 06:44. www.tianya200.com/90277_1.html

Huli-shao-ye (Fox-young-master). 2005. Response to Kuaile-cuojue 2005. Posted on September 17 at 11:55:23.

Jue-zhan-dou-shi. 2005. Response to Kuaile-cuojue 2005. Posted on September 18 at 14:19:12.

Jun-fei-fan. 2005. Response to Kuaile-cuojue 2005. Posted on September 18 at 10:34:26. http://tianya.cn/bbs/post-funinfo-90652-1.shtml

KTV-ah-KTV. 2005. Response to Kuaile-cuojue 2005. Posted on September 16 at 12:02:20.

Kuaile-cuojue (Happy-illusion). 2005. *"Wan Ren Qianming Fandui GuangDianZongJu 'Gang-Tai Qiang' Shijian! 'Gang-Tai Qiang' He Zui zhi You?"* ("Tens of Thousands Signing to Protest SARFT 'Hong Kong-Taiwan Accent' Incident! What Crime Has 'Hong Kong-Taiwan Accent' Committed?"). Posted on September 16 at 11:41:00. http://tianya.cn/bbs/post-funinfo-90652-1.shtml

lakaya. 2005. Response to Kuaile-cuojue 2005. Posted on September 21 at 15:53:08.

Li, Fang. 2005. *"Boyin Zhuchi Weiyuanhui Fachu Changyi Dizhi Disu zhi Feng"* ("Committee of Broadcasters and Hosts Issues Initiative to Resist the Trend of Vulgarity"). *Renmin Ribo (People's Daily)*. July 20, 11.

Li, Muyang. 2009. *"Yangshi Gaiban: Wei Yansu Xinwen Chuanshang Shishang Waiyi"* ("CCTV Reform: Dressing up Serious News with Stylish Outfit"). http://media. people.com.cn/GB/9866237.html. Accessed August 20, 2009.

Ling, Wendao. 2009. *"'Gang-Tai Qiang' Cuo Zai Nali"* ("What Is Wrong with 'Hong Kong-Taiwan Accent'"). In *Changshi (Common Sense)*, 58–60. Guilin: Guangxi Shifan Daxue Chubanshe (Guangxi Normal University Publishing House).

174 Warring Standards

Liu, Xiaobo. 2000. *"Xinling Aiyue Biancheng Routi Huange"* ("The Sad Song of the Soul Becomes the Happy Song of the Flesh"). *Kaifang Zazhi (Open Magazine)*, December, No. 168. www.epochtimes.com/gb/1/1/2/n28824.htm. Accessed May 3, 2012.

Marklesgaybi. 2012. *"Beijing Qiang, Dongbei Qiang, Gang-Tai Qiang, 818 Naxie Bu Haohao Shuohua de Yirenmen"* ("Beijing Accent, Northeastern Accent, Hong Kong-Taiwan Accent, Gossip about Those Performers Who Don't Talk Normally"). Posted on March 22 at 10:23:00. www.tianya.cn/publicforum/content/funinfo/1/3194918.shtml. Accessed May 3, 2012.

Mei-suo-mi-ya. 2005. Response to Xing-xun-bi-gong. 2005a. Posted on September 1 at 14:55:48.

Ministry of Education. 2005. *"Guanyu Kaizhan Di Ba Jie Quanguo Putonghua Xuanchuan Zhou Huodong de Tongzhi"* ("Notice for Carrying out the Activities of the Eighth National *Putonghua* Promotion and Publicity Week"). June 3. www.moe.gov.cn/publicfiles/business/htmlfiles/moe/moe_307/200507/8708.html. Accessed November 8, 2011.

Nanfang Dushi Bao (Southern Metropolis Daily). 2004. *"'Gang-Tai Qiang' He Shang Daya?*" ("How Much Harm Can 'Hong Kong-Taiwan Accent' Do?"). May 14. http://news.xinhuanet.com/newmedia/2004-05/14/content_1476751.htm. Accessed April 2, 2006.

Ning, Xin. 2011. *"'Xinwen Lianbo' Xin Miankong Ouyang Xiadan he Lang Yongchun s hi Juepei."* ("The New Faces of 'Network News Broadcast' Ouyang Xiadan and Lang Yongchun are the Perfect Match"). September 26. http://news.china.com.cn/zhuanti/Calendar/2011-09/26/content_23494800_4.htm. Accessed September 30, 2011.

People.com.cn. 2005a. *"Guangbo Yingshi Quan Cao 'Gang-Tai Qiang' Zhuchiren Da Soucha"* ("Comprehensive Search of Radio and Television Hosts Speaking 'Hong Kong-Taiwan Accent'"). September 19. http://media.people.com.cn/GB/40606/3705843.html. Accessed April 2, 2006.

People.com.cn. 2005b. *"Meiti Piping: Zhuchiren 'Gang-Tai Qiang' gai bu gai Zao Da?"* ("Media Critique: Should Hosts' 'Hong Kong-Taiwan Accent' be Struck or Not?"). Initiated on September 18. http://media.people.com.cn/GB/40698/3704711.html. Accessed April 2, 2006.

Phoenix Television. 2004. *"Xiaozi: Tong bing Wunai zhe"* ("The Petite Bourgeoisie: Painful and without Alternatives"). Uploaded on September 7. http://phtv.ifeng.com/home/fashion/jjtd/200409/07/324065.html. Accessed July 6, 2005.

Pi-gu-jun-tuan (Buttocks-contingent). 2010. Response to Hen-jia-hen-hexie 2010. Posted on December 27 at 07:57:35.

Planelove. 2005. Response to Kuaile-cuijue 2005. Posted on September 17 at 01:08:08.

PSCSG. 2004. *Putonghonghua Shuiping Ceshi Shishi Gangyao* (*Implementation Guidelines for the Putonghua Proficiency Test*). Beijing: Shangwu Yinshu Guan (Commercial Press).

Qiang, Yi and Haifeng Wang. 2007. *"Shuli Meiti Shehui Zerengan Dizhi Guangbo Jiemu Disuhua"* ("Establish Media's Social Responsibility Resist Vulgarization of Radio and Television Broadcasts"). *Xinwen Zhanxian* (*News Frontline*) 7:46.

Ren-dan-di-shi-yi. 2003. *"Xiao Tai San Gang"* ("Bickering Three Times"). Posted on February 24 at 02:42:09. www.tianya.cn/techforum/content/93/396791.shtml

Rong-yan-lao-si-ji. 2007. Response to *"Xiwang Dalu Beifang Tongbao Buyao Zai Shuo Shenme Beifang Qiang, Gang-Tai Qiang de Wenti!!"* ("Hope Mainland Northern Compatriots Don't Discuss the Issue of Northern Accent and *Hong Kong-Taiwan* Accent Anymore!!"). Posted by Jiu-fen-bei-qing-cheng-shi on January 16 at 22:06:00. www.tianya.cn/publicforum/content/funinfo/1/289461.shtml

SARFT. 2002. "*Guangdian Zongju Tongbao: Zhizhi Yulexing Zongyi Jiemu zhong Buliang Qingxiang*" (SARFT *Circular: Prevention of Bad Tendencies in Entertainment Variety Programs*"). http://news.xinhuanet.com/zhengfu/2002-01/23/content_250076. htm. Accessed April 5, 2006.

SARFT. 2004. "*Guangbo Yingshi Jiaqiang he Gaijin Weichengnian Ren Sixiang Daode Jianshe de Shishi Fangan*" ("Implementation Plan for Strengthening and Improving the Spiritual and Moral Construction of [Chinese] Minors"). www.sarft.gov.cn/manage/publishfile/35/1716.html. Accessed May 20, 2005.

SARFT. 2005. "*Zhongguo Guangbo Dianshi Boyinyuan Zhuchiren Zilü Gongyue*" ("The Self-Disciplining Conventions of Chinese Radio and Television Broadcasters and Hosts"). www.sarft.gov.cn/manage/publishfile/35/3282.html. Accessed April 5, 2006.

softree. 2008. "*Huoda, Weisha Laoyou Wuzhi de Beijing Ren Shuo Wo Gang-Tai Qiang*?!" ("Infuriated, Why Are There Always Ignorant Beijingers Accusing Me of Hong Kong-Taiwan Accent?!"). Posted on June 27 at 15:14:00. www.tianya.cn/publicforum/content/free/1/1322158.shtml

Wang, Shuo, and Xia Lao. 2000. *Meiren Zeng Wo Menghan Yao* (*A Beauty Presents Me with Knockout Drops*). Wuhan, China: Changjiang Wenyi Chubanshe (Changjiang Literature and Art Publishing House).

Wang, Xiaobo. 2006 [1996]. "*Jingpianzi yu Minzu Zixinxin*" ("Beijing Vernacular and National Self-Respect). In *Wang Xiaobo Quan Ji* (*Complete Collection of Wang Xiaobo*), 159–161. Kunming Shi: Yunnan Renmin Chuban She (Yunnan People's Publishing House).

Wang, Xiaohui. 2000. "*Dalu Changdao Putonghua, Fandui Mofang Gang-Tai Qiang*" ("Mainland Promotes *Putonghua*, Opposes Imitating Hong Kong-Taiwan Accent"). China News Service. September 7. www.chinanews.com/2000-09-07/26/45264. html. Accessed June 7, 2005.

Wang, Yuewen. 1998. "*Mei Zhe Huishi*" ("There Is No Such Thing"). In *Mei Zhe Huishi* (*There is No Such Thing*), 312–351. Changsha, China: Hunan Wenyi Chuban She (Hunan Literature and Art Publishing House).

Wu-ren-zhi-shan. 2005. Response to Kuaile-cuojue 2005. Posted on September 18 at 14:13:18.

Xiandai Hanyu Cidian (*Modern Chinese Dictionary*). 1993. Beijing: Shangwu Yinshu Guan (Commercial Press).

Xing-xun-bi-gong (Extorting-confessions-by-torture). 2005a. "'*Gang-Tai Qiang' 'Taiwan Qiang'—Juanshe Zhemen Shengzao Chulai de Gongji Gongju*" ("'Hong Kong-Taiwan Accent' 'Taiwan Accent'—Attacking Tool Fabricated by Tongue-Curling People"). Posted on September 1 at 1:57:00. www.tianya.cn/publicforum/content/funinfo/1/85683.shtml

Xing-xun-bi-gong (Extorting-confessions-by-torture). 2005b. Response to Kuaile-cuojue (Happy-illusion). 2005. Posted on August 24 at 00:16:43.

Xing-xun-bi-gong (Extorting-confessions-by-torture). 2005c. "*Qianglie Fangan Lingren Exinde Beifang Fangyan—Zhichi Gang-Tai Qiang*" ("Strongly Oppose Disgusting Northern Dialects—Support Hong Kong-Taiwan Accent"). Posted on August 21 at 23:56:00. www.tianya.cn/publicforum/content/funinfo/1/79492.shtml

Xinhuanet. 2009. "*Yangshi Xinwen Gaiban Huan Piaoliang Nü Zhuchi: 'Zhao Wen Tianxia' Da Bianlian*" ("CCTV News Reform Brings out Pretty Female Anchor: 'Morning News' Big Face Change"). http://news.xinhuanet.com/newmedia/2009-07/28/content_11785347.htm. Accessed July 31, 2009.

176 Warring Standards

Xu, Min. 2005. *"Boyin Zhuchijie Ding Gongyue Dizhi Disu Feng Zhuchiren Buneng Guyi Mofang 'Gang-Tai Qiang'"* (Radio and Broadcast Sector Sets Conventions to Resist Trend of Vulgarization Hosts Prohibited from Deliberate Imitation of 'Hong Kong-Taiwan Accent'"). *Renmin Ribao (People's Daily)*. September 15, 11.

Yang, Meiju. 2011. *"Yangshi Xinshengdai: Tamen shi Gexing, ye shi Lichang"* ("CCTV's New Generation: They Are Personality as well as Position"). *Shidai You Kan (Times Biweekly)* 158:18–19. www.shidaiyoukan.com/shehui/sxbt/2727.html. Accessed December 7, 2012.

Yi-ming. 2005. Response to Kuaile-cuo-jue 2005. Posted on September 18 at 10:52:57,

Yi-shi-ma-li (Ishmael). 2008. *"Putonghua yu Wenhua Shawenzhuyi"* (*Putonghua* and Cultural Chauvinism). Posted on January 21 at 08:41:05. http://blog.sina.com.cn/s/blog_4c7cf4fa010086tr.html

Yu, Jie. 2010. *"Gang-Tai Qiang" yu "Beijing Qiang"* ("'Hong Kong-Taiwan Accent' and 'Beijing Accent'"). In *Xianggang Chenmo (Hong Kong Sinking)*. http://blog.boxun. com/hero/200801/yujie/76_1.shtml. Accessed April 20, 2012.

Yu-rong-qiu. 2009. Response to fedent 2009. Posted on November 14 at 21:47:41.

Yun-an. 2005. Response to Xing-xun-bi-gong 2005c. Posted on August 22 at 23:47:47.

Zao-chun Qingchen (Early spring morning). 2010. *"Jiaoqing de Kouyin"* ("The Accent Which Is Affectedly Unconventional to Appear Superior"). Posted on August 31 at 19:55:35. http://blog.sina.com.cn/s/blog_4c0820a50100le6b.html

Zhang, Aijing. 2002. *"Qingdiao Xiaozi Nüren de Shishang Shenghuo"* ("Fashionable Life of the Sentimental Petite Bourgeoisie Women"). *Meirong Shishang Bao (Beauty and Fashion Magazine)*. April 4. www.people.com.cn/GB/shenghuo/77/117/20020404/702045. html. Accessed May 16, 2004.

Zhang, He. 2005. *"Disu zhi Feng, Shui zhi Guo?"* ("The Trend of Vulgarization, Whose Fault?"). *Renmin Ribao (People's Daily)*. August 29, 11.

Zhang, Miaoyang. 2011. *"Gang-Tai Qiang zhen shi Hongshui Mengshou ma?"* ("Is Hong Kong-Taiwan Accent Really a Scourge?"). www.zhangmiaoyang.com/thread-14502-1-1.html. Accessed December 8, 2011.

Zhang, Xuejun. 2005. *"Zhuchiren Fabiao 'Zilü Gongyue' Ming Zui Tui 'Zilü Shisi Tiao'"* ("Hosts Publish 'Self-Disciplining Conventions' Famous Hosts Promote '14 Self-Disciplining Items"). *Beijing Yule Xinbao (Beijing Entertertainment)*. July 20. http://news.xinhuanet.com/ent/2005-07/20/content_3241713.htm.

Zhao, Nannan. 2005. *"Guangdian Lingdao Tongchen Jiemu Disu"* ("SARFT Leader Harshly Criticize Vulgar Programs"). *Jinghua Shibao (Jinghua Times)*. August 27, A23.

Zhen-mo-ming-qi-miao (Really-baffling). 2008. Response to softree 2008. Posted on October 21 at 10:22:42.

Zhong, Yan. 2002. *"Hanwei Zuguo Yuyan de Chunjie"* ("Safeguarding the Purity of Homeland Language"). *Renmin Ribao (People's Daily)*. September 29, 12.

Zhuang, Liwei. 2005. *"Gang-Tai Hua Yeshi Zhongguo Hua"* ("Hong Kong-Taiwan Speech Is Also Chinese"). Posted on September 15. http://zhuangliwei.blogchina. com/89362.html. Accessed April 24, 2012.

Zhu-yue-yue. 2011. Response to *"Weishenme Daduoshu Ren Ting Dongbei Weir Putonghua Hui Ganjue Tu huo Bu Shufu, Ting Gang-Tai Qiang Putonghua jiu Juede Haihao?"* ("Why Most People Think Northeastern *Putonghua* Sounds Rustic or Uncomfortable, but Hong Kong-Taiwan Accented *Putonghua* Is Alright?"). Posted on November 13. www.butno.net/14686. Accessed April 24, 2012.

6

A STYLE-BASED APPROACH TO SOCIOLINGUISTIC CHANGE

6.1 Introduction

On New Year's Day 2015, another stylistic move caught my attention and that of reportedly billions of Chinese netizens (Li 2015). This time the stylistic agent was the President of China, Xi Jinping. The speech event was his 2015 New Year Celebration Address, broadcast and published on all mass media platforms across China.[1] About three and a half minutes into the speech, he said:

> 为了做好这些工作，我们的各级干部也是蛮拼的。当然，没有人民支持，这些工作是难以做好的，我要为我们伟大的人民点赞。
>
> *Weile zuohao zhexie gongzuo, womende geji ganbu yeshi **man pinde**. Dangran, meiyou renminde zhichi, zhexie gongzuo shi nanyi zuo haode, wo yao wei women waidade renmin **dianzan**.*
>
> To perform these tasks well, our cadres at various levels have **given it their best shot**. Of course, these achievements would not have been possible without the support of the people. I would like to give our great people a **thumbs-up**.[2]

What caught my attention and that of the Chinese media and many Chinese netizens was the unusual use of two popular expressions highlighted in the quotation above. 蛮拼的 *man pinde* means 'quite hardworking', or 'giving it one's bestshot'. Accredited to Cao Ge (Gary Chaw), a Malaysian Chinese singer-songwriter in a popular celebrity reality show on Hunan Satellite Television, the phrase was taken up by social media and became one of the top 10 most popular Internet buzzwords in 2014 (Gui 2014; Liu 2015).[3] The adverb *man* 'very' or 'quite' in *man* + adjective is one of the lexical innovations I discussed in Chapter 4 (see example (4) in Table 4.2). The other expression, 点赞

178 A Style-Based Approach to Sociolinguistic Change

dianzan 'click/touch like', originated from social media, referring to the action of giving a "like" or thumbs-up to a post. It was one of the top 10 most popular expressions in 2013 (Editorial Office 2014). It is now widely used in other domains as well as in the form of "*wei ... dian zan*" as in Xi's speech, meaning to praise, approve, or give a thumbs-up.

Xi's use of such trendy expressions incited tremendous attention because they are unexpected in such a ritual speech. The New Year Celebration Address of Chinese Presidents is serious and lofty, with formulaic expressions such as *gezu renmin* 'people of all ethnicities', *nuli* 'strive', *shixian* 'realize', *jianchi* 'adhere to' and *gao ju* 'uphold'. The 2015 address had all of them. It was delivered in Standard PTH with a measured speed and was punctuated by pauses between intonation units, stereotypic of what is known as *lingdao jianghua* 'leader speech' or *guan qiang* 'official talk' (see also Xu and Callier 2016).[4] The two buzzwords bring about something new and different in the stately persona of the *Guojia Zhuxi* 'National Chairman' in such a national speech event. Being new and popular in social media, the expressions' informality and trendiness shorten the social distance between the President and the people and brings him up to date. This stylistic move was widely recognized and responded to with great enthusiasm. People on social media reciprocate by giving him "a thumbs-up" and praising him for "giving his best shot" (e.g., Liu 2015; Wu and Li 2015). In their comments, many Chinese netizens refer to Xi with the endearment term *Xi Dada* 'Uncle Xi', and perceive him in the speech as *qinhe* 'amiable', *jie diqi* 'down-to-earth', *shishang* 'stylish/trendy', and even *mengmeng da* 'adorable' (e.g., China News 2015; Wu et al. 2015).[5] The last two descriptors are not the typical attributes associated with the image of the country's top leader.

Thus, in addition to enacting new images and personae as in the case of the Beijing yuppies and the lifestyle TV hosts in earlier chapters, enregistered linguistic innovation, as we see from this example, can also be recruited to give a new twist to an enduring social image. The example from Xi's speech also highlights the contrast between the use of individual, albeit salient, linguistic elements in fleeting moments of stylistic moves and the combination of linguistic elements constitutive of a style, or more precisely, an enregistered style. In other words, despite Xi's use of *man*, one of the components of CM, his speech style is still overwhelmingly conservative Standard PTH with stereotypical indexicals of "leader speech" mentioned earlier.

In Section 6.2, I reiterate and clarify crucial aspects of CM that define its distinction from the conventional standard "common speech." Section 6.3 summarizes the major findings of this study and revisits the central question raised at the beginning of this book, that is, "how 'style' has a particular role to play in effecting change" (Coupland 2007, 100; See Chapter 1 of this book). Section 6.4 concludes the chapter with a discussion on prospects of CM and Standard Mandarin in China.

6.2 What Makes Cosmopolitan Mandarin Distinctive

Based on analyses developed in Chapters 3 through 5, we can define CM as a supraregional linguistic style consisting of a fluid set of linguistic features, the combination of which is distinctive from the Beijing-Mandarin-based Standard PTH. Four aspects of this description are crucial. First, by emphasizing the *compositional fluidity* of CM, I reject a treatment of linguistic style as a closed system consisting of a fixed inventory of linguistic features whose distinctiveness is demarcated by discrete linguistic boundaries.[6] As I argue in Chapter 1, style is both bricolage and a sociohistorical process of enregisterment. Thus, CM is not only a clustering of linguistic features but also an *open-ended* process of meaning making that takes place through linking variable linguistic features to recognizable characters and social personae (including behaviors and attributes). Such compositional fluidity is demonstrated through its use by the Beijing yuppies and the television hosts. In each case, I describe the range of linguistic features that makes their speech distinctive from a conservative style of Bejing-Mandarin-based PTH. The analysis reveals the linguistic distinctiveness of CM, particularly the combination of the two most salient sound features used by both the yuppies and the TV hosts, namely de-rhotacization and full tone in a neutral tone environment.[7] The analysis also highlights the *variable* use of the components to create meanings of distinction by particular social actors as they engage in different stylistic projects. Thus, I expect that future studies will find variable use of specific components as well as additional linguistic forms that are not discussed in this study (see more discussion in Section 6.4). Furthermore, all such additional linguistic features should contribute to the distinctiveness of CM against a conservative style of Beijing-Mandarin-based PTH.

Second, despite its fluidity, the distinctiveness of CM depends crucially on co-occurrence of its linguistic components and the contrast that results from such co-occurrence in relation to its counterpart. Isolated use of any (one type of) innovative linguistic form, particularly the use of lexical items, such as the use of *man* + adjective in Xi's speech, does not mean that one is using the CM style (see more discussion in Section 6.3.2). In this respect, based on the analysis of production data in Chapters 3 and 4, the co-occurrence of de-rhotacization and full tone are found to be of primary importance in constituting the distinctiveness of CM (see n7).

Third, in addition to co-occurrence, similarity in patterns of linguistic variation such as the ones examined in this book (see Figure 3.3 in Chapter 3) is particularly important with regard to how CM sounds different from Beijing-Mandarin-based PTH. It is likely that future quantitative studies will find such similarity in variation patterns across different types of linguistic features (see discussion below in Section 6.4 on "*you* + VP").

Fourth, the difference between CM and its conservative counterpart, Beijing-Mandarin-based PTH, is not categorical but is rather frequency-based

180 A Style-Based Approach to Sociolinguistic Change

(see Figure 3.3 and Table 4.4). In other words, there is not a rigid linguistic boundary separating CM from a Beijing-Mandarin-based Standard PTH style. What distinguishes the two is a set of distinctive features, which varies in the number of specific features and the extent to which they co-occur. As shown in Chapters 3 and 4, the Beijing yuppies and the TV hosts draw on an overlapping set of linguistic features to enact distinction, but they do not sound the same because they use the linguistic features variably (see more detail in Section 6.3). Many factors contribute to the variability of CM, for example, emergent properties of communication events, participant roles in those events, the stylistic project in which the speakers are engaged, the range of features used and how they are combined, and last but not least, the local political economies where the speakers participate, which, as explained in Chapter 3, contribute to potential differences in their individual sociolinguistic biographies.

6.3 "How 'Style' Has a Particular Role to Play in Effecting Change"

The investigation of CM in the preceding chapters tracks its emergence as a stylistic resource as well as how it participates in dismantling the pre-reform socialist stylistic regime organized around conformity, egalitarianism, and the configuration of a postsocialist stylistic regime that valorizes differentiation. Such social-ideological transformation involves changes in content, form, meaning; style, as exemplified in the case of CM, includes all three dimensions. This is the answer to the central question of "how 'style' has a particular role to play in effecting change" (Coupland 2007, 100). In the rest of this section, I summarize the major findings of the book to elaborate the answer, with attention to changes in content (What is changed or new?), form (How is it different or changed?), and meaning.

6.3.1 Content: What is Changed or New?

With regard to change in content or "What is it that is changed or new?" CM is itself a new linguistic style whose emergence participates in diversifying the semiotic landscape of contemporary China. In addition, as an innovative stylistic resource, CM becomes part of the semiotic repertoires (Agha 2007) of other changes in content, such as new social identities and personae, and more broadly new ways of being and feeling. Specifically, this study locates its emergence in particularly salient sites, in the international business sector in Beijing and television programs, which are supposed to be strongholds for Beijing-Mandarin-based "common speech" and where new social distinctions are produced. Chapter 3 provides the primary and initial evidence for its emergence and use in the late 1990s by a group of Beijing yuppies, members of a rising social-economic elite in the country's capital city. The analysis depicts

A Style-Based Approach to Sociolinguistic Change **181**

the linguistic details of this innovative way of speaking Mandarin. What makes CM distinctive from the conventional Standard PTH is significantly decreased use of the most salient sound features of Beijing Mandarin—rhotacization, lenition, and neutral tone—but more use of their nonlocal variants. Chapter 4 examines its use in the mid-2000s by the hosts of a consumption-lifestyle TV program, metacultural experts who interpret meanings and values of signs that constitute new (life)styles. In addition to frequent de-rhotacization and full tone, the hosts use a larger range of linguistic forms, particularly lexical variation, and English expressions. Their linguistic style sounds more advanced, or stylistically more daring or flamboyant, than that of the yuppies in that they break norms in prescriptively obligatory environments for the neutral tone (as in the case of nouns with -zi), and in linguistic and pragmatic environments favoring rhotacization (e.g., see Table 4.5).

6.3.2 Form: How Is It Different or Changed?

With respect to form, or "How is it different or changed?," style is the very material and resource to display and bring about the "how" in multiple ways. Chapters 3 and 4 demonstrate that CM affords the yuppies and the TV hosts a resource through which new social distinctions are effected. The "newness" is created by bricolaging not only "new" linguistic martials, such as neologisms and English (a relatively new code in interactions among Chinese speakers), but also, and crucially, *stable* linguistic variation that has had a long history in regional variation between Northern Mandarin and Southern varieties. Furthermore, the recognition and construals of the social significance of CM and its salient components revealed in Chapter 5 means that these enregistered linguistic elements become themselves stylistic resources and even linguistic stereotypes, or stylistic shibboleths, that can be taken up by anyone in new stylistic moves in social interactions. Xi's use of *man* + adjective in his New Year Speech is a case in point: *Man* is no longer a signal of one's southern Chinese affiliation but is an element of (linguistic) trendiness that adds freshness or contemporariness to the ritual speech and makes the persona of China's President "amiable," "stylish," and "adorable" (as described in Section 6.1).

The new distinctions are created in multiple ways with regard to form. First, stylistic differentiation is established through intergroup contrast of aggregated use of linguistic variation. As shown in Chapter 3 (see Figure 3.3), the less use of conventional and local variants by the yuppie group distinguishes them from the state professional group. Second, more specific and pungent differentiation is created through more explicitly breaking conventional and prescriptive rules of variation, i.e., use of innovative variants in linguistically disfavoring environments (e.g., Example 11 and Table 4.5 in Chapter 4); or breaking a conventional rule in a pragmatically salient environment or form

182 A Style-Based Approach to Sociolinguistic Change

(e.g., de-rhotacization in minimal response *meicuo* 'right' instead of *meicuor* in Chapter 4). Third, differentiation is created through other strategic contrasts in moments of interaction where elements of CM and/or its counterpart are used to perform voicing contrasts (as in the case of stylization in Excerpt 15 in Chapter 4). Fourth, sequential contrast is another way to produce distinction whereby different contrasting linguistic forms, or variants, occur in sequence (as shown in examples 7, 8, and 10 in Chapter 4). Finally, distinction can also be created through content and form synchronism, that is, (clustering of) salient linguistic elements (of CM or its counterpart) in certain parts of the discourse and in salient lexemes (e.g., Excerpts 3.5, 3.7, 3.11, and 3.12 in Chapter 3, Excerpts 12 and 13 in Chapter 4). In such cases, the denotational meaning may not be necessarily by itself relevant to distinction or newness, but the use of stylistic elements, such as de-rhotacization (rhotacization) and full tone (neutral tone), highlight or vivify the social distinction intended to be conveyed through the content. In other words, stylistic resources create the link between the content and a persona or attributes of distinction.

6.3.3 Change in Meaning

These multiple ways through which distinctions are created through (elements of) CM are indeed how meanings of distinction are made. Style is fundamentally about constructing meanings of distinction. As stylistic resources such as CM emerge, new meanings about distinction emerge. The analyses in previous chapters reveal how CM is used to create such meanings. In addition, Chapter 5 shows that the emergence of CM involves change in the indexical meaning of existing linguistic forms, specifically shifting indexical orders and changing indexical fields. As illustrated in Table 5.3, the indexicality of de-rhotacization and full tone shifts from an n-th order indexicality of southern regional association to an $n+1$st order indexicality of supraregional social significance. This shift in indexical order—integral to the emergence of CM—affords possibilities of effecting other changes. For example, if Beijing-Mandarin-based PTH has been a stylistic resource for constructing meanings about supraregional Chineseness, CM expands the semiotic repertoires, making it possible to bring about different and more diversified ways to be Chinese and meanings of Chineseness (compare the positive $n+1$st indexical values of the two in Table 5.3).

Hence, the shift in indexical order is not merely changes in the social indexicality (i.e., social meaning) of linguistic forms. The analysis in Chapter 5 reveals that such indexical movement comes as a result of *changing ideologies* about language as well as larger sociopolitical issues that are themselves part of social change. I conclude the discussion on a style-based approach to sociolinguistic change in the next section by revisiting the central goal of this book: CM is a powerful resource for *undoing "commonness"* (see Section 1.2.1).

A Style-Based Approach to Sociolinguistic Change **183**

6.3.4 Undoing "Commonness" through Cosmopolitan Mandarin

In Chapter 1, I specified two ways of undoing commonness through CM (see Section 1.2.3.3): (1) through its use to produce new social distinctions and (2) through its construals that help shape the configuration of the postsocialist stylistic regime. The first way is demonstrated through the analysis undertaken in Chapters 3 and 4. As summarized in Sections 6.3.1–6.3.3, CM is a crucial resource to bring about new social distinctions that are transforming the socialist stylistic regime organized around conformity and egalitarianism. Furthermore, as pointed out in the previous section, the emergence of CM involves changes in not only the social meaning of linguistic forms but also changes in language ideologies. Style is fundamentally ideological (Eckert 2008; Irvine 2001), and the emergence of CM is mediated by ideology. In other words, what makes CM distinctive is not only the salient linguistic features such as de-rhotacization, full tone, and *man* 'quite, very', but equally important, changing beliefs about sociolinguistic normativity and construals of those linguistic features. As I explain below, changes in (language) ideology comprise the second way through which CM undoes "commonness."

This shift in language ideology is observable, first, in practice, or the production of style, and second, in the construals of CM. As explained in detail in Chapters 3 and 4, the conventional Standard PTH—a supraregional standard language—would be a "normal" resource at the disposal of both the Beijing yuppies and the TV hosts when enacting their identity and persona that are not based locally. However, their deployment of CM in practice breaks linguistic norms, which must be motivated by change in the belief about the appropriateness and adequacy of Beijing-Mandarin-based PTH as a resource for making their identity and persona meaningful in the social interactions in which they are engaged. The change in language ideology is also clearly observable in the construals of CM and its salient features revealed in the metalinguistic data in Chapter 5. The contesting interpretations found there (Table 5.3) provide strong evidence for rising awareness and recognition of the arbitrariness of the legitimacy and normativity of Beijing-/Northern-Mandarin-based "common speech"; such recognition, according to Bourdieu (1991), can destruct its symbolic power. In addition, as I point out in Section 5.3, the conflicting construals about the new style vis-à-vis the conventional PTH impact the indexical field of the "common speech." In this way, the emergence of CM dismantles "commonness" through undoing the "common speech" in both *practice* (disrupting its linguistic norms) and in *construal* (disrupting beliefs out of Standard PTH and reshaping its indexical field).

Finally, the multiple construals summarized in Table 5.3 are not merely about language but about changing ways of being and feeling, and evaluations of such changes mediated, again, by conflicting/changing ideologies about

184 A Style-Based Approach to Sociolinguistic Change

"appropriateness," "normativity," "authenticity," "morality," and so on. Hence, the positive and negative evaluations of CM and Beijing-Mandarin-based PTH provide evidence that Beijing, and by extension the North, is not the single center of evaluation but that multiple centers of evaluation are emerging. Furthermore, the emergence of CM and the reshaping of the indexical field of "common speech" (see Section 5.3) means that the status of the "common speech" as the single voice for a modern, globalizing China is being challenged. All of these—changing ways of being and feeling, emergence of multiple centers of evaluation, and multiple voices for modern Chineseness—are part of the transition to a postsocialist stylistic regime. Thus, the examination of the emergence of CM sheds light on how such a stylistic regime is coming into being (see Section 1.2.2).

In conclusion, a style-based approach to sociolinguistic change, taking the emergence of CM as a case study, enables an integrated treatment of language and social-ideological change. Linguistic change as emergent stylistic resources constitutes the content of "What is changed"; it affords the resource for making new social distinctions by bringing about "How it is different"; and it constructs the meanings of distinction. Such an approach embeds linguistic change within larger social-ideological processes.

6.4 Looking Forward: Prospects of Cosmopolitan Mandarin and Standard Mandarin

This study examines an early phase of the enregisterment of CM and focuses on a few phonological and lexical features that distinguish CM from its conservative counterpart, Beijing-Mandarin-based PTH. Two sound features, namely, de-rhotacization and full tone, are particularly salient distinctive components. Drawing on my findings, summarized in the preceding sections, I now turn to predictions about CM and Standard Mandarin: What is the future of CM and how does this new Mandarin style shape the future of Standard Mandarin in China? Following Agha's (2007) discussion on the three dimensions of register change, I predict that CM is going to expand in its constitutive forms, social domains, and range of indexical values.

First, CM is likely to expand in terms of the number and types of linguistic forms. Similar to the above distinctive features found in this study, the stable variation between Northern Mandarin and Southern Chinese are likely to remain a major source of such forms. This is because Mandarin is a dominant form of linguistic capital in the transnational Chinese linguistic market, and as found in this study, Beijing-/Northern-Mandarin-based PTH is no longer the only legitimate Mandarin in the market. Although English is recognized as a global language and is, as shown in the data, used to a limited extent, because it does not have a history of use in public and private domains, it is likely to remain a minor role in the development of CM. More southern-influenced

A Style-Based Approach to Sociolinguistic Change **185**

Chinese variants are likely to become components of CM by undergoing an indexical movement from a southern geographical association to supraregional social indexicality just as I noted for the sound features in this study. Evidence for the enregisterment of such forms will necessarily come from production data to show that they are being used to create supraregional social meanings and from metapragmatic discourse to reveal the recognition of their distinctiveness and linkage to a set of values as found in this study (see Table 5.3). In my personal observations, I have noticed two such forms that may be undergoing enregisterment. One of them is a syntactic feature, namely, the use of *you* 'have' as a perfective aspect marker in the structure "*you* + VP" 'have done something'. A feature shared among many Southern varieties, its use is increasing among Northern Mandarin speakers (e.g., Cui 2013; Yang and Dong 2003). The second one is a phonological feature: reduced degree of retroflexion (or fronting) of the alveolo-palatal retroflex onsets *zh*, *ch*, and *sh*, the same set of consonants that are lenited in the yuppies data set. The fronting results in their realization approximating the English postalveolar /dʒ/, /tʃ/, and /ʃ/ respectively.

Second, the social domains of CM will grow as more and more Chinese speakers recognize and take up features associated with CM in their linguistic practices. The expansion in social domains, particularly the increase in social groups adopting CM, depends on positive role alignment with the characters, personae, and indexical values enacted through the linguistic style (Agha 2007). Positive evaluations of CM found in the metalinguistic data in Chapter 5 offer strong evidence for role alignment in terms of perception but not production. Regarding the latter, this study focuses on speakers whose native dialects are Beijing and Tianjin Mandarin, but southern speakers are likely to take up CM more readily in their stylistic projects. Just as Northern Mandarin speakers have an advantage in speaking the conservative Standard PTH by virtue of shared linguistic features in their native dialects, the emergence of CM gives southern speakers an advantage because its salient components, as found in the current study, are part of their native dialects. Such salient southern features, including non-rhotacization and full tone, can be used (a) as part of a Southern dialect and (b) by anyone to enact stereotypical southern characters and to express *n*+1st order indexicalities motivated by beliefs about southerners. However, to distinguish speaking PTH with a southern accent from using full tone and de-rhotacization as part of CM, evidence needs to be found regarding when a southern Chinese speaker uses these features among other linguistic resources to create nongeographical, particularly non-southern, social indexicalities.[8]

Finally, CM is likely to expand in its indexical values, including types of social characters and personae, social relations, and attributes and the occasions in which it is used. Although this study does not examine CM's use in everyday, casual interaction, the results found support the likelihood of

186 A Style-Based Approach to Sociolinguistic Change

speakers drawing on distinctive features of CM in such occasions. Specifically, its indexical potential in enacting a nonlocal-based personae and affective stances that combine conviviality, youthfulness, and ebullience (as found in Chapters 4 and 5) enables CM to become incorporated into the casual registers of Standard Mandarin.[9] The consequence of such incorporation is the expansion of both the linguistic repertoires—with CM as one of the enregistered Mandarin styles—and the indexical range of the spoken standard language. Such expansion in Standard Mandarin is most palpably manifested in mass media, particularly in radio and television entertainment programs, despite the government's efforts in reinforcing linguistic norms based on Northern Mandarin. Based on the foregoing discussion, the trend is *diversification*, with CM and its constitutive elements becoming an increasingly salient stylistic resource rather than becoming the next phase of Standard Mandarin (cf. Li 2004). In other words, with regard to spoken Standard Mandarin in mainland China, the salient sound features of CM, de-rhotacization (or loss of rhotacization), and full tone replacing neutral tone are not likely to categorically replace rhotacization and neutral tone to become the next "new" norm, replacing the Beijing-/Northern-Mandarin-based standard (as Li 2004 suggests). For this to happen, there would have to be a much more drastic ideological shift that, on the one hand, completely stigmatizes the $n+1$st order indexicalities of rhotacization and neutral tone and, on the other, wipes out the negative indexical values of de-rhotacization and full tone. Such a drastic ideological shift is unlikely to happen in the near future.

Notes

1 Xi Jinping's 2015 New Year Celebration Speech can be viewed within China on all the state mass media platforms, including the CCTV website, http://tv.cntv.cn/video/C10420/1e58107053f649519eb3438fe87586e1. It can also be viewed at the CCTV official news channel on YouTube, www.youtube.com/watch?v=6u_K3npTaIc.

2 The full text of the speech is published in *People's Daily* on January 1, 2015, accessible at http://paper.people.com.cn/rmrb/html/2015-01/01/nw.D110000ren-mrb_20150101_2-01.htm. The English translation is adapted from Xinhua (2015) and Ministry of Foreign Affairs of the People's Republic of China (2015).

3 The popularity of *"ye shi man pinde"* 'working pretty hard' or 'give it one's bestshot' was accredited to Cao Ge (Gary Chaw), a Malaysian Chinese singer-songwriter who established his music career in Malaysia, Singapore, and Taiwan (e.g., Liu 2015). He became a celebrity in mainland China through participating in the second season of *I Am a Singer*, a popular singing competition show on Hunan Satellite Television, one of the most popular television stations in the country. He then participated in the second season of another popular celebrity reality show *Dad, Where Are We Going?* on the same television station. It was reported that *"ye shi man pinde"* was used often by him on the show to express his frustration in exerting himself to perform various arduous tasks with his two children, sometimes without being successful (Liu 2015). The popularity of the show garnered it many fans, and they helped make the expression a catchphrase widely used on social media. Similar to

many buzzwords on social media, humor and (self) mockery are often part of the intended connotations of the expression (ibid.). In Xi's speech, *"man pinde"* expresses the President's compliment to the cadres' hard work with no mockery intended.

4 In contrast to the heavily accented PTH of older generations of Chinese leaders, Xi Jinping's speech in Standard PTH at the first news conference after being elected as the General Secretary of the CCP Central Committee received enthusiastic reactions on Chinese social media (e.g., Wertime 2012; Xintianyou 2012).

5 The expressions used by the netizens to characterize Xi's use of the two terms are also mostly popular expressions originated from social media. *Jie diqi* 'down-to-earth' is one of the most popular buzzwords in 2012 (Editorial Office 2013), and *mengmengda* 'cute, adorable' is among the top 10 most popular expressions in 2014 (Editorial Office 2015). The kinship term *Xi Dada* 'Uncle Xi', originated from a Chinese Weibo blog account *Xuexi Fensituan* 'Study Fans Club' in 2012, has since become a popular address term for Xi Jinping (Ding and Feng 2015; Xinhua 2014).

6 Thus, it is not a goal of this study to offer a closed list of linguistic features constituting CM. Benor's conceptualization of ethnolinguistic repertoires (2010) also supports moving away from a fixed inventory approach to "ethnolects" to an emphasis on the compositional fluidity of linguistic resources.

7 The current study strongly suggests that the combination, or co-occurrence, of de-rhotacization and full tone in a neutral tone environment is of primary importance in creating the linguistic distinction of CM. However, perception experiments are needed to determine if phonological features are perceived to be more salient than other types of forms, such as lexical features.

8 These other linguistic resources include avoidance of features specific to the speaker's regional dialect, for example, the merger of alveolo-palatal retroflex onsets *zh*, *ch*, and *sh* with dental sibilants *z*, *c*, and *s*, and the merger of approximant and nasal onsets *r*, *l*, and *n*.

9 I am using the term "casual registers" here to emphasize the repertoire and utterance aspects of Agha's (2007) re-theorization of *register* formation and change as sociohistorical processes of enregisterment. In other words, the term register is used here in its more traditional sense, emphasizing the use of particular varieties of Standard Chinese, in both written and spoken forms, to serve particular functions in particular situations, ranging from formal and ritual domains to casual and everyday social interactions. We need to bear in mind that, as Woolard (2016) notes, the actual use and recognition of particular registers are mediated by language ideologies that can erase and "strip" them from the linguistic repertoires of a (standard) language as demonstrated in the case of Castilian and Catalan in Catalonia (see also Frekko 2009).

References

Agha, Asif. 2007. *Language and Social Relations*. Cambridge: Cambridge University Press.

Benor, Sarah Bunin. 2010. "Ethnolinguistic Repertoire: Shifting the Analytic Focus in Language and Ethnicity." *Journal of Sociolinguistics* 14 (2):159–183.

Bourdieu, Pierre. 1991. *Language and Symbolic Power*. Translated by Gino Raymond, and Matthew Adamson. Cambridge, MA: Harvard University Press.

China News. 2015. *"Xi Jinping 'dianzan' renmin renmin 'dianzan' Xi Dada"* ("Xi Jinping 'Gives Thumbs-Up' to the People, the People 'Give Thumbs-Up' to Uncle Xi"). www.chinanews.com/gn/2015/01-02/6930614.shtml. Accessed January 9, 2015.

Coupland, Nikolas. 2007. *Style: Language Variation and Identity*. Cambridge: Cambridge University Press.

188 A Style-Based Approach to Sociolinguistic Change

Cui, Na. 2013. *"Xiandai Hanyu Putonghua zhongde 'You + VP' Jushi"* ("The 'Have + VP' Syntactic Form in Modern Chinese *Putonghua"*.) *Duiwai Hanyu Jiaoxue yu Yanjiu (Chinese as a Foreign Language Teaching and Research).* 4:49–55.

Ding, Gang, and Xuejun Feng. 2015. *"2014, Shijie cong Zhe 6 ge Ci zhong Du Zhongguo: 'Xi Dada' Yici Fanyicheng le sha?"* ("2014, The World Understands China from These 6 Expressions: How is 'Xi Dada' Translated?"). http://politics.people.com. cn/n/2015/0106/c1001-26332767.html. Accessed January 9, 2015.

Eckert, Penelope. 2008. "Variation and the Indexical Field." *Journal of Sociolinguistics* 12 (4):453–476.

Editorial Office. 2013. "2012 Shida Liuxing Yu" ("2012 Top Ten Buzzwords"). *Yaowenjuezi (Overfastidious about Words)* 2013 Issue 2:4–6.

Editorial Office. 2014. "2013 *Shida Liuxing Yu*" ("2013 Top Ten Buzzwords"). *Yaowenjuezi (Overfastidious about Words)* 2014 Issue 2:4–6.

Editorial Office. 2015. "2014 *Shida Liuxing Yu*" ("2014 Top Ten Buzzwords"). *Yaowenjuezi (Overfastidious about Words)* 2015 Issue 2:4–6.

Frekko, Susan E. 2009. "'Normal' in Catalonia: Standard Language, Enregisterment and the Imagination of a National Public." *Language in Society* 38 (1):71–93.

Gui, Jie. 2014. *"'Shijian Dou Qu Na le' Lingpao 2014 Nian Shi Da Wangluo Yongyu"* ("'Where Has the Time Gone' Leads in the 2014 Top Ten Internet Buzzwords"). *Zhongguo Qingnian Bao (China Youth Daily),* December 23, 2014, 9. http://zqb.cyol. com/html/2014-12/23/nw.D110000zgqnb_20141223_1-09.htm. Accessed January 5, 2015.

Irvine, Judith. 2001. "'Style' as Distinctiveness: The Culture and Ideology of Linguistic Differentiation." In *Style and Sociolinguistic Variation,* edited by Penelope Eckert, and John R. Rickford, 21–43. Cambridge: Cambridge University Press.

Li, Chris Wen-Chao. 2004. "Conflicting Notions of Language Purity: The Interplay of Archaising, Ethnographic, Reformist, Elitist and Xenophobic Purism in the Perception of Standard Chinese." *Language & Communication* 24 (2):97–133.

Li, Zhengqiong. 2015. *"'Xi Dada Mengdong Zhongguo' Gandong Zhongguo Yiwan Wangyou Dianzan"* ("'Uncle Xi Adorably Moving China' Affects China: Billions of Netizens Giving It a Thumbs-Up"). http://news.youth.cn/wztt/201501/t20150105_6384517. htm. Accessed January 5, 2015.

Liu, Dongze. 2015. *"Li shuo 'ye shi man pinde'"* ("Examples and Explanations for 'Giving It One's Best Shot'"). *Yaowenjuezi (Overfastidious about Words)* 2015 Issue 2:9–11.

Ministry of Foreign Affairs of the People's Republic of China. 2015. "Chinese President Xi Jinping's 2015 New Year Message." http://news.xinhuanet.com/english/ china/2014-12/31/c_133890353.htm. Accessed January 5, 2015.

Wertime, David. 2012. "Finally, a Chinese Leader Who Speaks Intelligible Mandarin." *The Atlantic,* November 19, 2012. www.theatlantic.com/international/archive/ 2012/11/finally-a-chinese-leader-who-speaks-intelligible-mandarin/265409/. Accessed December 15, 2012.

Woolard, Kathryn A. 2016. *Singular and Plural: Ideologies of Linguistic Authority in 21st Century Catalonia.* Oxford and New York, NY: Oxford University Press.

Wu, Chu, and Li Zhengqiong. 2015. *"Qingnian dianzan Xi Dada xinnian heci: 'Nin yeshi man pinde!'"* ("Youth Give Thumbs-Up to Uncle Xi's New Year Celebration Speech: 'You've also Given It Your Best Shot!'"). http://picture.youth.cn/qtdb/201501/ t20150101_6377456.htm. Accessed January 9, 2015.

Wu, Chu et al. 2015. *"Dianzan renmin man pin mengxiang: Xi Dada mengdong Zhongguo"* ("Giving People Thumbs-Up, Working very Hard on Dreams: Uncle Xi Adorably Moves China"). http://news.youth.cn/wztt/201501/t20150101_6378311.htm. Accessed January 9, 2015.

Xinhua 2014. *"2014 nian shi da xinwen fabu: Xi Dada cheng re ci"* ("2014 Top Ten Internet News: Uncle Xi Becoming a Buzzword"). http://news.xinhuanet.com/politics/2014-12/31/c_1113839291.htm. Accessed January 9, 2015.

Xinhua. 2015. "President Xi Stresses More Reform, Rule of Law in New Year Address." http://news.xinhuanet.com/english/china/2014-12/31/c_133890353.htm. Accessed January 9, 2015.

Xintianyou. 2012. *"Guanyu xin zong shuji jizhe jianmianhui de jianghua dajia dou zengme kan a?"* ("How Does Everyone View the News Conference of the New General Secretary?"). www.vbol.cn/forum.php?mod=viewthread&tid=165548. Accessed December 15, 2012.

Xu, Robert, and Patrick Callier. 2016. "Exploring Prosodic Variability of Character Types in Mainland Mandarin." Paper presented at *New Ways of Analyzing Variation Asia Pacific*. Chiayi, Taiwan.

Yang, Wenquan, and Dong Yuen. 2003. *"Hanyu 'You + VP' Ju Jianxi"* ("Concise Analysis of Chinese 'Have + VP'"). *Yuwen Jianshe Tongxun (Philology Construction)* 75:27–32.

INDEX

accent 29–30, 61–2, 64, 151; Beijing accent 15, 16, 54, 65, 67, 69, 83, 85, 148, 158, 160; *boyin qiang* 'broadcasting accent' 120; local accents in Standard *Putonghua* (Standard PTH) 64, 74–5, 82–4, 187n4; Northeastern Mandarin accent 126–7, 140; oily accent 68; southern (Mandarin) accent 155, 158, 185; *see also Gang-Tai qiang* 'Hong Kong-Taiwan accent'

Agha, Asif 28, 31, 33, 64, 66, 106, 107, 125, 129, 129n2, 129n3, 134–8, 150, 167n1, 180, 184–5, 187n9

"alley saunterer" 71–2, 76, 78; gender and 71, 72, 86; interdental realization of (*ts*) and 66, 72–3, 76, 78, 86, 94

Androutsopoulos, Jannis 20

Auslander, Leora 24–5, 36n3

authentication *see* authenticity

authenticity 25, 30, 161, 184; Beijing Mandarin (BM) and 65, 73, 145–6, 158; code-mixing (Mandarin–English) and 114–15; enregisterment and 31, 158; *Gai-Tai qiang* 'Hong Kong-Taiwan accent' as inauthentic 151, 153, 155, 166; Southern varieties and 158–9; Standard *Putonghua* (Standard PTH) and 155, 157, 166

Bakhtin, Mikhail M. 29–30, 37n6, 88, 127

baofahu 'upstart/parvenu' 54–7, 96–7; *see also* Beijing yuppies

Bauman, Richard 30, 37n6, 37n7

Beijing Mandarin (BM) 9–10; Cosmopolitan Mandarin and 62, 80, 84, 181, 186; historical and cultural significance of 64–5, 69; lenition of (*sh*) 66, 69–71, 74–5, 181; neutral tone 74, 95, 116, 130n8, 181; rhotacization 68–9, 73, 89, 96, 115–16, 100n16, 130n8, 149, 157–9, 166, 181; phonological basis for *Putonghua* (PTH) 7–8, 80, 82–4, 100n16, 151, 157; Standard *Putonghua* (Standard PTH) and 10, 62–4, 83–4, 95, 117, 161, 181; *see also* accent, authenticity; Cosmopolitan Mandarin (CM); *Gang-Tai qiang* 'Hong Kong-Taiwan accent'; full-tone realization of a neutral tone; personae; *Putonghua* (PTH)

"Beijing smooth operator" 63, 66–7; gender and 67, 88; lenition of (*sh*) and 66, 69–71, 76, 88; rhotacization (*r*) and 63, 66, 67–71, 88; smoothness of Beijing speech and 67–8

Beijing yuppies, 14, 35, 46–9; aesthetic labor and 49, 58n3, 87, 99; contrast with *baofahu* 'upstart/parvenu' and local nouveau riche 54–7, 95–9; contrast with state professionals 48–51, 63, 86, 91, 99; Cosmopolitan Mandarin (CM) and 14–15, 28, 61, 63, 84–5, 98–9, 181; cultured cosmopolitans 52–8, 96; English and 61–2, 89–90, 92, 97–8, 181; gender variation and 77, 78; linguistic innovation and 35; linguistic styling and 61–2, 85–95, 97; patterns of variation

192 Index

76–9; topic variation and 76, 78–9; transnational Chinese linguistic market and 83–5; *waiqi* 'foreign enterprise' professionals and 48; *see also* full-tone realization of a neutral tone; gender; identity; interdental realization of (*ts*), lenition of (*sh*); personae (social); rhotacization (*r*)/non-rhotacization/de-rhotacization; social distinction; state professionals; *waiqi* 'foreign enterprises' professionals

Bell, Allen 22, 30

Bourdieu, Pierre 24, 25, 27, 53, 57, 80, 82, 83, 84, 106, 107, 122, 183

bricolage 14, 28–9, 58, 61, 64, 75, 98–9, 134, 179; *see also* style

Bucholtz, Mary 22, 24, 25, 29, 30, 88, 98, 124, 151

Cantonese (*Yue*) 7, 28, 62, 64–6, 68, 74, 80, 157, 159, 168n19; Hong Kong Cantonese 28, 66, 73, 75, 112–13, 156

capitalism 3, 8

Chao, Yuen Ren 68, 70, 74, 82

character types 15, 64–6, 71–3, 75–6, 88, 99, 143; *see also* "alley saunter"; "Beijing smooth operator"; "Cosmopolitan Chinese"

Chen, Ping 7, 9–11, 16n4, 16n7

China Central Television (CCTV) 16, 130n10, 156, 163, 168n17; CCTV Spring Festival Gala 139, 144, 161; Cosmopolitan Mandarin (CM) and 139, 144, 146, 150, 154, 161; news anchors and broadcasters 120, 129, 154; news programs 154; Standard *Putonghua* (Standard PTH) and 98, 120, 129, 159–60

Chinese (Chinese language) 6–9, 12–13, 16n4, 82–3, 112, 157, 159, 187n9; Modern Standard Chinese (Standard Chinese) 6, 8–9, 13, 16n4, 82, 157, 187n9; Northern varieties of 7, 159; Southern varieties of 7, 65, 74, 75, 100n6, 112–13, 137, 158–9, 181, 184–5; *see also* authenticity; Cantonese; language standardization; Mandarin; Min; *Putonghua* (PTH); Wu

Chinese Communist Party (CCP) 5, 8–10, 12, 49, 108, 150

code-mixing (Mandarin–English) 34, 80, 110, 114; *see also* authenticity; Cosmopolitan Mandarin (CM); English;

linguistic innovations; *Putonghua* (PTH); television (TV) hosts

Common Language Law 82, 110, 150

"common speech" 6, 8, 10, 14, 23, 98, 157, 165; contrast with Cosmopolitan Mandarin (CM) 30, 32, 178, 180, 183–4; semiotic inadequacy of 12–13, 16n2, 98; *see also Putonghua* as "common speech"

"commonness", undoing commonness 23–4, 32, 98, 182–4; *see also* Cosmopolitan Mandarin (CM)

communism and communists 5, 10, 71, 108

conformity 2, 11–13, 27–8, 72, 180, 183

consumer revolution 3, 5, 108

consumerism 2, 5, 56, 105, 107; *see also* social distinction; trendiness/trendy

"Cosmopolitan Chinese" 73–6, 137, 166; full-tone realization of a neutral tone 74, 76, 80, 98, 137

Cosmopolitan Mandarin (CM) 2; changing economy and 81–5; code-mixing (Mandarin–English) and 34, 80, 110, 114–15; compositional fluidity of 179, 187n6; contrasted with local style of state professionals 79–8; cosmopolitanism and 99, 128; definition of 80, 179; difference between Beijing-Mandarin-based *Putonghua* (PTH) and 80, 82, 179–81; distinctiveness of 62, 80, 144, 150, 98, 179–80, 187n7; exemplary speakers of 73, 89, 110, 129; indexical values of 36, 107, 128, 137–8, 165, 167, 182, 184–5; lexical features/items 80, 110–14, 124, 179, 184, 187n7; linguistic innovations and 20, 34; local features used with 95–8; mediatization of 99; normativity of 136, 144; phonological/sound features 15, 66, 115–29, 184, 187n7; popular media and literary representations of 139–47; prospects for future and 184–6; as resource for undoing commonness 23, 32, 182–4; as sociolinguistic change 20, 32, 34, 184; as symbolic/linguistic capital 28, 48, 80, 82–4, 87, 184; symbolic value of 80, 82, 83–4; transnational Chinese linguistic market and 35, 63, 80, 82, 83–5; *see also* Beijing Mandarin (BM); Beijing yuppies; China Central Television (CCTV); "common speech," English; counter-enregisterment; enregisterment; *Gang-Tai qiang* 'Hong

Kong-Taiwan accent'; identity; intensifier; linguistic markets; linguistic variables; personae; *Putonghua* (PTH); social distinction; stylistic resources; supraregional; television (TV) hosts

cosmopolitanism 99, 112, 114–15, 125, 128; *see also* Cosmopolitan Mandarin (CM); English; identity; personae; trendy/trendiness

counter-enregisterment 144, 157, 159–60, 164–6; Cosmopolitan Mandarin (CM) and 150–4; *see also* enregisterment; *Gang-Tai qiang* 'Hong Kong-Taiwan accent'

Coupland, Nicholas 2, 20–4, 27–8, 34, 36n1, 107, 116, 135, 158, 178, 180

cultural intermediaries 106–7; television (TV) hosts as 107, 109

De Francis, John 7, 9, 16n4, 157

de-eliticization 11, 25

Deng, Xiaoping 1, 2, 10, 16n1, 28

denotational meaning 4–6, 112, 120, 182

dental sibilants 62, 72, 140–1, 143, 187n8

dialogic, dialogism 14, 29–31, 64, 134; decontextualization and recontextualization 37n6; intertextuality and interdiscursivity 37n7; style as sociohistorical process 14, 28–9

discourse analysis 15, 35

discursive practice, metadiscursive practice 21, 34, 138

Dong, Jie 2, 10, 28

double-voicing, vari-directional 127

ebullience, ebullient: Cosmopolitan Mandarin (CM) and 128–9, 137, 166; persona and 15, 109, 120, 126, 128–9, 152, 186

Eckert, Penelope 21–2, 24–5, 29, 31, 36n1, 129, 135, 137, 183

egalitarianism *see* socialist egalitarianism

English 3–6, 15, 25, 34, 48–50, 57, 61; Cosmopolitan Mandarin (CM) and 80, 98, 140–1, 181, 184; cosmopolitanism and 114–5; *Gang-Tai qiang* 'Hong Kong-Taiwan accent' and 149; television (TV) hosts' use of 111–15, 124–5, 129n1, 181; *see also* authenticity; Beijing yuppies; code-mixing (Mandarin–English)

enregisterment 2–3, 13, 31–3, 122, 135–8, 150, 164–7, 179, 187n9; battle

over 15; characterological figures and 135, 138, 145–6, 149; Cosmopolitan Mandarin (CM) and 35, 129, 135–8, 144, 149, 154, 164, 167n5, 180, 184–5; indexical order and 136–7; (ideological) contestation 26–7, 31, 34, 68, 136, 138, 165–6; *Putonghua* (PTH) and 169n31; relational and contrastive process 165; sociohistorical process 23, 28, 32, 134–5, 148; *see also* counter-enregisterment; *Gang-Tai qiang* 'Hong Kong-Taiwan accent'; personae; social distinction; style; trendiness/trendy

erasure (erasing) 7, 11–12, 49, 138, 187n9

Ferguson, James 24, 25

fractal recursivity 146, 162; recursive construals 178, 180; recursive interpretations 164; recursive projections 172; recursive renderings 178

full-tone realization of a neutral tone 74–5, 78, 139, 182; Beijing yuppies and 76–81, 179; Cosmopolitan Mandarin (CM) and 80, 91–2, 94, 149, 179, 183–6, 187n7; *Gang-Tai qiang* 'Hong Kong-Taiwan accent' and 148–9, 155, 166; gender and 7–9, 77–8, 86, 88, 94; as innovative phonological/sound feature 115–16, 118–20; local variant 75, 94–5, 120; patterns of variation 76–9; Southern varieties and 74; state professionals and 77; television (TV) hosts and 179, 181; topic and 76–7, 79; *see also* Beijing Mandarin (BM); "Cosmopolitan Chinese"; *Gang-Tai qiang* 'Hong Kong-Taiwan accent'; identity; television (TV) hosts

Gal, Susan 5, 20–1, 23–4, 27, 33–4, 36, 36n3, 37n7, 67, 146, 148, 162

Gang-Tai qiang 'Hong Kong-Taiwan accent' 74, 145, 147; broadcasters and 145, 150; changes in culture and 165, 168n8, 169n26; characterological figures of 145–8; counter-enregisterment efforts and 150–4; as metapragmatic label for Cosmopolitan Mandarin (CM) 138, 147–9; public sphere metadiscourse about 154–65; Standard *Putonghua* (Standard PTH) and 147, 160–6, 165; television (TV) hosts and 152–3; full-tone realization of a neutral tone and 74, 147–50; *see also* authenticity; English; trendiness/trendy

194 Index

gender: career trajectories of *waiqi* 'foreign enterprises' professionals and 50–1, 87–8, 99, 100n12; identity and 14, 50; *see also* "alley saunterer"; "Beijing smooth operator"; Beijing yuppies; Cosmopolitan Mandarin (CM), linguistic variables, *waiqi* 'foreign enterprises' professionals

Great Proletariat Cultural Revolution (Cultural Revolution) 11–13, 16n10, 23, 28, 71, 169n30

Guevara, Che 4–5

Guojia Guangbo Dianying Dianshi Zongju see State Administration of Radio, Film, and Television (SARFT)

guoqi 'state-owned enterprises' 14, 47; gender and 49–50

guoqi 'state-owned enterprises' professionals: see state professionals

Hanser, Amy 2, 23, 58n3

Hanyu see Chinese (Chinese language)

Hebdige, Dick 25

Hill, Jane H. 20–1, 26, 138, 146

Hong Kong and Taiwan accent: *see Gang-Tai qiang* 'Hong Kong-Taiwan accent'

Hymes, Dell 20

iconization 67–8

identity: of Beijing yuppies 62, 63, 99; Chinese identity, Chineseness 137, 155, 166–7; of corporation 49; cosmopolitan 62, 73, 80, 99; Cosmopolitan Mandarin (CM) as resource for 80, 183; indexical order and 75; linguistic market and 80; professional 14, 63, 80, 121–2; Standard *Putonghua* (Standard PTH) and 137, 155, 166, 183; television (TV) hosts and 183; *see also* gender

ideologies 23–7, 33, 36n3, 75, 106, 122, 128, 135, 138, 144, 146, 183; of differentiation 14, 24, 32; ideological shift 2, 10, 13, 20, 27, 186; of socialist egalitarianism 23; *see also* sociolinguistic change; style

Implementation Guidelines for the Putonghua Proficiency Test (PSCSG) 74, 115–16, 119, 130n8, 150

indexical congruency 33, 125–8

indexical field 35, 137–8, 166–7, 183–4

indexical incongruency 127

indexical meaning 97, 112, 114, 125, 136, 152, 182; *see also* indexicality (social)

indexical order 34, 36, 136–8, 175, 182; indexical movement 137, 182, 185; n-th order indexicality 136–8, 151, 153, 155, 166; n+1st order indexicality 136–8, 150, 152–5, 165–6, 182, 186; *see also* Cosmopolitan Mandarin (CM); Mainland Standard *Putonghua* (MSP); enregisterment

indexical potential 99, 167, 186

indexicality (social) 29, 100n8, 126, 136, 162, 165; fluidity of 34, 136; indexical values 112, 114, 128, 136, 138, 165, 167, 186; multiplicity of 34; *see also* Cosmopolitan Mandarin (CM); identity; indexical order; social distinction; social meaning; supraregional

Inoue, Miyako 21, 26–8, 33, 37n8, 106, 138

interdental realization of (*ts*) 66, 71–3, 100n5; Beijing yuppies and 77–9, 81; gender and 78, 86; local variant 66, 75; state professionals and 76–8; topic and 77–9; *see also* "alley saunterer"

internal constraints 76–8

interviews, sociolinguistic 35, 52, 63, 67

Irvine, Judith 5, 24–5, 36, 67, 146, 162, 183

Ji, Fengyuan 12–13

Johnstone, Barbara 22, 30, 135, 137–8, 167n1

Kroskrity, Paul V. 24, 36n3

Labov, William 20, 22, 27, 36n3, 37n4

language change 1, 2, 13–14, 20–1, 34; *see also* linguistic change; sociolinguistic change

language ideologies 9, 14, 25, 27, 31–4, 36, 66, 182–3, 187n9; *see also* ideologies

language standardization 2, 6, 8–9, 13; politics of 6; of Modern Standard Chinese 6, 8–9; as process of de-eliticization 8, 11–12, 25

legitimacy 13, 15, 25–8, 30–1, 68, 82, 136, 151

Lei Feng 4–5, 127

lenition of (*sh*) 66, 69–71, 78, 97; Beijing yuppies and 76–9, 81, 86, 88, 92; Cosmopolitan Mandarin (CM) and 92, 94; *Gang-Tai qiang* 'Hong Kong-Taiwan accent' and 149; gender and 77–8, 81, 88, 94; local variant 75, 92, 94–5, 97; patterns of variation 76–9; state professionals and 77–8; topic and 76–7,

79; *see also* Beijing Mandarin (BM); "Beijing smooth operator"
Lévi-Strauss, Claude 28–9
linguistic anthropology 14, 20–1, 32, 37n7
linguistic change 11, 14, 20, 22, 24, 34, 37n4, 64, 184; *see also* language change; sociolinguistic change
linguistic constraints 76; *see also* internal constraints
linguistic enregisterment 134; *see also* enregisterment
linguistic innovations 1, 3, 6, 13–14, 20, 22–3, 31–2, 35–6, 66, 75, 134, 136, 178; adverb *man* 'quite', 'very' 112–13, 124, 177, 179, 181, 183, 186n3; code-mixing (Mandarin–English) as 114; intensifier *hao* 'quite', 'very' 96, 113, 140, 147; lexical innovations 110–14; sound features 115–20; *see also* Cosmopolitan Mandarin (CM); linguistic variables
linguistic markets 80, 84–5; Mainland Standard *Putonghua* (MSP) linguistic market 82–3, 100n9; transnational Chinese linguistic market 28, 35, 48, 63, 80, 82–5, 98, 100n9, 184; *see also* Cosmopolitan Mandarin (CM); English; identity; state professionals
linguistic styling 61, 119; *see also* Beijing yuppies; *Gang-Tai qiang* 'Hong Kong-Taiwan accent'; social distinction; style
linguistic (sociolinguistic) variables 14–15, 22, 34, 63–4, 66–7, 74–6, 78–82, 86–8, 95, 99, 179; *see also* full-tone realization of a neutral tone; interdental realization of (ts); lenition of (sh); rhotacization (r)
Lu, Yunzhong 68–9, 74, 118–19

Mainland Standard Mandarin *see Putonghua*: Mainland Standard *Putonghua*
Mandarin *see* Beijing Mandarin (BM); Cosmopolitan Mandarin (CM); non-mainland Mandarin; Northern Mandarin; Southwestern Mandarin; Taiwan Mandarin (*Guoyu*); Tianjin Mandarin
mass media 66, 99, 105–7; *see also* social distinction; popular culture; mediation; mediatization
Mazzarella, William 105–6
mediation 15, 34, 105–7, 129n3; media and 106; social distinction and 106; *see also* semiotic mediation; sociolinguistic change

mediatization 34, 106–7, 129n3; *see also* Cosmopolitan Mandarin (CM); social distinction; sociolinguistic change
Mendoza-Denton, Norma 22, 25, 30, 129
metacultural experts 106–7, 109, 181; *see also* cultural intermediaries
metalinguistic data 15, 32, 34, 35, 183, 185; *see also* metalinguistic discourse
metalinguistic discourse 15, 16n3, 32–6, 37n8, 64, 85, 135–6, 138, 144, 165, 183, 185
metapragmatic discourse: *see* metalinguistic discourse
metapragmatic function 136
metapragmatic label 138, 147, 149; *see also Gang-Tai qiang* 'Hong Kong-Taiwan accent'
metapragmatic messages 125, 135–6, 143–4, 150
metasemiotic discourse 15, 32, 35, 94, 99, 105–7, 120–8, 139
middle classes, Chinese 2, 26, 47–9; middle-class consumer 14, 106–7, 109, 120–7; middle-class identities 106; middle-class lifestyle 14, 99
Min 7, 74; Southern Min (Taiwanese) 7, 74, 156–7, 159, 168n19; *see also* Chinese (Chinese Language); Southern varieties
methodology 32–6

non-mainland Mandarin varieties 48, 66, 79, 84 98; *see also Putonghua* (PTH)
Norman, Jerry 7, 16n4, 69–70, 74, 159
normativity 31, 34, 127, 144
Northern Mandarin 7–8, 66, 119, 130n8, 130n11, 139, 147, 151, 156; basis for *Putonghua* (PTH) 8, 10, 164, 186; variation between Southern varieties of Chinese and 181, 184–5; *see also Putonghua* (PTH)

Ong, Aihwa 75, 88
order of indexicality *see* indexical order

People's Republic of China (PRC) 2, 7–10, 13, 49, 184; pre-reform, socialist, Maoist 23, 92, 97–8, 164–5, 180; postsocialist, contemporary 26, 28, 122, 180; socialism 3, 92; *see also* Great Proletariat Cultural Revolution (Cultural Revolution); stylistic regime
personae (social): Beijing yuppies 15, 35, 85, 89, 178; cosmopolitan 33, 75, 99, 109, 120; Cosmopolitan Mandarin

196 Index

(CM) as a resource for 15, 92, 95, 99, 179, 185–6; enregisterment and 129, 135; local features as a resource for 95; middle-class consumer 106, 109; Standard *Putonghua* (PTH) as a resource for 183; style and 135, 180–3, 185–6; television (TV) hosts and 33, 106, 108, 109, 124, 126, 128–9, 154, 178; *see also* ebullience; ebullient; trendiness/trendy

phonological variables 22, 34, 63–4, 185; *see also* linguistic variables; full-tone realization of a neutral tone; interdental realization of (*ts*); lenition of (*sh*); rhotacization (*r*)

pinyin 7, 11, 16n16, 74, 116

Podesva, Robert J. 22, 25, 30, 88

popular culture 73, 112, 114, 128; *see also* Cosmopolitan Mandarin (CM); *Gang-Tai qiang* 'Hong Kong-Taiwan accent'; mass media; trendiness/trendy

power: of language 1; style and 24–5; stylistic regime and 26, 36n3; symbolic 24, 27, 183

Putonghua (PTH) 48, 82, 87; Beijing Mandarin (BM) and 8, 63–4, 74–5, 83–5, 95, 129, 151, 157, 166–7, 179–185; Beijing-Mandarin-based *Putonghua* (PTH) 14, 24, 30, 32, 34, 36, 68, 75, 80, 84, 98, 107, 110, 129, 137, 150, 154, 157, 162, 164, 167, 179–80, 182–4, 186; code-mixing (Mandarin–English) and 114; as "common speech" 10, 12–13, 23, 98; conventional, conservative 26, 34, 110, 112, 118, 120–1, 178; Cosmopolitan Mandarin (CM) and 15, 32, 34, 36, 62, 73, 80, 107, 110, 112, 120–1, 125, 129, 137, 149, 165, 179; definition of 6–8; development of 8–13; exemplary speakers of 98, 110, 129, 150, 154; *Gang-Tai qiang* 'Hong Kong-Taiwan accent' and 147, 151, 153–164; Mainland Standard *Putonghua* (MSP) 8, 28, 48, 62–3, 68, 74–5, 80–7, 95–8, 100n9, 107, 110, 115–6, 154, 187; Mainland Standard *Putonghua* (MSP) features of 110, 112, 114–17, 119, 125, 130n8, 143, 147–9, 168n10, 185; Mainland Standard *Putonghua* (MSP) symbolic value of 82–3; non-mainland Mandarin and 74, 98; normativity of 154, 156, 165; Northern Mandarin and 66, 165, 166; *see also* accent; authenticity;Beijing Mandarin (BM);

China Central Television (CCTV);-Cosmopolitan Mandarin (CM), enregisterment, identity, linguistic market, linguistic variables, Northern Mandarin, personae, state professionals

Putonghua Proficiency Test (PSC) 74, 82, 110, 115–16, 119, 129n8, 130n8

Putonghua Shuiping Ceshi 'Putonghua Proficiency Test' see Putonghua Proficiency Test (PSC)

Putonghua Shuiping Ceshi Shishi Gangyao 'The Implementation Guidelines for the Putonghua Proficiency Test' see Implementation Guidelines for the *Putonghua* Proficiency Test (PSCSG)

Qing Dynasty 9, 66, 158

qualitative analysis 34–6, 167

quantitative analysis 15, 34–6, 62–3, 76, 85, 87, 179

Rampton, Ben 22, 27, 147

Ramsey, S. Robert 7, 9, 13, 16n4, 74

repertoires 138; ethnolinguistic 187n6; linguistic 134, 138, 186, 187n9; semiotic 180, 182, 187n9

rhematization *see* iconization

rhotacization (*r*)/non-rhotacization/de-rhotacization, 61–2, 78, 99n1, 100n2, 139, 150, 168n25, 182; Beijing yuppies and 61–2, 76–9 , 86, 179; Cosmopolitan Mandarin (CM) and 80, 92, 94, 116–19, 121, 137, 140–1, 166, 179,182–6, 187n7; de-rhotacization as innovative sound feature 115–18; *Gang-Tai qiang* 'Hong Kong-Tawain accent' and 147–9, 155, 159, 161; gender and 77–8, 81, 86, 88, 94; local variant 66, 75, 97, 120; patterns of variation 76–9; Standard *Putonghua* (Standard PTH) and 98, 119, 129n8, 130n8, 150, 157–9; state professionals and 77; television (TV) hosts and 179, 181; topic and 77, 79 *see also* Beijing Mandarin (BM); "Beijing smooth operator"; television (TV) hosts

Rickford, John R. 22, 36n1, 138

retroflex initials 62, 66, 69–71, 141, 143, 148–9, 157–8, 185, 187n8; *see also* lenition of (*sh*)

retroflex onsets *see* retroflex initials

S Qingbao Zhan 'S Information Station' 15, 108–10, 120, 124–5, 128, 130n8, 154; constructing new middle-class

consumer 120–7; Cosmopolitan
Mandarin (CM) used in 15, 106–7, 120,
122, 125, 128; *see also* television (TV)
hosts
Schilling-Estes, Natalie (Schilling, Natalie)
22, 30, 36n1
script reform 9, 10–11, 16n2; simplified
characters 11
semiotic mediation 106, 128, 129n2
semiotic resources 3, 5, 15, 22, 24, 28–9,
32, 58, 64, 74–5, 109
Shopping Mall: 8 Miles New Culture
Plaza 4, 5, 8
signs 15, 33, 35, 58, 99, 106, 107; metasign
33, 106
Silverstein, Michael 27, 32–4, 36–7, 75,
121, 136
simplified characters 4, 6, 16n2, 16n9; *see
also* script reform
social change 1–3, 6, 14, 20–1, 23, 34,
106, 134, 182; social-ideological,
sociocultural, socioeconomic, and
sociopolitical transformations 1–3, 8, 10,
13, 14, 23, 26–7, 30, 35, 143, 180, 184;
valorization of difference 2, 26, 105; *see
also* language change; linguistic change
social constraints: gender 76; professional
group 76; topic 76
social distinction, new 2, 3, 13, 26, 32,
106, 181–182; consumerism 107;
Cosmopolitan Mandarin (CM) and 14,
20, 23, 99, 106, 134, 181–3; indexical
order and 137, 155, 166; linguistic
innovation as resource for 20, 26;
linguistic styling of Beijing yuppies and
58, 61–2, 98; mediatization of 99, 106,
107; metasemiotic discourse and 105,
120, 128; mass media's role in 105–7,
134; strategy of distinction 26–7, 53; *see
also* style; mediation
social index 4, 33
social meaning 5, 15, 21–2, 28, 30–1,
33–4, 37n7, 75, 106, 128, 134–6, 165;
indeterminacy of 37n5; meaning-
making resources 14, 21–2, 24–5, 28–32,
61–4, 109, 120, 128; multiplicity of
37n5; *see also* indexicality (social)
socialist egalitarianism 1, 2, 8, 10, 13–14,
19, 23, 98, 137, 155, 166, 180, 183; *see
also* ideologies
sociolinguistic change 20–1, 27, 34, 107,
167, 184; ideologies and 22; mediation
and mediatization of 34; style-based
approach to 2, 14, 20, 22, 26, 28,

167, 182, 184; *see also* Cosmopolitan
Mandarin (CM); language change;
linguistic change; style
sociolinguistic variation 22, 27, 34, 63; as
meaning-making resources 21–2; *see also*
linguistic variables
Southern dialects *see* Southern varieties
Southern varieties 7, 64–5, 74–5, 159, 185;
Cosmopolitan Mandarin and 185; *see
also Gang-Tai qiang* 'Hong Kong-Taiwan
accent', authenticity
Southwestern Mandarin 7, 68
Standard *Putonghua* (Standard PTH) *see
Putonghua* (PTH): Mainland Standard
Putonghua (MSP)
State Administration of Radio, Film, and
Television (SARFT) 110, 151–3, 155,
168n14
state professionals (Beijing) 15; aesthetic
labor and 86; contrasted with Beijing
yuppies 49–51, 63, 86, 91, 99; gender
variation and 77–8, 86; Mainland
Standard *Putonghua* linguistic market
and 82–3; patterns of variation
76–80; Standard *Putonghua* (Standard
PTH) and 83; topic variation and
77–9, 81–2; *see also* gender; linguistic
variables; *waiqi* 'foreign enterprises'
professionals
style: as accommodation to audience
types 22; as attention paid to speech
22; as bricolage 31, 179; change in
content and 14, 180–1, 184; change
in form and 14, 112, 134, 180, 181–2,
184; change in meaning and 14, 180,
182, 184; clothing style 11, 25, 27;
co-occurrence styles 125, 128, 134–5,
179–80; cosmopolitan vs. local 79–81;
cosmopolitan as innovative 4, 80;
definition of 14, 23–4; enregistered 38,
178, 186; enregisterment and 31–2, 179;
furniture style 24, 36n3; as ideological
system of distinction 24–7, 183;
ideologies and 22–6, 183; indistinction
and 26, 27; pre-reform, socialist 23;
as sociohistorical process 27–32, 134;
sociolinguistic change and 2, 22, 23,
180; strategic stylization 116, 127, 134,
182; *see also* personae; power; social
distinction
stylistic regime 24–6, 31, 34, 36n3;
postsocialist 32, 36, 166, 180, 183, 184;
pre-reform, socialist, Maoist 23–6, 31,
34, 180, 183; *see also* power

198 Index

stylistic resources: Cosmopolitan Mandarin as emergent/emerging 1–2, 14–15, 20, 22, 24, 136, 138, 165, 167, 180–2; linguistic change and innovation as emergent/emerging 24, 28, 30, 32, 134–5, 184
stylistic variation 22, 27, 36n2, 135
supraregional 5, 48, 62, 120, 155, 182, 183; Chinese identity, Chineseness 155, 166–7, 182; Cosmopolitan Mandarin (CM) and 80, 99, 120, 137, 150, 179; indexicality and 136–7, 185; *see also* identity

Taiwan Mandarin (*Guoyu*) 8, 13, 16n11, 48, 66, 74–5, 80, 84, 159
television (TV) hosts 15, 99, 106–9; code-mixing (Mandarin–English) and 114–15; Cosmopolitan Mandarin (CM) and 105–7, 128–9, 134, 181; de-rhotacization 116–18; full-tone realization of a neutral tone 118–20; innovative lexical items 110–14; innovative phonological/ sound features 115–20; new middle-class consumer 120–8; *see also* Beijing Mandarin (BM); Cosmopolitan Mandarin (CM); cultural intermediaries; English; enregisterment; *Gang-Tai qiang* 'Hong Kong-Taiwan accent'; identity; linguistic variables; personae; *S Information Station;* trendiness/trendy
Third Wave approach to variation 21, 24
Tianjin Mandarin 113, 116–17, 130n8, 185
traditional characters 4, 6, 16n2, 16n9
trendiness/trendy: Cosmopolitan Mandarin (CM) and 15, 61–2, 73, 99, 113, 128, 137, 140, 166; *Gang-Tai qiang* 'Hong Kong-Taiwan accent' and 150–3,

161, 163–4; persona and 15, 99, 112, 126, 129, 143

Urban, Greg 37n7, 106

variationist sociolinguistics 21, 24, 26, 32, 35, 36n1–2, 134; *see also* Third Wave approach to variation

waiqi 'foreign enterprises' 14, 47; gender and 48–51, 58n4
waiqi 'foreign enterprises' professionals 14–15, 46–9; *bai-ling liren* 'white-collar beauty' 48–9, 61–2; gender and 15, 48–51, 58n4, 76–9, 99; *see also* Beijing yuppies; gender
Wang, Jing 23, 105, 109, 168
Woolard, Kathryn A. 20, 25, 27, 32, 138
Wu 64; Shanghai *hua* 64–5, 74, 112

Xi, Jinping 177, 178, 186n1, 187n4, 187n5
Xiaopin 'theatrical or comic skits', skit 139–40, 143–6, 150, 161, 167n2–3, 167n6–7
Xinhua Dictionary of New Expressions (XXCC) 110, 111, 113
Xinhua Xin Ciyu Cidian see *Xinhua Dictionary of New Expressions* (XXCC) 110–11, 113

Yan, Yunxiang 47–8
Yang, Mayfair Mei-hui 23, 50, 75

Zhang, Li 2, 23
Zhang, Lihang 65, 67, 72
Zhang, Qing 27, 29–30, 67, 76, 86
Zhongwen see Chinese (Chinese Language)